The Economics of International Transfers

Since the famous debate between Keynes and Ohlin on German reparation payments after World War I, international transfers have attracted the attention of economists. Today the subject is of even greater importance with billions of dollars flowing between nations as unilateral transfers. However, the emphasis has shifted from balance-of-payments issues to the welfare consequences following a transfer, and in particular the welfare issues arising from aid to developing countries. In *The Economics of International Transfers* Professors Brakman and Van Marrewijk present a complete overview of transfers (including the history of transfers and current transfer flows), and their own unified framework in which they describe important and original research. Subjects considered include welfare effects, distortions, third parties, rent-seeking, the "trade or aid" discussion, multilateral agencies, tied aid and imperfect competition.

STEVEN BRAKMAN is Associate Professor at the Department of Economics, University of Groningen. He has published widely in the field of international economics, and has developed scientific television programs for Dutch television.

CHARLES VAN MARREWIJK is Associate Professor at the Department of Applied Economics, Erasmus University. He has published on various topics focusing attention on international economics and economic agglomeration.

The Economics of
International Transfers

Steven Brakman and
Charles van Marrewijk

CAMBRIDGE
UNIVERSITY PRESS

PUBLISHED BY THE PRESS SYNDICATE OF THE UNIVERSITY OF CAMBRIDGE
The Pitt Building, Trumpington Street, Cambridge CB2 1RP, United Kingdom

CAMBRIDGE UNIVERSITY PRESS
The Edinburgh Building, Cambridge, CB2 2RU, UK
  http: //www.cup.cam.ac.uk
40 West 20th Street, New York, NY 10011–4211, USA   http: //www.cup.org
10 Stamford Road, Oakleigh, Melbourne 3166, Australia

First published 1998

Printed in the United Kingdom at the University Press, Cambridge

Typeset in Times 10/12pt   [CE]

A catalogue record for this book is available from the British Library

Library of Congress Cataloguing in Publication data

Brakman, Steven.
The economics of international transfers / Steven Brakman and
Charles van Marrewijk.
        p.   cm.
Includes bibliographical references (p.   ).
ISBN 0 521 57214 2 hb
1. Balance of payments.   I. Marrewijk, Charles van.   II. Title.
HG3882.B72   1998
382′.17 – dc 21   98–3809   CIP

ISBN 0 521 57214 2 hardback

Contents

Figures

Tables

Preface

Few economic problems have attracted as much of the attention of the world's leading economists and stirred up such lively debates between them as the transfer problem. Classical writers such as David Ricardo, David Hume and others, had heated debates with contemporaries on the consequences of balance-of-payments disequilibria (a temporary transfer). The most famous debate, however, was the discussion between John Maynard Keynes and Bertil Ohlin, which led to the first systematic treatment of the consequences of transfers as such. This debate was also primarily directed at the causes and consequences of possible balance-of-payments disequilibria. The early attention on balance-of-payments problems following a transfer is somewhat in contrast with today's interest in the transfer problem, which is mostly concerned with welfare effects. For example, the welfare effects associated with development assistance have been considered by Jan Tinbergen (1976), who regards development aid from the North to the South as a means of obtaining greater equality between nations. Moreover, he is convinced that development aid is necessary to increase welfare levels in the developing world. Needless to say, there is no general agreement between economists on the influence of development aid on welfare. Nor is there agreement on whether or not development assistance is necessary in the first place in order to put a country on a more rapid path to development. There are not only disagreements and discussions on the practical consequences of transfers, but also disagreements between modern theorists on the effects of transfers and how to model them. This is illustrated, for example, in the sometimes heated debate involving Graciela Chichilnisky, Jagdish Bhagwati and T. N. Srinivasan, Jan Willem Gunning and others.

Most textbooks on international trade theory contain a section on the transfer problem. It is often used to illustrate the fact that income adjustments in international economic relations are very important, or that terms-of-trade adjustments are only part of the adjustment process.

Furthermore, the transfer problem can easily be analyzed in Keynesian-type models, such as the Mundell–Fleming model. Textbooks use the 1929 debate between Keynes and Ohlin only to illustrate differences between the two main channels of adjustment: price adjustments and income adjustments. To summarize, however, this approach to the transfer problem, by simply restating the famous debate between Keynes and Ohlin in a "Keynesian" framework, ignores the fact that since the 1980s the literature on international transfers and international trade theory has witnessed a minor revolution. Not only have the analytical tools to analyze transfer problems changed, but the issues themselves have also changed.

Duality theory is a very powerful tool in reformulating various topics of importance in the literature on economic development and international economic theory. Most importantly, using duality theory it is possible to analyze the welfare consequences of various phenomena and economic policies in a systematic way. This enables us to make explicit welfare comparisons. The general equilibrium nature of duality theory also makes it very clear that the traditional partial equilibrium insights on the transfer problem can be misleading.

The "new" trade theory stresses the fact that the world is also characterized by increasing returns to scale and imperfect competition. It is by now well known that these developments in international trade theory imply that some of the traditional problems have to be reanalyzed. This also holds, as we will show, for the transfer problem. Economic welfare and economic development can be influenced in many ways; for example, by economic distortions, the wasting of valuable resources, rent-seeking, etc. The main focus of this book is how these aspects influence the welfare effects of transfers.

We do not expect the reader to have a thorough knowledge of international trade theory, but some knowledge of the basic results in international economics is recommended. Moreover, we expect the reader to know intermediate microeconomics, since we will frequently use microeconomics to explain our results. A short refresher course on the most important concepts is offered in the mathematical appendix. This appendix is also useful for becoming acquainted with our notation.

The plan of the book is as follows. Chapter 1 gives a brief overview of the history of the transfer problem and some information on transfer flows. It highlights the fact that it was traditionally considered to be a problem of balance-of-payments adjustments. Chapter 2 summarizes the debate on German war reparations payments between Keynes and Ohlin in 1929. It is important from an historical point of view, as the disagreement between Keynes and Ohlin paved the way for a systematic treatment of the transfer problem. One could argue that the modern literature on transfers takes this debate as a starting point. Chapter 3 presents the core material of this book. It not only illustrates that the transfer problem is not a problem in the Keynesian sense, but also introduces the main analytical tools of this book. Most chapters are relatively self-contained, but we advise the reader always to read chapter 3 before reading any of the other analytical chapters, because the conclusions serve as a benchmark for the results developed in other chapters. Chapter 4 generalizes the findings of chapter 3. The conclusions of chapters 3 and 4 change, in general, if distortions, such as tariffs or rent-seeking, are present. These are analyzed in chapter 5. In chapter 6 it is shown that, rather surprisingly and for reasons that may not be intuitively obvious, transfer paradoxes are possible in a perfectly competitive Walrasian-stable world if a third country (the bystander) is introduced. Chapters 7 and 8 generalize the results of the earlier chapters in a number of ways. Does it matter, for instance, if aid is given by multilateral agencies? Or does it matter that, in practice, aid is often given as tied aid? Note, that chapters 3 to 5 analyze a two-country world, whereas chapters 6 to 8 analyze a three (or more)-country world. Chapter 9 analyzes imperfect competition and economies of scale, alone and in combination with tied aid. It is shown that welfare is not only influenced by income and price effects, but also by a "love-of-variety" effect. Furthermore, and most importantly, it is shown that profits are possible in this context, even in equilibrium, if aid is tied to a specific sector or commodity. Finally, transfers are frequently given to alleviate balance-of-payments disequilibria (often by means of foreign exchange). In fact, this is a basic task of the International Monetary Fund. Moreover, aid is given to put developing countries on a higher path of development. Both issues require that a dynamic framework be introduced to analyze the consequences of aid. This is done in chapter 10.

The following people were helpful at various stages in writing this book: Filip Abraham, Peter van Bergeijk, Andries Brandsma, Willem Buiter, John Chipman, Richard Gigengack, Catrinus Jepma, Murray Kemp, Thijs Knaap, Jan Pen, Leendert Punt, Zvi Safra, Teun Schmidt, Albert Schweinberger, Georg Tillman, Edward Tower, Jean-Marie Viaene and Casper de Vries. They commented on parts of the manuscript or on our earlier work on the transfer problem. We also received useful comments from seminar participants at the University of Melbourne, New York University, Purdue University, Erasmus University Rotterdam, the University of Groningen and the University of Leuven, and from participants at conferences of the Econometric Society (Munich,

1989), the European Association of Development Institutes (Oslo, 1990 and Berlin, 1993) and the European Economic Association (Dublin, 1992).

We would also like to thank Patrick McCartan and Ashwin Rattan of Cambridge University Press for their stimulating comments and encouragements during the writing of this book. Finally, our thanks go to Chris Doubleday for his prompt, precise and educational editorial assistance.

1   General overview and stylized facts

1.1   What is a transfer?

All economic exchanges involve transfers. In fast food restaurants, for instance, you will exchange cash for a hamburger. This is a bilateral transfer. It is bilateral because most fast food chains do not give hamburgers for free, nor are you willing to give up hard-earned dollars without being able to bite into a burger. The large majority of economic transfers are bilateral. Nowadays, it is usually goods or services for money, be it dollars, guilders, pounds or yen, or barter trade. This book is not about such transfers.

This is a book about unilateral transfers. It involves money sent to alleviate some of the distress after earthquakes or famines, or money sent to help a friend or relative, etc. In these instances the donating party helps the recipient without getting anything in return, save perhaps the good feeling of helping someone. For that reason it is called unilateral, because you get nothing in exchange for your dollars. Of course, one might also be on the receiving side of a transfer, for example if the state helps you to pay for university, or if you "enjoy" unemployment benefits. It is easy, but admittedly rather boring, to come up with an endless list of examples of unilateral transfers.

We analyze the economic consequences of international unilateral transfers. Why did we not state this more explicitly in the title of our book? Force of habit. For many years prominent economists have discussed "the transfer problem" with reference to international uni-lateral transfers (Eichengreen 1992).[1] The former is, of course, a more succinct term with a better ring to it than the latter.

---

[1] Although we will discuss transfers in an international context, the methodology developed can easily be applied to all types of unilateral transfers, such as between economic agents within a single country.

1.2 Definitions

We analyze international unilateral transfers. In principle all such transfers should be recorded in the balance-of-payments statistics. This is by no means straightforward, because the balance-of-payment statistics are based on a bookkeeping system, which requires that an offsetting entry should follow each transaction.[2] In the case of unilateral transfers no offsetting transaction exists. However, the International Monetary Fund (IMF) requires that the balance of payments shows all economic values, including those without a quid pro quo, provided by residents of one country to residents of another country. The IMF publishes on a regular basis data on the balance of payments and makes a distinction between capital and current transfers.

Capital transfers consist of the transfer of ownership of a fixed asset or the forgiveness of a liability by a creditor when no counterpart is received in return. Furthermore, a transfer of cash is a capital transfer if it is linked to, or conditional on, the acquisition or disposal of a fixed asset (for example, an investment grant). A capital transfer should result in a commensurate change in the stock of assets of one or both parties in the transaction. Capital transfers can further be separated into those by the official sector and those by the private sector.

An example of a capital transfer by a government is debt forgiveness. When a government creditor in one country agrees with a debtor in another country to forgive all, or part, of the obligations of the debtor to that creditor, the amount forgiven is the capital transfer. Other capital transfers include investment grants, to finance all or part of the costs of acquiring fixed assets. In this case the recipients are obliged to use investment grants for purposes of (gross) fixed capital formation and are in this sense tied to specific investment projects. Investment grants in kind consist of transfers of transport equipment or machinery, or the direct provision of buildings or other structures such as docks, roads, airfields, hospitals, etc. Taxes are also included, for example inheritance taxes and gift taxes, and also compensation payments for damages such as oil spills and explosions. Examples of capital transfers by those not in the government sector are migrant transfers and debt forgiveness by such people or organizations. In principle, the items distinguished for the government sector can also be distinguished for other sectors.

Current transfers are, not surprisingly, all transfers that are not capital transfers. They directly influence the level of disposable income and

---

[2] This section is based on the fifth edition of the balance-of-payments manual (International Monetary Fund, 1996).

Table 1.1. *Net unilateral transfers ($ billions)*

| | 1989 | | 1994 | |
	Current	Capital	Current	Capital
Australia	0.0	1.9	−0.4	0.6
Canada	−0.8	1.1	−0.3	1.0
France	−7.6	−1.0	−8.3	−4.8
Germany	−16.7	0.1	−37.9	0.7
Italy	−3.5	0.9	−7.1	1.3
Japan	−4.3	n.a.	−7.5	n.a.
Netherlands	−1.9	−0.3	−5.3	−0.9
Sweden	−1.8	−0.3	−1.8	−0.1
United Kingdom	−7.5	n.a.	−8.2	n.a.
United States	−26.3	0.2	−35.2	−0.6

Note: Net transfers are credit minus debit transfers.
Source: International Monetary Fund, *Balance of Payments Statistics Yearbook*, various issues.

influence the consumption of goods and services. As in the case of capital transfers a distinction between government and non-government transfers can be made. Government transfers, in cash or in kind, comprise transfers to finance current expenditures of the receiving government, gifts of food, clothing or medical supplies, gifts of military equipment, the contributions by governments to international organizations or by international organizations to governments, and also fines, penalties and interest on late payment of taxes. Basically the same examples can be given for non-government transfers. Remittances by migrants are also important.

Table 1.1 gives an indication of the size of the different kinds of transfers, as derived from the balance-of-payment statistics. The outflow of unilateral transfers is particularly large in Germany and the United States. Moreover, unilateral capital transfers tend to be smaller than unilateral current transfers.

1.3 An early example of transfers: Alexander the Great

Although transfers are now regular transactions and routinely described in the balance-of-payments statistics, the first sizable "international" transfers were most likely of an involuntary nature, dating far back in history. After losing a war or a battle, a country, region, city or tribe was likely to be forced to pay reparations or be plundered on the spot. That is how it used to be, and in many cases that is how it still is. We will encounter more examples of reparations payments in the remainder of this chapter, but we will begin with a particularly successful and vivid example: Alexander the Great. Alexander financed his war efforts by taking gold and silver and goods in kind from the many conquered peoples. He gave this to his soldiers directly, or after converting the bullion to coins.[3] Bosworth (1993, pp. 241–2) summarizes this as follows:

> Alexander himself was not greatly concerned with the regular payments of tribute. He relied on periodical influxes of bullion to finance the expenses of his campaigns and drew prodigally upon the accumulated reserves he discovered at Sardes, Damascus, Susa and, above all, Persepolis. Ultimately no less than 180,000 talents were concentrated at Ecbatana, a truly colossal sum which freed him from any budgetary constraints.

To put this wealth in proper perspective, Hammond (1989) writes: "We may recall for comparison that the output of Philip's mines at Philippi alone had been 1,000 talents a year, regarded then as a huge sum" (p. 157). Or, to give some more perspective, when Alexander is campaigning in the east in 331 BC he is accumulating enough reserves to stop a rebellion back home: "He sent to Antipater 3,000 talents, a large sum, with which to buy support and mercenaries" (p. 160). Apparently, this was enough: "Antipater won the ensuing battle near Megalopolis, in which Agis and 5,300 of his army were killed, and obtained the capitulation of the enemy, Sparta providing hostages" (p. 160).

1.4   Transfers and the balance of payments

The history of transfers is long and varied. As the previous section illustrates, early examples were often concerned with battles and wars. These transactions are interesting from an historical point of view but do not contribute much to the understanding of the economic consequences of transfers. The first examples of economic analyses with respect to transfers deal with balance-of-payments problems. In the so-called classical theory of balance-of-payments adjustments, transfers are important because a current account disequilibrium can be seen as a unilateral transfer within a single period, that is a current account surplus or deficit which has to be settled in a future period; see also sections 10.2 and 10.3. The classical theory assumed that capital was more or less immobile and the adjustment had to come from changes in exports and imports accompanied by changes of the terms of trade and movements along given demand and supply curves. Although the language of the classical

---

[3] Of course, part of the gold and silver given to the soldiers may have been spent in the country of origin, but it was always a transfer between individuals of different nations.

writers can sometimes be confusing to a present day reader the theory can be summed up as follows. Suppose a country has a current account surplus and there is a strict relation between gold reserves and the stock of money. Assuming that the quantity theory of money holds, this surplus causes an increase in prices and therefore reduces the demand for exports; see also Wicksell (1918).[4] In the deficit country the opposite happens. The adjustment of prices gradually eliminates the surplus and the deficit. This theory of balance-of-payments adjustments can easily be stated in terms which are found in the transfer literature and thus gives one of the first theoretical analyses of the transfer problem. The first and most complete statement of this theory is often associated with the name of David Hume.

1.4.1 David Hume

The mechanism equilibrating the balance of payments in the gold exchange standard under normal circumstances originates from the Scottish economist David Hume. His objective was to demonstrate the automatic nature of this so-called price–specie–flow mechanism, that is it did not require the "benefit" of (mercantilist) government intervention (Hume 1985 [1752]):[5]

Suppose four-fifths of all the money in Great Britain to be annihilated in one night, and the nation reduced to the same condition, with regard to specie, as in the reigns of the Harrys and the Edwards, what would be the consequence? Must not the price of all labor and commodities sink in proportion, and everything be sold as cheap as they were in those ages? What nation could then dispute with us in any foreign market, or pretend to navigate or to sell manufactures at the same price, which to us would afford sufficient profit? In how little time, therefore, must this bring back the money which we had lost, and raise us to the level of all the neighboring nations? Where, after we have arrived, we immediately lose the advantage of the cheapness of labor and commodities; and the farther flowing in of money is stopped by our fullness and repletion.

Again, suppose that all the money in Great Britain were multiplied fivefold in a night, must not the contrary effect follow? Must not all labor and commodities rise to such an exorbitant height, that no neighboring nations could afford to buy from us; while their commodities, on the other hand, became comparatively so

---

[4] Note the close resemblance of this theory to the monetary approach to the balance of payments, although in the monetary approach the adjustment also comes about by the direct influence of the stock of money on expenditure.

[5] This chapter and the next will be exceptional in their rather frequent use of quotations. We have done so deliberately in this "historical" part to "let the authors speak for themselves." It is useful to keep in mind T. S. Eliot's words: "Someone said: 'The dead writers are remote from us because we know so much more than they did.' Precisely, and they are that which we know."

cheap, that, in spite of all the laws which could be formed, they would run in upon us, and our money flow out; till we fall to a level with foreigners, and lose that great superiority of riches which had laid us under such disadvantages?

Changes in relative prices and their influence on the volume of exports and imports are therefore, according to Hume, the chief driving force behind equilibrating the balance of trade. In addition, and to a limited extent, exchange rate changes within the limits of the gold points serve the same purpose. Thus, according to the price–specie–flow mechanism a unilateral transfer should reduce prices to produce an export surplus. The main purpose of Hume was, however, not to develop a theory of transfers, but to react to what he considered to be gross errors by contemporary writers; that is, the mercantilists. His goal was to show that the mercantilists were wrong when they stated that if England ran a balance-of-payments deficit (or current account deficit) the outflow of gold would drain the entire gold reserves of the country.

1.4.2 Adam Smith

War has been a frequent motivation for transfer payments and it was also the driving force behind the discussion of a transfer problem by the Scottish economist Adam Smith. In this particular instance it was not for reparations payments or indemnities, but for subsidies to Great Britain's allies against France in the Seven Years War (1756–63). Smith (1981 [1776], pp. 441–2) first gives information on the enormous size of the transfer:

The last French war cost Great Britain upwards of ninety millions ... More than two-thirds of this expense was laid out in distant countries; in Germany, Portugal, America, in the ports of the Mediterranean, in the East and West Indies ... Let us suppose, therefore, according to the most exaggerated computation which I remember to have either seen or heard of, that, gold and silver together, it [the circulating gold and silver in Great Britain] amounted to thirty millions. Had the war been carried on, by means of our money, the whole of it must, even according to this computation, have been sent out and returned again at least twice, in a period between six and seven years.

Smith concludes that such a rapid circulation of money was impossible so that payments must have been made in terms of commodities. For this he gives the following explanation (Smith 1981 [1776], p. 443):

The transportation of commodities, when properly suited to the market, is always attended with a considerable profit; whereas that of gold and silver is scarce ever attended with any. When those metals are sent abroad in order to purchase foreign commodities, the merchant's profit arises, not from the purchase, but from the sale of the returns. But when they are sent abroad merely to pay a debt,

Table 1.2. *Britain's foreign trade 1796–1816, compared with unilateral foreign payments (annual averages in £ millions)*

	1793–1805	1796–1805	1806–16
Exports	n.a.	47.3	54.5
Imports	n.a.	53.2	63.0
Trade volume	n.a.	100.6	117.5
Foreign payments	3.0	2.3	10.9
Payments/exports	6.4%[a]	4.9%	20.1%
Payments/imports	5.7%[a]	4.4%	17.4%
Payments/trade volume	3.0%[a]	2.3%	9.3%

Note: [a] Calculated with reference to trade in 1796–1805.
Source: Machlup 1966.

he gets no returns, and consequently no profit. He naturally, therefore, exerts his invention to find out a way of paying his foreign debts, rather by the exportation of commodities than by that of gold and silver.

This explanation of balance-of-payments adjustment is remarkable in that the higher profitability of sending goods rather than specie is inconsistent with Smith's own doctrine of the equality of profit in the employment of different capitals.

1.4.3   The bullionist controversy

The famous bullionist controversy started with the large payments of Great Britain to continental Europe during the Napoleonic wars. Detailed information on Great Britain's balance of payments is lacking, but it seems that these transfers were large relative to exports, but rather small relative to GDP. With respect to the transfer problem (see chapter 2) it is interesting to note that during the period in which the largest payments were made, 1806–16, Britain's terms of trade deteriorated by about 30 percent (Imlah 1958). This debate was one of the first in which large payments to "over-sea countries" gave rise to economic analyses of the issues involved.

On February 27, 1797, Great Britain's war with France had brought a suspension of gold payments by the Bank of England, which was now authorized to refuse payments for its notes in gold to save it from a state of chronic insolvency. Subsequent renewals prolonged the restriction until 1821. At this time Great Britain was involved in heavy remittances to its allies (see tables 1.2 and 1.7), and the government was involved in large-scale borrowing. Simultaneously, a remarkable series of bad harvests led to large-scale imports of wheat and disturbed the balance of payments. Inconvertibility combined with rising prices resulted in a premium for gold in the market over the quoted mint price. With convertible paper this obviously cannot occur because then the exchange rate between two currencies is determined by the ratio of the gold prices plus or minus the cost of shipping and handling gold.

The "bullionists," among them the English economists Henry Thornton, David Ricardo and John Wheatley, advocated resumption of specie payments by the Bank of England at the earliest possible date. In general the "excessive" issue of irredeemable bank-notes was considered to be responsible for the evil of inflation, although Thornton's analysis following the Hume type of explanation was considerably more cautious in listing the many causes, consequences and symptoms of inflation. Thornton investigated, in particular, a crop failure which necessitated increased imports of grain and arrived at a shift in the terms of trade against the paying country. As will become clear in due course, a crop failure can be analyzed in terms of transfers; see chapter 5. Ricardo (1810) denied that a crop failure or subsidy would disturb the balance of payments at all and questioned any need for a mechanism of adjustment with the peculiar reasoning that it would be a waste of effort to first send specie abroad only to have it returned at a later time:

The ultimate result then of all this exportation and importation of money, is that one country will have imported one commodity in exchange for another, and the coin and bullion will in both countries have regained their natural level. Is it to be contended that these results would not be foreseen, and the expense and trouble attending these needless operations effectually prevented, in a country where capital is abundant, where every possible economy in trade is practiced, and where competition is pushed to its utmost limits? Is it conceivable that money should be sent abroad for the purpose merely of rendering it dear in this country and cheap in another, and by such means to insure its return to us?

There is no need to comment on the implied omniscience and capabilities of individual agents in abstaining from sending money abroad because it will ultimately return to the country of origin. Suffice it to say that many years later some authors give Ricardo more credit than he probably deserves for claiming that a relative price change is not necessary. As Blaug (1978, p. 219) puts it:

Oddly enough Ricardo's argument is correct if we assume that he was thinking of the modern Keynesian theory of transfer payments and assumed it to be operative immediately. In other words, if a failure of harvest would immediately and automatically bring about a proportionate change in reciprocal demands of countries for each other's products, no alteration whatever would take place in the exchanges. On this ground some authors have credited Ricardo with extraordinary prescience ... The whole argument is somewhat forced, and Ricardo would hardly have adopted it had he not been so anxious to attribute the entire "premium on bullion" to an excessive issue of Bank Notes. To improve his presentation by crediting him with a Keynesian theory of transfers seems to miss the point.

Schumpeter (1954, p. 704, n. 13) and Silberling (1924) give similar views. The latter is also useful for a more detailed account of the bullion controversy.

Wheatley (1807) deserves perhaps more credit in this respect for pointing out income effects in addition to price effects by maintaining that crop failures or subsidies would alter the relative demands of two countries and their ability to purchase each other's goods:

If, then, it be correct in theory, that the exports and imports to and from independent states have a reciprocal action on each other, and that the extent of the one is necessarily limited by the extent of the other, it is obvious, that if no demand had subsisted in this country from 1793 to 1797 for corn and naval stores, the countries that furnished the supply would have possessed so much less means of expending on our exports, as an inability to sell would of course have created an equal inability to buy. It is totally irregular, therefore, to infer, that our exports would have amounted to the same sum, had the import of the corn and naval stores been withheld, as those who provided the supply would have been utterly incapable of purchasing them.

In the discussion several elements can be recognized which will later also dominate other debates involving transfers: the influence of transfers on the balance of payments; whether or not balance-of-payments disequilibria would give rise to terms-of-trade changes; and how this could come about. In the bullionist controversy the inconvertibility of paper money for gold resulted in a rise in the price of gold relative to its mint price; the implied depreciation of paper money meant a terms-of-trade depreciation (see, for a related discussion, Taussig [1917, 1918] and Hollander [1918]). As we will see in chapter 2, this debate resembles the famous Keynes–Ohlin debate on the consequences of transfers; both debates failed to put the transfer problem in a general equilibrium context.

1.4.4 John Stuart Mill

The English economist John Stuart Mill, in his authoritative *Principles*, attributes to relative price changes almost sole responsibility for restoring equilibrium in the balance of payments. Only on one occasion does Mill mention a relative shift of income as an equilibrating force; on both points, see Viner (1955, p. 300). Thus, the conventional wisdom in those days that a transfer of funds from one country to another will worsen the paying country's terms of trade, thereby creating a secondary burden is argued by Mill (1848, book III, ch. XXI, para. 4) as follows (our emphasis):[6]

The supposed annual remittances being made in commodities, and being exports for which there is to be no return, it is no longer requisite that the imports and exports should pay for one another: on the contrary, there must be an annual excess of exports over imports, equal to the value of the remittance. If, before the country became liable to the annual payment, foreign commerce was in its natural state of equilibrium, it will now be necessary, for the purpose of effecting the remittance, that foreign countries should be induced to take a greater quantity of exports than before: which can only be done by offering those exports on cheaper terms, or, in other words, by paying dearer for foreign commodities. The international values will so adjust themselves that, either by greater exports, or smaller imports, or both, the requisite excess on the side of exports will be brought about; and this excess will become the permanent state. *The result is that a country which makes regular payments to foreign countries, besides losing what it pays, loses also something more, by the less advantageous terms on which it is forced to exchange its productions for foreign commodities.*

The idea that a country which makes a transfer abroad suffers a *secondary burden* because of a deterioration of its terms of trade (that is, the classical theory of transfers) was termed the "orthodox" view by Ohlin (1928a).

1.4.5   Charles Bastable's critique

At first glance, and partly as a result of its eloquent wording, Mill's argument in the previous subsection may sound convincing. The main weakness in the analysis was pointed out most explicitly for the first time by Charles Bastable in 1889. After discussing a few examples, in one of which the two countries engaged in the transfer are not involved in any trade such that there cannot be a secondary burden, Bastable cuts to the heart of the matter (1889, p. 15):

He [Mill] has, however, omitted an important qualification. B [the recipient], having got 100,000 quarters without cost, is the better able to purchase: her sum of income is higher. It is therefore possible that she may desire to take a greater quantity, – say 200,000 quarters, purchasing 100,000. This increased demand would affect the terms of trade to her [the recipient's] disadvantage, and would so far counteract the loss incurred by A [the donor].

---

[6] The argument here is for the case of barter trade. Mill goes on to argue that there is no difference if money is introduced or transferred instead.

In short, the recipient's income is higher as a result of the transfer. This increases the recipient's demand for goods in general and for the donor's export goods in particular, which in turn potentially improves the donor's terms of trade and facilitates the required generation of an export surplus for the donor.

The conclusion of the debates discussed in this section is that from early on it has been recognized that balance-of-payments disequilibria or transfers lead to terms-of-trade effects and quantity adjustments. The primary attention in the discussion is on terms-of-trade effects, rather than on quantity adjustments. The subsequent literature did not add much to our understanding of the transfer problem, and we had to wait until 1929 for a renewed interest in and more systematic treatment of the problem. This is discussed in the next chapter.

1.5 German transfer problems

France and Germany were the main participants in two well-known war-related international transfer schemes that attracted a lot of analytical and political attention. The first scheme involved a transfer payment from France to Germany after the war in 1870–1. The second scheme involved a transfer payment from Germany to France (and other allied forces) after World War I, some fifty years later.

1.5.1   Franco-German indemnity of 1871

Taussig (1927) notes that the frequent reference in his days to the ease with which France fulfilled its indemnity obligations after the Franco-Prussian War of 1870 is quite misleading owing to the exceptional circumstances of this case.[7] France was required to pay 4,976 million francs (5 billion in indemnity, plus 301 million in interest on postponed payments, minus 325 million for the railroads of Alsace-Lorraine, which were taken over by the German Empire and whose owners were reimbursed by France). Unlike most cases (the Chinese Boxer indemnities of 1901, the Turkish indemnity of 1878 or Germany after World War I) the period for the arrangement of the transfer was so short that it was almost like a lump sum being handed over at once, and this appeared to impose a formidable burden on France in relative terms; see table 1.3. The first task of financing was astoundingly successful; France floated two great loans (1.5 billion in 1871 and 3 billion in 1872), the latter being oversubscribed more than tenfold. The French bonds were purchased to

---

[7] This subsection is based on chapter 22 of Taussig (1927).

Table 1.3. *French foreign trade 1872–5,*
compared   with   indemnity   payments
(annual averages in million francs)

Exports	4,159
Imports	3,649
Trade volume	7,808
Indemnity (one-fourth)	1,248
Indemnity/exports	30.0%
Indemnity/imports	34.2%
Indemnity/trade volume	16.0%

Source: Machlup 1966.

a large extent by foreigners and by French investors who disposed of their foreign investments. The second task of transferring the funds to Germany, mainly in the form of bills of exchange, was equally successful. Taussig (1927, p. 266) attributes this to a reduction in French foreign investments:

The one adequate resource was the great mass of accumulated French invest-ments in foreign countries. These investments existed chiefly in the form of foreign securities held by Frenchmen. It was their sale that supplied most of the funds for the great loans and for the bills of exchange, the funds both for the domestic and foreign tasks.

Taussig (1927, p. 268) concludes: "What happened under these circum-stances (so fortunate for France) gives hardly any clue to what might happen under such conditions as would ordinarily have to be faced by a country required to pay a great lump-sum indemnity ... The French experience helps hardly at all for the purposes of verification."

1.5.2   German payments after World War I

Germany was obliged by the Treaty of Versailles in 1919 to pay reparations to the victorious nations after World War I.[8] However, the Allied nations could not agree on a total reparations sum at the Paris Peace Conference in 1919. As a practical solution to the resulting stalemate situation they asked the Germans to suggest a proposal for a settlement. The Allied nations hoped this procedure would lead to a speedy solution. Germany, quite understandably, tried to strike as hard a bargain as possible. A number of conferences were held to solve the

---

[8] This subsection is based on chapter 15 of Machlup (1966).

problem of calculating the total sum of the reparations. The climax of these conferences was reached in 1921 in London. Germany made an offer the Allied nations had to refuse and after an ultimatum this situation led to the occupation of three towns in the Ruhr. In April 1921 the Reparations Commission finally came up with a total figure. They recommended a total liability of 132 billion marks (6,600 million pounds) payable in annual installments of 2 billion marks (100 million pounds). This annual figure amounted to about 25 percent of German exports at the time, and also meant that the last installment had to be paid in 1988! Hesitantly, the Germans began paying their debt. This did not imply that they agreed to the huge reparations. On the contrary, the prime minister (Joseph Wirth) and the minister of reconstruction (Walter Rathenau) hoped that by attempting to pay the annual installments they could show their economic impossibility. At first Germany tried to pay the installments by borrowing on the international capital market, which led to a sharp fall of the mark in the exchange markets. Repeatedly the Germans asked for moratoria. Again the Allied nations could not agree and in 1923 French and Belgian troops entered the Ruhr in order to secure "productive guarantees." Germany stopped all payments and broke off all diplomatic relations. Workers went on strike in the Ruhr and the burden of paying wages to those on strike proved too formidable for the German economy; a period of hyperinflation started. At the beginning of 1923 a dollar was worth about 18,000 marks. In November, 4 billion marks had to be paid for a dollar! A detailed account of how all this helped to pave the way for Hitler can be found in Carr (1987).

Before 1924 payments were chiefly in kind (materials and equipment). These were, not surprisingly, appraised at low values by the recipients and at high values by Germany. The Dawes Plan of 1924 scheduled annual payments of increasing magnitude. After five years, the payments would also depend on an index measuring Germany's prosperity. This was revised in 1929 under the Young Plan. In response to the world depression of 1929 and dwindling world trade, actual payments were suspended in 1931 and officially stopped in June 1932. Table 1.4 presents payments statistics from 1925 to 1932.

In the early years, from 1925 to 1927, large amounts of foreign (mainly American) loans were received by Germany. The excess of these loans over the reparations payments could be used to incur import surpluses. After 1929, until the Hoover moratorium of 1931, reparations payments exceeded capital imports. In relative terms the demands imposed on the German economy do not seem exceptional. Indeed, if we compare the payments relative to either exports, imports or the trade volume in tables 1.2, 1.3 and 1.5 of Britain in 1796–1816, France in 1872–5 and Germany

Table 1.4. *German reparations payments 1925–32 (million Reichsmarks)*

	Payments in RM for deliveries in kind	Payments in RM for armies of occupation	Payments in foreign currencies	Total
1924–5	414	208	271	893
1925–6	658	102	416	1,176
1926–7	617	82	683	1,382
1927–8	725	71	943	1,739
1928–9	985	49	1,419	2,453
1929–30	515	32	728	1,275
1930–1	464		921	1,385
1931–2	214		747	961
Total				11,264

Note: Data are for "annuity years" ending July 31.
Source: Machlup 1966.

Table 1.5. *German foreign trade 1925–32, compared with reparations payments (annual averages in million Reichsmarks)*

	1925–8	1929–32
Exports	10,840	10,214
Imports	12,224	8,808
Trade volume	23,064	19,022
Trade balance	−1,384	1,406
Reparations payments	1,182	1,498
Reparations/exports	10.9%	14.7%
Reparations/imports	9.7%	17.0%
Reparations/trade volume	5.1%	7.9%

Note: Trade data are for calendar years. Reparations data are for "annuity years" ending on July 31 in the corresponding calendar year.
Source: Machlup 1966.

in 1925–32 the German payments show a relatively modest ratio. Machlup (1966, p. 385) even remarks: "It is hard to understand why some economists in the late 1920's made such a fuss about the supposed severity of the German transfer problem." This is, we think, a quite unfair criticism which does not take into consideration the exceptional circumstances of France in 1871 (see subsection 1.5.1), the dismal circumstances of Germany after the world depression in 1929 or the simple fact that under the Young Plan, German reparations payments were scheduled to continue until 1988.

1.5.3 Current German transfer problems

In the last decade of this century Germany is again involved in a substantial unilateral transfer payment. Depending on one's perspective this is either a national or an international transfer, since we are referring to the payments from western Germany to eastern Germany after the German unification following the destruction of the Berlin Wall. On July 1, 1990, some three months before the official reunification on October 3, 1990, the D-mark was introduced in the German Democratic Republic (the former East Germany) and this initiated the process of economic unification.

While eastern Germany had a population of about 26 percent of that of western Germany, its output was only 8 percent of the latter's in 1991 (Welfens 1992). The costs to both western and eastern Germany of the unification were initially seriously underestimated (Welfens 1992, p. 174). The transfers from west to east are large by any standard. Almost immediately from the start of the unification it became clear to the German government that the infrastructure, the communication system, the sewerage system and the maintenance of buildings in general needed a complete overhaul. It is estimated that the net transfers to the eastern part of Germany amount to 4.25 percent of the GDP of western Germany on an annual basis. From 1991 to 1995 almost DM 900 billion were transferred from the western to the eastern part.[9] At the date of political unification, October 3, 1990, it was widely expected that closing the east–west income gap in Germany would take less than a decade, because of the massive transfers. But at present, the expected time-frame for closing the intra-German income gap is several decades rather than one, because the initial gap between eastern and western Germany turned out to be much larger than had been expected; see Brakman and Garretsen (1994).

The transfers from western Germany to the new *Länder* were quite substantial from a western German perspective. Most of this was used to support investment and develop the infrastructure. For eastern Germany these transfers were truly enormous, namely some 70 percent of national income in 1991, leveling off to about 50 percent in 1994 (Association of German Economic Research Institutes 1991–5). Nonetheless, the costs of

---

[9] Deutsche Bundesbank, *Monatsbericht*, October 1996, p. 26.

Table 1.6. *Eastern Germany relative to western Germany (western Germany = 100) and transfers*

	1991	1992	1993	1994	1995	1996
GDP per capita (1991 prices)	31.1	38.0	42.7	44.6	45.4	45.4
Unemployment as percentage of labor force	—	224	199	170.3	173	168.1
Unit wage cost	145.3	139.3	131.7	129.8	130.6	132.4
Transfers from West to East (billion DM)	129	253	198	165	143	—

Source: Deutsche Bundesbank, *Saisonsbereinigte Wirtschaftszahlen, statistisches Beiheft zum Monatsbericht*, various issues.

unification were substantial for eastern Germany. After the collapse in 1990–1, resulting in high unemployment, a strong (relative) recovery started, but from 1994 the eastern German catching-up leveled off (see table 1.6). After the initial collapse, the eastern German economy as a whole performed well in the period 1991–4, certainly compared to western Germany. The size of the transfer was very large, especially for the recipients in the East. For example, each man, woman and child received about DM 15,000 in 1992. Undoubtedly, given the enormous transfers from western Germany for investment and infrastructure, the eastern German economy would have done much better if the East German mark had not been exchanged one-for-one for the West German mark (for details, see Welfens [1992]) and if there had not been a politically inspired decision forcefully to increase eastern German wages to the western German level within a certain time-frame. Both decisions resulted in very high relative unit wage costs. These two policy decisions, in conjunction with the transition process in eastern Germany itself, from a centrally planned economy to a market economy, make it extremely difficult to gauge the contribution of the transfer scheme to the economic and social well-being of eastern Germany.

1.6   Evaluation of some historical transfers

In the preceding sections we briefly discussed some of the well-known examples of war reparations. The most famous is, without doubt, the reparations payments following World War I, because it inspired Keynes to write his *Economic Consequences of the Peace* and led to the Keynes–Ohlin debate discussed in chapter 2. It would be a mistake to think that all the attention given to the German reparations implies that

Table 1.7. *Historical examples of transfers*

	Trade balance	Transfer (T)	T/exports	T/GNP
Great Britain				
1793–1805	n.a.	£3.0 m.	6.4%	1.0%
1796–1805	n.a.	£2.3 m.	4.9%	n.a.
1806–16	n.a.	£10.9 m.	20.1%	n.a
France				
1867–71	FF − 119 m.	n.a.	n.a.	n.a.
1872–75	FF 510 m.	FF 248 m.	30.0%	5.6%
Germany				
1925–28	RM − 1,384 m.	RM 1,182 m.	10.9%	2.5%[a]
1929–32	RM 1,406 m.	RM 1,498 m.	14.7%	2.5%[a]
1953–59	$914 m.	$233 m.	2.0%	0.6%
1959–65	$1,275 m.	$573 m.	3.8%	0.9%
West to East Germany				
1991–95	n.a.	DM 900 b.	n.a.	4.25%
Finland				
1944–48	n.a	OM 7,832 m.	n.a.	4.0%
1948–52	OM 17,200 m.	OM 10,446 m.	8.7%	2.2%
Italy				
1947–56	$ − 682 m.	$23 m.	0.015%	0.002%
1956–65	$ − 1,078 m.	$15 m.	0.004%	0.001%
Japan				
1955–60	$ − 559 m.	$45 m.	1.5%	0.002%
1960–65	$ − 833 m.	$63 m.	1.1%	0.001%
United States				
1950–55	$2.4 b.	$4.4 b.	29.0%	1.5%
1956–61	$4.4 b.	$7.0 b.	31.1%	1.8%
1962–67	$5.4 b.	$8.1 b.	25.4%	1.5%

Notes: The table shows averages over the respective periods. [a] 1924–32 average.
Source: Stern 1973, p. 258; and Deutsche Bundesbank for West to East German transfers.

the actual payments were very large compared to the other examples described above. Table 1.7 gives some additional examples, and relates these to the size of the donor's exports and national income (see also Viner 1924).

The table shows four examples of relatively large payments in relation to exports and national income: (i) the reparations paid by France to Germany in the period 1872–5; (ii) the Finnish payments to the Soviet Union in 1944–8; (iii) the foreign transfers by the United States, which has since World War II made large payments, consisting mostly of military spending abroad and foreign aid; and (iv) the transfers from western to eastern Germany. Italy and Japan have made some reparations payments, but they have been relatively small compared to exports and national income. In retrospect, it seems that the attention the German reparations received after World War I can to a large extent be explained by the fact that it inspired Keynes and Ohlin to discuss the matter, rather than by the size of the transfer itself.

1.7   From war reparations payments to foreign aid

After World War II attention to transfers was no longer focused on reparations and balance-of-payments issues. The literature on balance-of-payments disequilibria shifted towards analyses with Mundell–Fleming-type models and related exercises with exchange rate models. These models could easily analyze the consequences of transfers and the debate between Keynes and Ohlin could simply be resolved by applying these models to transfers (this also implies that most economists thought that Ohlin was right and Keynes was wrong, because in the Mundell–Fleming-type models spending effects dominate the analyses).[10] At the same time, war reparations as such were not different from transfers in general and were sufficiently small that a separate analysis seemed unnecessary. What became important was that, in the slipstream of the decolonization process, the former colonial powers felt an obligation to give development aid (see, for example, Abrams and Lewis [1993] and Ansari and Singer [1982]). One of the first major examples was the aid given by the United States as a result of the Economic Cooperation Act of 1948, better known as the Marshall Plan. The main aim of the United States was to help its allies with reconstructing their economies after World War II. Many European countries received aid; from 1948 to 1954 the United States donated a total of $15 billion of which $13 billion was in the form of gifts. The remainder consisted mainly of loans. The Marshall aid per capita averaged about $39 for all recipients combined.[11]

The main objective of aid programs is to increase welfare in the developing world. The analysis therefore shifted from balance-of-payments issues to the welfare effects of transfers. This problem is also

---

[10] As will be made clear in the next chapter both types of reasoning, the classical and the Keynesian, are incomplete.

[11] See De Nederlandse Bank (1954, p.158). In a private correspondence on this matter, Jan Pen argues that the official figures understate the importance of Marshall aid for the recipients. First, the aid was at official parity, while the market value of the dollar was much higher. Second, Europe was confronted with a solvency constraint which threatened to severely hamper its imports. This constraint was removed or alleviated by Marshall aid.

Table 1.8. *Ten largest donors of net official development assistance (\$ billions); percentage of GNP shown in parentheses*

	1964	1974	1979	1984	1989	1994
Japan	0.1 (0.1)	1.1 (0.2)	2.7 (0.3)	4.3 (0.3)	9.0 (0.3)	13.2 (0.3)
United States	3.6 (0.6)	3.4 (0.2)	4.7 (0.2)	8.7 (0.2)	7.7 (0.2)	9.9 (0.2)
France	0.8 (0.9)	1.6 (0.6)	3.4 (0.6)	3.8 (0.8)	5.8 (0.8)	8.5 (0.6)
Germany	0.5 (0.4)	1.4 (0.4)	3.4 (0.5)	2.8 (0.5)	4.9 (0.4)	6.8 (0.3)
United Kingdom	0.5 (0.5)	0.7 (0.4)	2.2 (0.5)	1.4 (0.3)	2.6 (0.3)	3.2 (0.3)
Italy	0.0 (0.1)	0.2 (0.1)	0.3 (0.1)	1.1 (0.3)	3.6 (0.4)	2.7 (0.3)
Netherlands	0.0 (0.3)	0.4 (0.6)	1.5 (1.0)	1.3 (1.0)	2.1 (0.9)	2.5 (0.8)
Canada	0.1 (0.2)	0.7 (0.5)	1.1 (0.5)	1.6 (0.5)	2.3 (0.4)	2.3 (0.4)
Sweden	0.0 (0.2)	0.4 (0.7)	1.0 (1.0)	0.7 (0.8)	1.8 (1.0)	1.8 (1.0)
Australia	0.1 (0.5)	0.4 (0.6)	0.6 (0.5)	0.8 (0.5)	1.0 (0.4)	1.1 (0.4)

Note: Figures also include donations to multilateral organizations.
Source: OECD, Development Assistance Committee, *Development Co-operation*, various issues.

central in this book. In table 1.8 we give some data on development aid in recent years for the ten largest donors.

This shows that the largest donors are to be found among the "old" industrial powers. Large countries contribute the most, but relatively small countries like the Netherlands, Sweden and Australia also belong among the largest donors. Over time, Japan has become the largest donor in absolute terms, rising from a share of 2% in 1964 to 25% in 1994. It took over the first place from the United States, which fell from a share of 62% in 1964 to 19% in 1994. Comparing the data with United Nations Resolution No. 2626, which states that the developed countries should give at least 0.7 % of GNP in development assistance, it follows that only the small donors comply with the resolution (also among these countries are Norway and Denmark). This promise was renewed by the European Union donors at the "Earth Summit + 5" Conference held in New York in 1997.

Table 1.9 shows receiving countries, aggregated into larger areas. This clearly demonstrates that the largest recipients are to be found among the poorest regions in the world. Africa South of the Sahara, for example, received roughly a third of official development assistance in 1994. This is, of course, to be expected. The same holds *grosso modo* within each region: the poorest nations within a region receive the largest sum of development aid. The two tables together suggest that the main purpose of transfers is to relieve the burden of poverty in the poorest regions in

Table 1.9. *Total net development assistance from DAC countries, including multilateral organizations ($ billions)*

	1969	1974	1979	1984	1989	1994
Europe	0.3	0.1	0.8	0.4	0.4	2.2
Africa, North of Sahara	0.3	1.5	2.4	2.5	2.5	3.9
Africa, South of Sahara	1.3	2.7	6.7	8.2	14.8	18.9
North & Central America	0.3	0.6	1.6	2.3	2.6	3.2
South America	0.5	0.7	0.9	1.1	1.8	2.5
Middle East	0.2	1.5	5.1	3.5	2.3	4.4
South & Central Asia	1.4	2.8	4.1	4.6	6.3	7.9
Far East Asia	1.5	2.3	2.2	2.9	6.3	8.4
Oceania	0.2	0.5	0.9	1.0	1.4	1.8
LDCs unspecified	0.4	1.3	4.8	4.8	7.7	7.8
Total	6.3	14.1	29.5	31.1	46.1	60.9

Source: OECD, Development Assistance Committee, *Development Co-operation*, various issues.

the world, that is the objective is to increase the recipients' welfare. Moreover, donors and recipients can be found all over the world.

Finally, we want to point out that international transfers are also made within institutionalized frameworks other than the United Nations, the World Bank or the International Monetary Fund. The European Union (EU), for example, levies contributions from its fifteen members which, after the deduction of operating expenses, are redistributed among the members (Grilli and Riess 1992). This redistribution in essence leads to international unilateral transfers and is mainly based on (i) agricultural policy and (ii) structural funds to assist poorer regions. Table 1.10 gives an overview of the share of the total funds the member countries contribute to and receive from the EU. Germany and the Netherlands are (relatively) the largest net contributors, both paying about twice as much as they receive. Greece, Spain, Ireland and Portugal are (relatively) the largest net recipients, each receiving more than twice as much as they contribute.

For the relatively largest net recipients, the transfers from the EU can be substantial, certainly if we compare their relative size with the evaluation of the historical transfers in section 1.6 (see the last column of table 1.7). Ireland, for example, contributed on average 1.5 percent of its GNP annually to the EU in the period 1990–6, while receiving on average 7.1 percent of its GNP annually from the EU in the same period. Over these seven years net receipts were therefore equal to 7.1–1.5=5.6

Table 1.10. *Payments in the European Union 1996 (percentages of total)*

	contribution to EU	receipts from EU
Austria	2.6	2.4
Belgium	3.9	3.1
Denmark	1.9	2.3
Finland	1.4	1.5
France	17.5	17.7
Germany	29.2	14.8
Greece	1.6	7.6
Ireland	1.0	4.4
Italy	12.7	11.4
Luxemburg	0.2	0.2
Netherlands	6.2	3.0
Portugal	1.2	5.4
Spain	6.4	15.6
Sweden	2.8	1.9
United Kingdom	11.6	8.8

Source: European Commission.

percent of GNP annually. According to the International Monetary Fund (1997, pp. 62–3) these substantial net transfers from the EU explain at least partly the impressive growth performance of Ireland in the 1990s.

1.8 Conclusion

In this chapter, we briefly discussed international unilateral transfers and gave a broad overview of the evolution of its discussion in economic terms over time. Different transfers gave rise to various discussions: from balance-of-payments problems during the Napoleonic wars to the welfare implications of aid. As we shall see later, these issues can be analyzed within a single consistent framework. We concluded by giving an overview of some of the best-known international transfers and the current size and structure of official development assistance.

2   The Keynes–Ohlin controversy

2.1 Introduction

The undisputed highlight among controversies involving international transfers is the discussion in 1929 between the Englishman John Maynard Keynes and the Swedish economist Bertil Ohlin. In March of that year Keynes published an article in the *Economic Journal*, of which he was editor. Keynes argued that the reparations payments imposed on Germany after World War I were too high a burden on the German economy. According to Keynes the required price and cost cuts for the German export sector were virtually impossible to achieve. Bertil Ohlin responded in the same journal later the same year by claiming that only limited export price changes, or none at all, were necessary for the expansion of the German export sector.

For a long time, starting with David Hume and John Stuart Mill and continuing up to the beginning of this century, changes in price levels played the predominant role in economic analyses in bringing about the necessary adjustment of trade balances following a transfer from one country to another. This partial equilibrium analysis ignored an important equilibrating factor: the influence of income changes in the paying and receiving countries on the demand for goods. As we shall see later, the changed demand for goods due to income changes as a result of a transfer might make relative price changes entirely unnecessary under certain circumstances. Bertil Ohlin was the main catalyst for this realization, notably in his heated debate with John Maynard Keynes.[1]

---

[1] The reader should not be confused in this chapter by the fact that in the discussion on the transfer problem Keynes himself still acted as a classical economist (Garretsen 1992; Skidelsky 1992), instead of as a "Keynesian" economist.

2.2   The issues in the debate

2.2.1 Keynes's original argument

In a classic paper in the March 1929 issue of the *Economic Journal*
Keynes argues that the reparations payments demanded from
Germany after World War I impose a heavy burden on the battered
German economy. In principle, Keynes (1929a, p. 2, our emphasis)
acknowledges the fact that: "*If £1 is taken from you and given to me
and I choose to increase my consumption of precisely the same goods as
those of which you are compelled to diminish yours, there is no Transfer
Problem.*"

However, he claims that the Germans, in transferring funds, do not
choose to diminish consumption in precisely the same goods as the
recipients of the transfer, say the English, choose to increase theirs as
a result of receiving the transfer. He points, in particular, at the small
proportion of German goods consumed by the English (on the
limitations of such observations, see section 2.3.2). Added to this
observation Keynes notes that one of the main problems of Germany
is that:

For the last two or three years the Transfer Problem has been temporarily solved
by Germany borrowing abroad ... Clearly this process of borrowing abroad
cannot go on indefinitely ... when foreign borrowing (of Germany) comes to an
end, it will be a question, not of reducing current consumption in Germany, but
of transferring labour from capital works in Germany to the export trades ...
where the outcome of capital improvements ... is not in exportable form (and
much of it will not be in such a form), the diversion of production out of other
employments into export trades ... will have to be on a greater scale than is
required by the payment of the Reparations alone ... (p. 3)

Keynes concludes that:

the solution of the Transfer Problem must come about, in the main, not by the
release to foreign consumers of goods now consumed by Germans (e.g. wheat,
sugar, cotton), but by the diversion of German factors of production from other
employments into the export industries. (p. 3)

The diversion of German factors of production from other uses in
other sectors to the export industries should, according to Keynes's
calculations, raise the value of German exports by some 40 percent. This,
he argues, is simply impossible if the price elasticity of demand is less
than unity, for then a cut in the price of German export goods reduces
rather than raises the value of exports. Even if the price elasticity of
demand for German export goods exceeds unity, Keynes claims, the
required price, and hence cost, cuts are so large that they are virtually

impossible to achieve: "if a reduction in price of 10 per cent. stimulates the volume of trade by 20 per cent., this does not increase the value of the exports by 20 per cent., but only by 8 per cent. (1.20 × 0.90 = 1.08)." (p. 5)

2.2.2   Ohlin's critique

Ohlin criticizes Keynes's argument and conclusion in the preceding subsection in the June issue of the *Economic Journal*.[2] He makes two general points which are of interest to us. First, he notes that past observations of imports and exports for Germany cannot be used to gauge whether or not it is difficult for Germany to create an export surplus large enough to fulfill the needs of the reparations payments. This follows from the simple fact that Germany had until that time been borrowing more capital from abroad than required for the reparations payments such that, if anything, a reverse transfer had taken place (see subsections 1.5.2 and 2.2.1). Second, and most importantly, Ohlin (1929a, p. 172) writes: "His reasoning ignores, however, one very important side of the problem."

This very important side of the problem is the change in the conditions of the demand for goods which might suffice to produce the required export surplus and, in any case, does not presume the necessity for a reduction in the price of export goods. It is surprising that Keynes, who will put so much emphasis on the demand side of the economy in the *General Theory* (1936), almost completely ignores changes in demand conditions when analyzing the transfer problem. At this point we simply emphasize that the price elasticity of (excess) demand is *not* the factor determining the direction of the change in the terms of trade, but income elasticity is (as implied by Ohlin). In retrospect, it is also clear that the Keynes–Ohlin discussion would have been much simpler and more transparent if the authors had used a simple economic model to convey their main arguments. Moreover, the discussion is clouded by empirical observations which are not crucial to the issue at hand, such as Keynes's emphasis on the small proportion of foreign goods consumed by the Germans (on this, see section 2.3.2) and both Keynes's and Ohlin's attention to the importance of non-traded goods (on this, see chapter 4). With respect to the latter, Ohlin's conclusion regarding the importance of the presence of non-traded goods for the terms-of-trade effect of a transfer is also correct (1929a, p. 174):

---

[2] The transfer problem had already caught the attention of Ohlin (1928a).

Home market prices tend to rise in A [the recipient] and fall in B [the donor], relative to prices of export and import goods and prices of the goods which compete with import goods ... It is not necessary that A's *export* prices should rise and B's fall. Thus, B need not offer its goods on cheaper terms of trade to induce A to take a greater quantity of them. Indirectly, however, it is probable that a certain shift of the terms of exchange will take place.

2.2.3   Keynes's reply

Keynes wrote a reply to Ohlin's critique in the same issue of the *Economic Journal*. He was uneasy with the fact that the discussion moved to theoretical aspects of the problem, whereas he was more concerned with its practical side.[3] He partially agrees with Ohlin that there will be income effects to take into consideration (1929b, p. 181):

In so far as Germany can, for my reasons, pay Reparations without borrowing, these payments will, it is true, react on the levels of income abroad, causing them to move slightly upwards. Not necessarily by the full amount, because the increase in German exports may be partly at the expense of unemployment amongst her competitors and of using their resources less effectively.

The total absence of positive multiplier effects, indeed rather the suggestion of negative multiplier effects, in Keynes's arguments so shortly before the publication of the *General Theory* is quite remarkable. Indeed, the fact that Keynes in the discussion of the transfer problem followed the classical or orthodox view, and not what was later to be called the "Keynesian" model, has, quite understandably, been cause for confusion. In view of the minimal importance granted by Keynes to Ohlin's income effects in the quotation above it is not surprising that he does not change his mind (1929b, p. 181): "I conclude, therefore, as before, that Germany must mainly depend, particularly in the first instance, on cutting her prices ... ".

2.2.4   Ohlin's rebuttal

The September issue of the *Economic Journal* again addresses the transfer problem. Ohlin (1929b) seems to lose his patience with Keynes, as his tone of voice shows irritation: "Is it not obvious that the buying power of a country, like that of an individual, will exceed its (his) income by the amount of gifts and loans, quite independently of any price changes? Mr. Keynes' answer to this question is in the negative ... To make clear why I think this is profoundly wrong ... " (p. 400).

---

[3] In his final reply to Ohlin, Keynes writes (1929c, p. 404): "the controversy ... moves quite inevitably, from the particular (German war-reparation case) to the general."

Ohlin argues that Keynes focuses attention almost exclusively on the supply side of the economy and, like Keynes before him, does not change his mind: "In conclusion, therefore, I must uphold my contention that reactions on the demand side play their very important part in the mechanism of international capital movements just as well as reactions on the supply side." (p. 403)

2.2.5   Other participants

Other authors, usually at somewhat later stages and inspired by Keynes and Ohlin, also contribute to the discussion and analysis of the transfer problem. In the September 1929 issue of the *Economic Journal*, Jacques Rueff (1929) argues that there is no transfer problem and gives France as an example:

the decision suddenly taken by Great Britain and the United States at the beginning of 1919 to cease granting France the sterling and dollar credits which had previously enabled France's balance of payments to be kept in equilibrium ... removed from the credit side of this balance of accounts an item of approximately 20 milliards of francs ... If this had been so [that is, if Keynes were right], the deficit in France's balance of payments would have been approximately 20 milliards of francs per annum. The facts show, however, that this was by no means the case. In 1919 the deficit in France's commercial balance was approximately 23 milliards of francs. In 1920 it was approximately the same. But in 1921 it had been reduced to approximately 2 milliards of francs, and remained more or less at that level during 1922 and 1923. (p. 392)

In retrospect, Rueff's contribution is most interesting for the remark in which he argues, contrary to Keynes, that: "the commercial balance has shown a tendency to adjust itself to the necessities of the balance of payments, whatever they might be and whatever their origin." (p. 394)

This makes Rueff an early advocate of the monetary approach to the balance of payments. After further discussing the history of France, he concludes: "What is remarkable in the case of France after 1870 is that a surplus appeared in the commercial balance at precisely the moment when theory would lead one to expect it. This only constitutes a presumption – but a very strong presumption – in favor of the said theory." (p. 395)

In the period following the Keynes–Ohlin discussion various authors develop the terminology that a transfer can be "overeffected" or "under-effected," as explained in the appendix to this chapter. Pigou (1932, 1950) holds on to the "orthodox view" and argues that a "secondary burden," that is a deterioration of the paying country's terms of trade, is "extremely likely." His argument is, however, largely based on the *a priori* assumption that both countries are completely specialized in the production of one good. This is pointed out by Elliot (1938), who in addition draws attention to non-traded goods (called domestic goods) and third parties. As we shall see later, Elliot is wrong on both counts since he argues that the presence of third parties without non-traded goods makes no difference (see, on the contrary, chapter 6), and that the presence of non-traded goods makes the orthodox view more likely (see, however, chapter 4).

2.3 Some problems resolved

This section clarifies two important points. First, we argue (subsection 2.3.1) that the confusion between Keynes and Ohlin on the effects of an international transfer arises from implicit reasoning within a partial equilibrium framework. Second, we demonstrate (subsection 2.3.2) that Keynes's observation that only a small proportion of foreign goods is consumed by the Germans, and similar observations by many other authors, are not relevant for the analytical question to be addressed.

2.3.1 *Partial equilibrium*

We give here a rudimentary graphical analysis. A more exact analysis, including many complications, can be found in subsequent chapters. Consider the excess-demand curves in figure 2.1. The downward-sloping curve D_0D_0 represents Foreign's net demand for Home's export goods, while the upward-sloping curve S_0S_0 represents Home's supply of such goods. In the absence of any transfers the market equilibrium occurs at point E_0 with a price for Home's export goods at P_0. Suppose that Home (that is, its government) wants to transfer 4 units to Foreign. This could be represented in figure 2.1 as a rightward shift of the S curve by 4 units. We do not follow that approach but instead require a gap between S and D of 4 units.

Keynes follows the classical partial equilibrium reasoning that such a transfer requires a substantial deterioration of Home's terms of trade along the old D_0D_0 and S_0S_0 curves from P_0 to P_{Keynes}. Thus, the transferring country, in the terminology of John Stuart Mill, "besides losing what it pays, loses also something more, by the less advantageous terms on which it is forced to exchange its production for foreign commodities." It is obvious, as argued by Keynes in subsection 2.2.1, that the price elasticity of net demand is crucial in determining the required size of the export price cut.

Ohlin, on the contrary, emphasizes the shift in net demand and (to a

Price

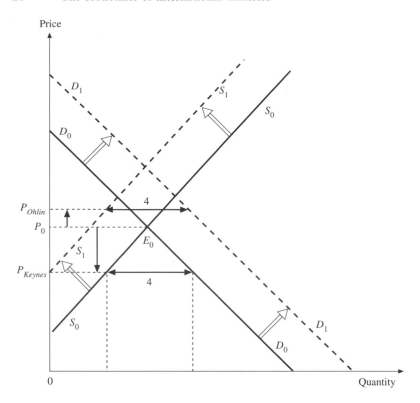

Figure 2.1   *Keynes and Ohlin compared*

lesser extent) net supply curves as a result of the transfer of purchasing power. Thus, Foreign's demand for Home's export good increases as a result of the increase in income, which in figure 2.1 shifts curve D_0D_0 to D_1D_1, while curve S_0S_0 shifts to S_1S_1. Consequently, in figure 2.1, the price of Home's export good rises from P_0 to P_{Ohlin} rather than falling from P_0 to P_{Keynes}. Obviously, whether or not the price of Home's export good rises or falls depends on the extent of the shift of the D and S curves. These shifts, in turn, depend on the propensity to consume Home's export good and not on the price elasticity of demand.

2.3.2   Small expenditure on foreign goods

Suppose there are two countries, Home and Foreign, which both produce two goods, guns and butter. The price of both guns and butter is 1. Home produces 30 guns and 70 butter, while Foreign produces 50

Table 2.1. *Production and consumption patterns*

	Pre-transfer					
	Production		Consumption		Export guns	Income
	Guns	Butter	Guns	Butter		
Home	30	70	40	60	−10	100
Foreign	50	50	40	60	10	100
	Post-transfer					
	Production		Consumption		Export guns	Income
	Guns	Butter	Guns	Butter		
Home	30	70	38	57	−8	95
Foreign	50	50	42	63	8	105

guns and 50 butter. Both Home and Foreign consume 40 guns and 60 butter. Obviously, this implies that Home exports 10 butter to Foreign and imports 10 guns. The information is summarized in Table 2.1.

We assume that both Home and Foreign always spend 40 percent of their income on guns and 60 percent of their income on butter. It is important to note that Home (and Foreign, for that matter) spends only a small fraction (10 percent) of its income on Foreign's goods. Now suppose that, for whatever reason, Home transfers 5 units of its income to Foreign. At the old unity prices this fall in income level for Home (from 100 to 95) reduces Home's demand for guns by 2 and for butter by 3. At the same time Foreign, which receives Home's transfer, has a rise in income (from 100 to 105) which increases its demand for guns by 2 and for butter by 3. Evidently, the total world demand for guns and butter remains the same such that no change in prices (of guns or butter) or production level (at Home or in Foreign) whatsoever is required. Only the final trade flows differ, because Home now exports 13 butter in exchange for 8 guns, where 5 units of butter are given to Foreign as a transfer. It is also obvious that the fact that before the transfer Home only spends 10 percent of its income on Foreign's goods is entirely irrelevant. The crucial parameters are the marginal propensities to consume guns and butter at Home and in Foreign. In this respect we advise the reader to re-read Keynes's first quote in subsection 2.2.1.

2.4 Conclusions

The debate between Keynes and Ohlin is important for two reasons. First, it led to a systematic treatment of the transfer problem (Metzler

1942). Second, it showed that the discussion was not as instructive as it could have been. The lack of a formal analysis of the problem made the discussion unnecessarily complicated. A formal treatment could have led to an agreement between the participants in the discussion. Keynes had trouble in admitting, or so it seems, that his analysis failed to include income effects of transfers. This was pointed out forcefully by Ohlin. Historically, the debate ended in the sense that Ohlin's insights were incorporated into "Keynesian" Mundell–Fleming type models, which stress income effects and balance-of-payments issues. Both the classical (that is Keynes's) and the Keynesian (that is Ohlin's) analyses are partial equilibrium ones (see also the appendix to this chapter and chapter 3).

2.A   Appendix: over- and undereffected transfers

The debate between Keynes and Ohlin was about the balance-of-payments consequences of transfers. The debate ended in favor of Ohlin and in later analyses the effects of transfers were usually analyzed in demand-type (that is "Keynesian") models, like the Mundell–Fleming model and variants thereof. The "transfer problem," as it is known in this type of analysis, consists of calculating whether or not a transfer results in a balance-of-payments disequilibrium (known as the primary burden). If so, some equilibrium-restoring mechanism must start to work. Usually, the terms of trade must change (known as the secondary burden). There are in principle three possible cases (all from the donor's point of view):

- The donor's trade balance (in the absence of interest payments) improves by less than the amount of the transfer. The current account deteriorates and the transfer is called *undereffected*.
- The donor's trade balance improves exactly by the amount of the transfer. The current account balances and the transfer is called *effected*.
- Finally, the donor's trade balance improves by more than the amount of the transfer. The current account improves and the transfer is called *overeffected*.

The transfer problem consists of an analysis of the conditions which lead to one of these possibilities. The standard literature distinguishes between two types of models: classical and Keynesian.

The classical model assumes that prices are constant. Furthermore, income is completely spent on goods, that is, nothing is saved or invested. How will the balance of trade change in such a model, which consists of two goods: numéraire x and y?

Assume that μ_x^A is donor A's marginal propensity to consume good x, which it imports, and μ_y^B is the recipient B's marginal propensity to consume good y. Three effects can be distinguished: the initial deterioration of A's current account due to the transfer T, an improvement due to the reduction of the donor's imports $\mu_x^A T$, and an increase of A's exports of good y due to the income transfer $\mu_y^B T$. The change of the current account of country A, ΔTB, thus equals

$$\Delta TB = -T + \mu_x^A T + \mu_y^B T = T(\mu_x^A + \mu_y^B - 1)$$

Depending on whether $\mu_x^A + \mu_y^B \lesseqgtr 1$, the transfer is over-, under- or exactly effected. In the case where a transfer is not exactly effected the terms of trade will have to change in order to restore equilibrium.

In the Keynesian analysis it is no longer necessary that the income changes in both countries correspond to the amount of the transfer. It is, for example, possible that the donor's savings diminish to "finance" part of the transfer, or that the recipient's savings increase in order to absorb part of the transfer. These income changes give rise to multiplier effects, both for the donor and the recipient. The change of the current account in the donor country equals

$$\Delta TB = -T + \mu_x^A \Delta Y^A + \mu_y^B \Delta Y^B$$

where ΔY^A and ΔY^B are the income changes in both countries following the transfer. These terms depend on the multipliers in the model and can be quite complicated, depending on the level of sophistication of the model in use. As in the classical model, some adjustment process starts if the transfer is not effected. For example, an exchange rate adjustment, which changes the relative prices between the donor and the recipient, may take place.

Both models assume that the transfer problem can be split into two distinct phases for analysis, the first being the effect on the balance of trade and the second the adjustment mechanism to restore equilibrium, usually a terms-of-trade change. This procedure is not valid for large transfers and the corresponding large terms-of-trade effects (as transfers will only rarely be effected). The analyses performed are thus not truly marginal comparative analyses, because in both types of models terms-of-trade changes (or exchange rate changes) will have some effect on the marginal propensities to consume and therefore on the conditions for the over-/undereffectiveness of transfers themselves (see also Dixit and Norman [1980, p. 256]). A correct analysis should incorporate the adjustment channels right from the beginning.

3   Welfare effects: Samuelson's theorem

3.1   Transfers: more than a balance-of-payments problem

The appendix of the preceding chapter discussed over- or undereffected transfers, that is whether or not there is excess demand or supply at given prices, which results in a secondary burden if markets have to clear. The initial motivation for this research was the fear that transfers could lead to serious balance-of-payments difficulties in the donor country. After World War II this issue became less important, although it was still in the mind of many economists; see, for example, Johnson (1955, 1956). The dominant reason for making international transfers is no longer war reparations payments but development assistance. The old colonial powers feel obliged to help their former colonies and other less developed countries on the path to development. The relevant question with respect to the effects of international transfers therefore shifts from whether or not the donor has difficulties in financing the transfer to whether or not the recipient benefits from the gift. A related question is, of course, what the welfare effects are for the donor.

Development aid has two basic functions: first, to give a "big push" to the developing world or, to put it differently, to set a country on the path to self-sustained growth; and second, to alleviate poverty in the receiving countries. The latter function of aid will be the main topic of this chapter. We do not define "poverty" explicitly, but assume that the poverty problem is alleviated if the recipient's welfare level rises as a result of the transfer. We therefore ignore the many (inequality) problems underlying the microeconomic foundation for this macroeconomic concept (see, however, chapter 7). The donor transfers a part of its income to the recipient. We derive the welfare effects of such transfers in a systematic and unified general equilibrium framework. The reader should bear in mind that the analysis is basically static, although it can be given a rudimentary dynamic interpretation; see below and chapter

10. The amount of the transfer can be varied at the policy maker's will. Markets are competitive and complete. Furthermore, we abstract from problems of aggregation over households, which might arise with the introduction of "social" or economy-wide utility functions; basically, we assume households to be identical. This means that we do not address some important issues, such as the "optimal timing" of aid, whether aid can be used to stimulate growth, distributional effects which might arise when many different types of households are considered and whether or not the recipient can "absorb" the transfer, no matter how big the transfer is. We therefore concentrate purely on the welfare analysis of transfers within a comparative static framework.

The main method of analysis throughout the remainder of this book will be the so-called duality approach; see, for example, Silberberg (1990). This approach uses the fact that there is a fundamental relationship between technical possibilities and economic decision-making, such as between production functions and cost functions and between utility functions and expenditure functions. For example, if we are given a (technical) production function and define the (economic) cost function as the minimum cost to produce a certain level of production at given input prices, then it is in principle possible, if we only have the cost function, to retrieve the concomitant production function; see, for example, Varian (1992, ch. 1). In this respect the cost function not only summarizes all relevant economic information, but also incorporates the technological structure underlying the economic decisions. Using the dual functions (the cost function, the revenue function or the expenditure function) is usually simpler than working with production functions or utility functions. The mathematical appendix to this book states the most important duality results, while the appendix to this chapter relates these results to *net* demand and offer curves.

We address the following questions in this chapter. Do international transfers affect the terms of trade and the recipient's or donor's welfare level? The analysis demonstrates that the Keynes–Ohlin discussion (chapter 2) was unnecessarily complicated as a result of the lack of a clear mathematical formulation of the problem. It is relatively straightforward to shed light on the Keynes–Ohlin debate in a duality framework. There are in principle two effects associated with an international transfer: a direct income effect (the transfer of purchasing power) and a change in the terms of trade. In particular, we show that any difference in spending pattern between donor and recipient results in terms of trade adjustments (see also Li and Mayer [1990]). This change in the terms-of-trade can be in the donor's favor. This raises the following important question: if the terms of trade change in favor of the donor as a result of the transfer can the extent of this gain be so large as to improve the donor's welfare and/or worsen the recipient's welfare? That is, can it dominate the direct income effect? If so, why and under what circumstances? The first economist to pose and answer this question was Wasily Leontief.

3.2   The transfer paradox: Leontief's example

The analysis of the economic consequences of international transfers has been greatly stimulated by paradoxical examples. One of the first of such examples was given by Leontief (1936). His aim was to shed light on the potentially paradoxical welfare effects of a transfer of purchasing power. Other examples are given in chapter 6.

Leontief makes ample use of rather cumbersome tables. For ease of exposition his example is translated into figure 3.1. Consider two countries, A and B, consuming and producing two goods, meat and wheat. Country A makes a transfer to country B equal to the *value* of one unit of meat, collected and distributed in a non-distortive lump-sum fashion. The inhabitants of country A are not in any way compensated for their gift, and other reactions, such as reduced savings or investments to compensate for the loss in spending power, are ruled out. The same holds, necessary changes being made, for country B. The supply of money is constant in both economies so that the total value of traded quantities before and after the transfer must be the same. Furthermore, markets clear at all times.

As indicated in figure 3.1, the pre-transfer production points for wheat and meat are $P_0^A = (8, 13)$ for country A and $P_0^B = (10, 5)$ for country B, respectively. Similarly, the pre-transfer consumption points for wheat and meat are $C_0^A = (13, 8)$ for country A and $C_0^B = (5, 10)$ for country B. The pre-transfer relative price of meat in terms of wheat is 1. Since there are no distortions in this perfectly competitive economy the budget lines for countries A and B are tangential to the production possibility curves and indifference curves.

As also indicated in figure 3.1, the post-transfer production points for wheat and meat are $P_1^A = (6, 14\frac{1}{2})$ for country A and $P_1^B = (8, 6)$ for country B. The post-transfer consumption points for wheat and meat are $C_1^A = (13, 11\frac{3}{4})$ for country A and $C_1^B = (1, 8\frac{3}{4})$ for country B. The post-transfer relative price of meat in terms of wheat is 4. The income (= revenue) line generated by the production level in country A, which is tangential to country A's production possibility curve AA', is one unit of meat above A's expenditure line, which is tangential to A's indifference curve U^{A1}, because of the transfer of the equivalent of one unit of meat from A to B. This is indicated by the downward arrow in figure 3.1.

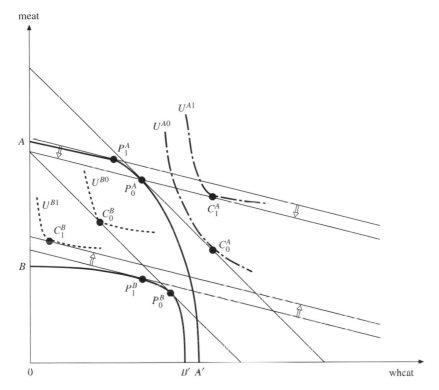

Figure 3.1   *Leontief's example of a transfer paradox*

Similarly, the revenue line generated by the production level in country
B, which is tangential to B's production possibility curve BB', is one unit
of meat below B's expenditure line, which is tangential to B's indifference
curve U^{B1}, because of the receipt of the equivalent of one unit of meat
from A. This is indicated by the upward arrow in figure 3.1.

Several important observations follow from Leontief's example. We
start by listing a few in its favor. The donor *gains* rather than loses from
the transfer because he is consuming the same amount of wheat and
more meat after the transfer. The recipient, on the other hand, *loses*
rather than gains from the transfer because he is consuming less of both
wheat and meat after the transfer. These two counter-intuitive results, for
this reason termed "paradoxes," have attracted a lot of attention.[1] The

---

[1] Sometimes the literature distinguishes between "weak" and "strong" paradoxes. A "weak"
paradox occurs if *either* the donor gains *or* the recipient loses, but not both simultaneously.
A "strong" paradox occurs if both the donor gains *and* the recipient loses.

reason for these paradoxes is that the relative price increase of meat favors the country which produces and exports a lot of meat, in this case country A. Note that the paradoxes do not arise from distortions in the economy. The utility functions and production possibility curves, which were not given by Leontief but drawn in by us, can satisfy a number of restrictions (see also Leontief [1936, p. 88, n. 2]). For example, the production possibility curve is concave, thus the production possibility set is convex, while the utility functions are increasing in both arguments and quasi-concave, such that the upper contour sets are convex.

To its disadvantage the Leontief example appears rather contrived for a number of reasons. The paradox of donor-enrichment and recipient-impoverishment results from an enormous change in the terms of trade as a result of the transfer, beneficial to the donor and detrimental to the recipient. The transfer of less than 2.8 percent of the world's income when evaluated at pre-transfer prices (or less than 4.2 percent of the world's income when evaluated at post-transfer prices) has resulted in a 400 percent increase in the relative price of meat! While this enormous price change has only a minuscule effect on the production points, as a consequence of the almost-kinked nature of the production possibility curves at the initial equilibrium, it has a large effect on the consumption points. In particular, even though the relative price of meat has increased fourfold both countries consume relatively more meat after the transfer than before. This peculiar and strongly non-homothetic nature of the countries' preferences, arising from strong income effects, is the source of the problem, as will become apparent later. It is also important to observe that Leontief's example involves substitution effects. This is in sharp contrast to Gale's example; see section 6.2. As pointed out in section 3.4 below, in a two-country world substitution effects in either production or consumption are necessary to get any welfare changes at all for donor or recipient as a result of a transfer.

> **Example 1** (Leontief) It is possible to construct an example involving two goods and two countries under perfect competition such that a transfer from one country to the other paradoxically benefits the donor and hurts the recipient.

3.3   Samuelson's claim

Exactly how contrived is Leontief's example in the previous section? The answer was given by Paul Samuelson. Perhaps the single most important result in the theory of unilateral transfers is what we will call the

"Samuelson theorem." This theorem states that in a perfect-equilibrium, two-good, two-country, distortion-free world a transfer will always reduce the donor's welfare and increase the recipient's welfare, provided the equilibrium is Walrasian-stable. Thus, this theorem implies that Leontief's example requires markets to be unstable. This was stated for the first time, by Samuelson (1947) on page 29 in a footnote (!), as follows:

Professor Leontief has produced a numerical example illustrating the possibility that a unilateral payment from one country to another may so shift the terms of trade in favor of the *paying* country as to cause it to be better rather than worse off as a result of the transfer . . . The example is carefully framed so as to guarantee indifference curves of the proper curvature for both countries. However, if one sets up an analytical system, along the lines of the numerical example, one will find that the *Leontief effect* can only happen for a system in which an increase in demand for a commodity lowers rather than raises its price. If the latter phenomenon is ruled out as being anomalous, or incompatible with stability (defined arbitrarily or in terms of a dynamic set up), then we can by the same action rule out the possibility of the *Leontief effect*.

The "dynamic set up" referred to in this quotation can be set up along the lines of Samuelson (1941); see subsection 3.4.1.

3.4   Samuelson's theorem: the model

Samuelson (1947) does not prove his claim that the donor loses and the recipient gains as a result of a transfer. Many years later, Mundell (1960) provides a complete proof, while Kemp (1964, p. 89, n. 11) wants the result derived in an exercise problem (see also Kemp [1992, 1995] and, for an early treatment, Jones [1970, 1975]). With the assistance of duality theory it is straightforward to prove Samuelson's claim. The reader is referred to the mathematical appendix to the book for general results in duality theory, but at this point we want to remind the reader of the derivative properties of dual functions:

(i)   the derivative of the expenditure function with respect to the price of the i-th good is equal to the compensated demand for the i-th good, and

(ii) the derivative of the revenue function with respect to the price of the i-th good is equal to the supply of the i-th good.

The mathematical appendix to this chapter gives some useful results on net demand, two goods and their relation to the "offer curve."

There are two countries, denoted A and B. Country B receives a transfer from country A. Both countries produce and consume two final goods, x and y. Good x is the numéraire, p is the relative price of good y,

E^J is the minimum expenditure to achieve utility u^J at relative price p and R^J is the maximum revenue obtainable using current technology and inputs v^J at price p, for $J = A, B$. Finally, T is the amount of the transfer. All variables are in terms of good x, the numéraire. The imports (net demand) in a country are usually denoted by the variable m. We will do the same by defining, throughout this book, the variable $m^J \equiv E_p^J - R_p^J$, where a subscript always refers to a (partial) derivative. From the derivative property of dual functions mentioned above m^J is the *difference* between compensated demand for and supply of good y in country J. Thus, m^J is equal to the *net* (compensated) demand for good y in country J and as such denotes the import of good y in country J if m^J is positive, while country J exports $-m^J$ units of good y if m^J is negative. Given this notation the international transfer model can now be very efficiently formulated as follows:

$$E^A(p, u^A) = R^A(p, v^A) - T \tag{3.1}$$

$$E^B(p, u^B) = R^B(p, v^B) + T \tag{3.2}$$

$$m^A(p, u^A, v^A) + m^B(p, u^B, v^B) = 0 \tag{3.3}$$

Equation (3.1) indicates that total expenditure E^A for the donor of the transfer is equal to the total revenue from production R^A minus the outlay for the transfer abroad T. The revenue of the latter is assumed to be raised from the inhabitants of the donating country through lump-sum taxes. Similarly, equation (3.2) indicates that total expenditure E^B for the recipient of the transfer is equal to the total revenue from production R^B plus the receipts of the transfer from abroad T. The latter is assumed to be distributed among the inhabitants of the receiving country in a lump-sum fashion. Equation (3.3) gives the market-clearing condition for good y, and thus by Walras's law for good x also. The effect of a transfer from country A to country B can be easily derived by totally differentiating system (3.1)–(3.3), where we normalize such that $E_u^J = 1$, for $J = A, B$, and, for notational convenience, define $M_p \equiv \sum_J m_p^J$ and $\Delta^{-1} \equiv -\sum_J \left(m_p^J - m^J m_u^J \right).$ [2]

$$\begin{bmatrix} m^A & 1 & 0 \\ m^B & 0 & 1 \\ M_p & m_u^A & m_u^B \end{bmatrix} \begin{bmatrix} dp \\ du^A \\ du^B \end{bmatrix} = \begin{bmatrix} -1 \\ 1 \\ 0 \end{bmatrix} dT \tag{3.4}$$

---

[2] Since preferences are ordinal and not cardinal we can use a strictly increasing monotone transformation of the utility function to ensure that the normalization holds without affecting the preference ordering.

Solving (3.4) using Cramer's rule gives the following results:[3]

$$\det = \sum_J \left(m_p^J - m^J m_u^J \right) \equiv \frac{-1}{\Delta} < 0 \tag{3.5}$$

$$\frac{dp}{dT} = \left(m_u^B - m_u^A \right) \Delta > 0 \quad \Leftrightarrow \quad m_u^B > m_u^A \tag{3.6}$$

$$\frac{du^A}{dT} = \left[M_p + (m^A + m^B) m_u^A \right] \Delta = M_p \Delta \leq 0 \tag{3.7}$$

$$\frac{du^B}{dT} = -\left[M_p - (m^A + m^B) m_u^A \right] \Delta = -M_p \Delta \geq 0 \tag{3.8}$$

$$\frac{du^A}{dT} + \frac{du^B}{dT} = M_p \Delta - M_p \Delta = 0 \tag{3.9}$$

3.4.1   Walrasian stability

The term $m_p^J = E_{pp}^J - R_{pp}^J$ is always non-positive, as this is simply the derivative of the *compensated* net demand for good y with respect to its own price in country J. If there is some substitutability at all in either demand or supply (or both) between good y and good x in country J the term m_p^J will be strictly negative. Similarly, the term $M_p \equiv m_p^A + m_p^B$ is always non-positive (hence the inequalities in equations [3.7] and [3.8] under the assumption of Walrasian stability, see below), while M_p is strictly negative if there is any substitutability at all in either demand or supply in either country A or country B. Equation (3.5) gives the determinant of the coefficient matrix on the left-hand side of equation (3.4), where the inequality follows from the assumption of Walrasian stability as we will now explain in somewhat more detail since this condition is used throughout the remainder of the book.[4]

Let $\dot{p}$ denote the change in the price of good y over time as a result of an imbalance in the demand and supply of good y. Consider the equations (3.1), (3.2) and the dynamic adjustment equation:

---

[3] The solution to the matrix equation $\mathbf{Ax = b}$ follows from Cramer's rule; $x_j = \det(\mathbf{A}_j)/\det(\mathbf{A})$, where $\mathbf{A}_j$ is obtained by replacing the j-th column of $\mathbf{A}$ by $\mathbf{b}$.

[4] Throughout this book we will use the concept of Walrasian stability, which is the standard in this type of analysis. Some economists have argued that in the case of imperfect competition and increasing returns to scale Marshallian stability might be more appropriate (see, for instance, Ide and Takayama [1990a]). As noted in Takayama (1994, p. 366), both Walras and Marshall had theories of production as well as those of pure exchange. The Marshallian quantity adjustment is often associated with the theory of production while the Walrasian price adjustment is more often associated with the theory of exchange. This is another reason why in the transfer literature the concept of Walrasian equilibria dominates.

$$\dot{p} = \Pi\big(m^A(p, u^A) + m^B(p, u^B)\big) \tag{3.10}$$

Since the function Π in equation (3.10), which is assumed to be continuously differentiable, depends on the world excess demand of good y we assume that the price of good y is rising if, and only if, the world excess demand for good y is positive, such that $\Pi(0) = 0$ and $\Pi'(0) > 0$. If we *linearize* system (3.1), (3.2) and (3.10) around equilibrium values of price and welfare, $\bar{p}, \bar{u}^A$ and $\bar{u}^B$ say, and use the normalization above we obtain

$$m^A(p - \bar{p}) + (u^A - \bar{u}^A) = 0$$
$$m^B(p - \bar{p}) + (u^B - \bar{u}^B) = 0$$
$$\dot{p} = \Pi(0) + \Pi'(0)\Big[m_p^A(p - \bar{p}) + m_u^A(u^A - \bar{u}^A) + m_p^B(p - \bar{p}) + m_u^B(u^B - \bar{u}^B)\Big]$$

Substituting $(u^A - \bar{u}^A)$ and $(u^B - \bar{u}^B)$ from above and using $\Pi(0) = 0$ gives

$$\dot{p} = \Pi'(0)\Big[\big(m_p^A - m^A m_u^A\big) + \big(m_p^B - m^B m_u^B\big)\Big](p - \bar{p}) = \Pi'(0)[\det](p - \bar{p})$$

For (local) Walrasian stability we want the price change of good y to be negative if p exceeds the equilibrium price $\bar{p}$ and to be positive if p falls short of the equilibrium price $\bar{p}$. Walrasian stability thus requires that $\det \equiv \frac{-1}{\Delta} < 0$, or $\Delta > 0$.

An alternative way of investigating the sign of the determinant is by using the results of duality theory directly. It is easy to show that $\frac{-1}{\Delta}$ is the slope of the uncompensated excess demand curve of good y, denoted $\tilde{y}$, which should be negative in a Walrasian-stable world. Let $v^J(p, I^J)$ be the indirect utility function for country J. The uncompensated global excess demand, $\tilde{y}$, can then be expressed as

$$\tilde{y}(p, I^A, I^B) = m^A\big(p, v^A(p, I^A)\big) + m^B\big(p, v^B(p, I^B)\big)$$

Differentiating this equation with respect to p gives

$$\tilde{y}_p = m_p^A + m_p^B + m_u^A v_p^A + m_u^B v_p^B$$

Using Roy's identity and our normalization, $E_u^J = 1$, allows us to write $v_p^J = -m^J$; substituting this in the expression for $\tilde{y}_p$ gives equation (3.5).

Finally, we can also use the dual Slutsky equations to net demand directly (see the appendix to this chapter, equation [3.19]). By analogy to $\tilde{y}$ introduced above, we can define $\tilde{m}^J$, to denote country J's *uncompensated* net demand for good y:

$$\tilde{m}_p^J = m_p^J - m^J m_u^J \quad \text{for} \quad J = A, B$$

$$\text{such that} \quad \det = \sum_J \left(m_p^J - m^J m_u^J \right) = \tilde{m}_p^A + \tilde{m}_p^B < 0$$

As above, the determinant is the derivative of uncompensated net demand for good y with respect to its own price, which should be negative in a Walrasian-stable world. It is vitally important to realize that in a two-country world Walrasian stability *can* be compatible with a backward-bending offer curve for one of the countries involved ($\tilde{m}_p^J > 0$ for J equal to A or B), provided the derivative of uncompensated net demand is sufficiently negative for the other country, such that $\tilde{m}_p^A + \tilde{m}_p^B$ is negative to assure Walrasian stability. This is explained in more detail in the appendix to this chapter. We will use Walrasian stability throughout the remainder of this book. To avoid the cumbersome need to remind the reader time and again that "det" is negative in discussing our various results we define det $\equiv -1/\Delta$ throughout what follows, such that Δ is positive.[5] We are now ready to analyze the economic consequences of an exogenous transfer in a two-country, general-equilibrium, Walrasian-stable world in the next section.

It is important to understand why we are only interested in stable equilibria. First of all, how could the economy, after a process of adjustment, possibly end up at an *un*stable equilibrium? This seems to be possible only by some fluke of nature such that it does not appear to be interesting to analyze such equilibria. Second, suppose that, for some unexplained reason, we are initially in an *un*stable equilibrium. By its very nature, any small perturbation in this initial equilibrium will not bring us back to the unstable equilibrium, but to a different and stable equilibrium, assuming that such a stable equilibrium exists. If the small perturbation in question is a change in the size of an international transfer, such as analyzed throughout this book, this implies that the process of comparative statics applied to the unstable equilibrium is grossly misleading in its results as it implicitly assumes that we go from one unstable equilibrium to another, whereas the process of adjustment would bring us from the unstable to a stable equilibrium. Therefore, it is only economically meaningful to analyze changes in stable equilibria. This is known as Samuelson's correspondence principle; see Samuelson (1947) and Ide and Takayama (1990b). It also implies that our, in principle, local analysis always applies to every stable equilibrium. For a

---

[5] To avoid excessive notation, the symbol $-1/\Delta$ is used for the determinant for all the different models in what follows except where it may be confusing, as for example in the case of endogenous transfers in chapters 4 and 6.

discussion of "local" and "global" equilibria, see Kemp and Shimomura [1991]).

3.5   Samuelson's theorem: the results

It follows from equation (3.6) that the price p of good y changes if, and only if, $m_u^B \neq m_u^A$. It is important to understand the precise meaning of this condition. It says that the relative price of good y changes, following an international transfer, if there is a *difference* in the marginal propensity to consume good y in the two countries.[6] More precisely, the relative price of good y increases under Walrasian stability if, and only if, the recipient's marginal propensity to consume good y is larger than the donor's marginal propensity to consume this good, that is if $m_u^B > m_u^A$. This condition makes perfect sense: if you give one dollar to me and I consume more of good y out of this dollar than you would have done, the price of good y rises. Thus, the price elasticity of export supply, of central importance in Keynes's discussion in the previous chapter, is not essential to determine the *sign* of the terms-of-trade change.

The result in equation (3.6) is partially in line with the finding in the appendix of the previous chapter that the international transfer is over- or undereffected if, and only if, the sum of the marginal propensities to import exceeds or falls short of unity, respectively. Although one should always be careful in comparing results from partial equilibrium models with results from general equilibrium models, the condition which implies that the donor's trade balance improves in the former model is identical to the condition which implies that the donor's terms of trade improve in the latter model. To clarify this point, let μ_i^J denote the marginal propensity to consume good $i = x, y$ in country $J = A, B$. Suppose country A imports good x and country B imports good y, then according to the appendix to chapter 2 the transfer is overeffected if the sum of the marginal propensities to import exceeds unity:

$$\mu_x^A + \mu_y^B > 1 \quad \text{or}$$

$$pm_u^B = \mu_y^B > 1 - \mu_x^A = \mu_y^A = pm_u^A \quad \Leftrightarrow \quad m_u^B > m_u^A$$

which is the same result as above in equation (3.6).

It is now easy to show that Samuelson was right when he pointed out that the numerical example constructed by Leontief was a very special

---

[6] The marginal propensity to consume good y is by definition the portion of additional expenditure spent on good y, that is $pm_u/E_u = pm_u$ using our normalization; see the mathematical appendix.

case. In a Walrasian-stable two-country world it is impossible to have perverse welfare effects. Since the compensated substitution effect M_p is non-positive we can easily sign the welfare effects in equations (3.7) and (3.8). It follows from equation (3.7) that the donor always loses, while it follows from equation (3.8) that the recipient always gains as a result of the transfer. If the marginal propensity to consume good y is identical in the two countries it follows from equation (3.6) that there is no terms-of-trade effect. In this special case we have, using equation (3.5),

$$\frac{du^B}{dT} = -\frac{du^A}{dT} = 1$$

which are the pure "income effects" as a result of the transfer. More generally, the welfare effects in equations (3.7) and (3.8) can be written as:

$$\frac{du^A}{dT} = -1 - m^A \frac{dp}{dT} \; ; \quad \frac{du^B}{dT} = 1 + m^B \frac{dp}{dT}$$

Thus, equations (3.7) and (3.8) show that if there are differences in marginal propensities to consume, that is if there are terms-of-trade effects, this will affect the donor's and recipient's welfare levels (either positively or negatively), but never to such an extent that it will dominate the pure income effect. Thus, Leontief's case was very special as his example involved Walrasian instability. Equation (3.9), finally, shows that the transfer is a reallocation from one Pareto-optimal allocation to another Pareto-optimal allocation, that is, it is impossible to improve country B's welfare without worsening country A's welfare.[7]

An interesting special case is that of an exchange economy with fixed proportion preferences, that is there is substitution neither in production nor in consumption. Under these circumstances the term $M_p \equiv m_p^A + m_p^B = E_{pp}^A + E_{pp}^B - (R_{pp}^A + R_{pp}^B) = 0$, such that from equations (3.7) and (3.8) it follows that neither the recipient's nor the donor's welfare is affected by the transfer. This result, which generalizes to an arbitrary number of goods (see chapter 4), shows that Leontief had to use substitution effects in his two-country example discussed above. To summarize the results in this section:

Proposition 1: (Samuelson's Theorem) In a perfectly competitive, two-good, two-country and Walrasian-stable world the donor

---

[7] We abstract from the utility which is derived from the satisfaction of helping a poorer nation; see, however, chapter 7.

always loses and the recipient always gains as a result of a transfer. The donor's terms of trade deteriorate, causing a "secondary burden," if, and only if, the donor's marginal propensity to consume its own export good is lower than the recipient's marginal propensity to consume the donor's export good.

Remark 1 *Leontief's example investigates an unstable equilibrium of the world economy.*

We want to clarify one more issue, which appears to be obvious but has given rise to confusion nonetheless; see, for example, Chichilnisky (1980) and the discussion following this article in issue 13 of the *Journal of Development Economics* (1983). The transfer is assumed to be given in terms of the numéraire good x. What if it is given in terms of good y instead? This makes no difference, as long as we evaluate at post-transfer prices.

Suppose that $\bar{p}, \bar{u}^A$ and $\bar{u}^B$ solve equations (3.1)–(3.3) if country A gives a transfer of T units of good x to country B, that is $\bar{p}$ is the post-transfer relative price of good y. The situation is illustrated for recipient B in figure 3.2, where BB' is country B's production possibility curve, P^B denotes its production point, C^B denotes its consumption point and the difference between the value of country B's consumption and the value of country B's production is equal to the value of the transfer received from country A. If country A had given $T/\bar{p}$ units of good y (T_y in figure 3.2) instead of T units of good x (T_x in figure 3.2) to country B, then at price $\bar{p}$ the production decisions would be the same (P^B does not change), so that the available income for the two countries and thus the consumption decisions would be the same as before (C^B does not change). Therefore $\bar{p}, \bar{u}^A$ and $\bar{u}^B$ would also have been an equilibrium of the system if country A had given $T/\bar{p}$ units of good y. The consequences of a transfer in terms of one good can always be restated as an equivalent transfer in terms of another good when evaluated at the appropriate post-transfer prices. If evaluated at pre-transfer prices (say $\tilde{p}$), however, the transfer of T units of good x will have different effects from the transfer of $T/\tilde{p}$ units of good y if the terms of trade change. This is most explicitly pointed out by Jan Willem Gunning (1983a).

Proposition 2: (Gunning) If $(\bar{p}, \bar{u}^A, \bar{u}^B)$ is an equilibrium for a transfer of T units of good x for equations (3.1)–(3.3), then $(\bar{p}, \bar{u}^A, \bar{u}^B)$ is also an equilibrium for a transfer of $T/\bar{p}$ units of good y. Note that the evaluation is at the post-transfer relative price.

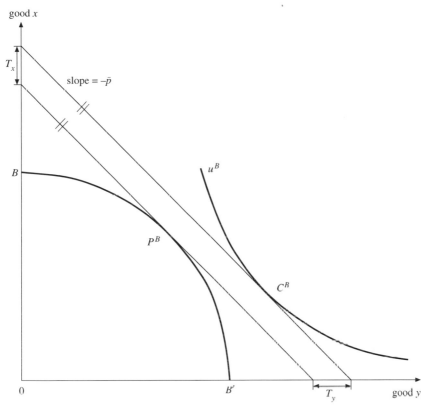

Figure 3.2   *Transfers and a change in numéraire*

To end this section we return to the Keynes–Ohlin debate. As we saw
in the previous chapter, the discussion between Keynes and Ohlin
included many aspects of the transfer problem. However, we can now
illustrate one aspect of the discussion, namely the remarks by Keynes
and Ohlin on the relevance of differences between the marginal propensities to consume between donor and recipient. Note that the terms-of-
trade change can be written as $dp/dT = -\left(m_u^B - m_u^A\right)/(\tilde{m}_p^A + \tilde{m}_p^B)$; see
the appendix to this chapter. Thus, translated into the variables of our
model Keynes says that there is no transfer problem if $m_u^B = m_u^A$. In this
case there are no terms-of-trade effects, only the pure income effects on
welfare for both countries. So, Keynes and Ohlin agree under these
special circumstances. Keynes argued, however, that "the transfer
problem will be a hopeless business" if "the demand of the rest of the

world for these articles has an elasticity of less than unity" (1929a, p. 2). In our view, he is both wrong and right. He is wrong because the *sign* of the terms-of-trade change is determined by differences in marginal propensity to consume, as argued by Ohlin, and not by price elasticities of exports. He is right, however, in the sense that price elasticities of exports play a prominent role in determining the *size* of the terms-of-trade change. Thus, under Keynes's presumption that the terms of trade change to the donor's disadvantage, low price elasticities of exports lead, other things being equal, to a large secondary burden for the donor. An, admittedly rather crude, summary of the Keynes–Ohlin debate, in view of the fact that the terms-of-trade change is given by $dp/dT = -\left(m_u^B - m_u^A\right)/\left(\tilde{m}_p^A + \tilde{m}_p^B\right)$, is to say that Ohlin stresses the importance of the numerator and Keynes emphasizes that of the denominator.

3.6   Conclusions

We have developed a basic general equilibrium transfer model, variants of which we will use often in the remainder of this book. The description of the transfer problem in a general equilibrium framework is relatively easy when we use standard results from duality theory. The terms of trade effects and the corresponding welfare effects for donor and recipient as a result of an international transfer are related to differences in the marginal propensities to consume.

Under Walrasian stability no perverse welfare effects, that is, donor-enrichment or recipient-impoverishment, can occur, no matter how special the marginal propensities to consume. If the marginal propensities to consume goods are the same for donor and recipient there are no terms-of-trade effects, only the welfare consequences of a pure income effect of the gift; the recipient gains one unit of welfare and the donor loses one unit of welfare following a gift of one unit of good x. Keynes was right in stating that the transfer problem for Germany was difficult if the rest of the world did not spend much of the transfer on German exports, in the sense that Germany would suffer from a decline in its terms of trade. He was wrong in claiming that under such circumstances the transfer problem would be a hopeless affair, in the sense that Germany would need ever-increasing terms-of-trade losses to sell extra units of exports.

3.A   Appendix: net demand and the offer curve

International economics based on duality theory uses *net* demand functions. To confuse matters, however, classical international eco-

nomics often uses offer curves. This appendix summarizes some
properties of net demand functions and briefly relates these to offer
curves.

3.A.1 Net demand

We assume that a country's expenditure level to reach utility u at prices $\mathbf{p}$
equals $E(\mathbf{p}, u)$, while that country's earnings (or revenue) at the price
level $\mathbf{p}$, given the vector of factor endowments $\mathbf{v}$, equals $R(\mathbf{p}, \mathbf{v})$. Since a
country's total expenditure cannot exceed its total revenue it follows
that:[8]

$$E(\mathbf{p}, u) = R(\mathbf{p}, \mathbf{v}) \tag{3.11}$$

We can also define a country's net expenditure function $Z(\mathbf{p}, u, \mathbf{v})$ as
the difference between the expenditure function and the revenue function:

$$Z(\mathbf{p}, u, \mathbf{v}) \equiv E(\mathbf{p}, u) - R(\mathbf{p}, \mathbf{v}) \tag{3.12}$$

The net expenditure function inherits its characteristics from the expenditure function and the revenue function (giving the minus sign in front of
the latter due consideration). Thus, for example, Z is homogeneous of
degree one in $\mathbf{p}$, concave as a function of $\mathbf{p}$, convex as a function of $\mathbf{v}$ and,
most importantly, the derivative property holds:

$$Z_{\mathbf{p}}(\mathbf{p}, u, \mathbf{v}) = E_{\mathbf{p}}(\mathbf{p}, u) - R_{\mathbf{p}}(\mathbf{p}, \mathbf{v}) = \mathbf{c}(\mathbf{p}, u) - \mathbf{x}(\mathbf{p}, \mathbf{v}) \equiv \mathbf{m}(\mathbf{p}, u, \mathbf{v}) \tag{3.13}$$

Thus, the derivative of country J's net expenditure function with
respect to price p^i gives country J's net demand for good i, that is the
difference between the demand for good i and the supply of good i in
country J. The net demand is denoted $\mathbf{m}$ in this book, the usual notation
for imports in the international economics literature. Obviously, good i is
only imported if m^i is positive, while good i is exported if m^i is negative.

---

[8] We investigate, of course, at great length the extent to which expenditure may exceed or
fall short of total revenue as a result of unilateral transfers. In the absence of such
transfers there may be a *temporary* difference between expenditure and revenue, where it
should be noted that temporary does not mean for a short time period. During the time
that a country's revenue exceeds its expenditure there is a surplus on the current account
and the country builds up claims on the rest of the world. It will later be remunerated for
such claims so that, in the future, expenditure may exceed revenue. In present-value
terms, that is, discounting all future values of expenditure and revenue to the present
using the appropriate discount rate, total revenue still equals total expenditure. This
interpretation is used here; see Dixit and Norman (1980) and chapter 10.

For concreteness, the remainder of this appendix will assume that there are only two goods (1 and 2, identified by superscripts), but most statements generalize easily. The arguments of functions will be suppressed in the following.

Since Z is homogeneous of degree one in prices $\mathbf{p}$ it follows that $\mathbf{p}'Z_{\mathbf{p}} = \mathbf{p}'\mathbf{m} = Z = 0$, or

$$p^1 m^1 + p^2 m^2 = 0 \tag{3.14}$$

This is, of course, an alternative way of stating that total expenditure equals total revenue. Thus, if a country is a net demander of good 2, that is $m^2 > 0$, it follows that it must be a net supplier of good 1, that is $m^1 < 0$.

Since Z is homogeneous of degree one in prices $\mathbf{p}$, it follows from Euler's theorem that $Z_{\mathbf{p}} \equiv \mathbf{m}$ is homogeneous of degree zero in $\mathbf{p}$. Therefore

$$p^1 m^1_{p^1} + p^2 m^1_{p^2} = 0 \tag{3.15}$$
$$p^1 m^2_{p^1} + p^2 m^2_{p^2} = 0 \tag{3.16}$$

If Z is twice continuously differentiable, as we assume throughout this book, it follows from Young's theorem (see, for example, Takayama [1994, pp. 51–2]) that $Z_{p^i p^j} = Z_{p^j p^i}$; that is, the compensated cross-price effect of net demand for good 1 as a result of a price change of good 2 is the same as the compensated cross-price effect of net demand for good 2 as a result of a price change of good 1, or

$$m^1_{p^2} = m^2_{p^1} \tag{3.17}$$

From the mathematical appendix to this book it follows that the marginal propensity to consume good i (μ_i) is given by:

$$\mu_i = \frac{p^i Z_{p^i u}}{Z_u} = \frac{p^i m^i_u}{E_u} \quad \text{and} \quad \sum_i \frac{p^i m^i_u}{E_u} = 1 \tag{3.18}$$

Differentiating the net expenditure function with respect to price p^i gives the *compensated* net demand function m^i for good i, that is, for a given utility level u. If we let the uncompensated net demand function for good i be denoted by $\tilde{m}^i$, then we have, analogously to the demand functions in the mathematical appendix, the following net demand dual Slutsky equation:

$$\widetilde{m}^i_{p^j} = m^i_{p^j} - \frac{m^j}{E_u}m^i_u = m^i_{p^j} - m^j m^i_u, \quad \text{if } E_u = 1 \tag{3.19}$$

The dual Slutsky equation will turn out to be useful in a number of applications, for example in analyzing properties of the offer curve.

3.A.2   The offer curve

Neoclassical international economics makes frequent use of the "offer curve" in its analysis. International trade is basically a supply of exports in exchange for imports, or an offer of exports in exchange for imports. Suppose there are two countries, A and B, and two goods, 1 and 2. Country J's compensated net demand for good i is denoted m^{Ji}, while its uncompensated net demand is denoted $\widetilde{m}^{Ji}$. The net demands depend, of course, on the goods prices, p^1 and p^2. Suppose that country A exports good 1 and country B exports good 2 in equilibrium. To determine this equilibrium first consider arbitrary prices $\mathbf{p} = (p^1, p^2)$. Given these arbitrary prices and using the budget constraint, country A is willing to export, or offer, $-\widetilde{m}^{A1}$ of good 1 in exchange for $-p^1/p^2\widetilde{m}^{A1} = \widetilde{m}^{A2}$ of good 2. As the prices $\mathbf{p}$ vary we can plot the export offers for imports in a (good 1, good 2) diagram. This is done in figure 3.3.

Figure 3.3 illustrates the explicit offers at three prices, $\mathbf{p}1$, $\mathbf{p}2$ and $\mathbf{p}3$, which leads to offers $A1$, $A2$ and $A3$, respectively, for country A and offers $B1$, $B2$ and $B3$, respectively, for country B. Note that the slope of a line through the origin indicates the price of good 1 relative to the price of good 2, that is p^1/p^2, and this is shown for the prices, $\mathbf{p}1$, $\mathbf{p}2$ and $\mathbf{p}3$ in figure 3.3. If we vary the relative price of good 1 continuously we can trace out all export supplies by country A of good 1 for imports of good 2. Doing this leads to country A's offer curve, the solid line $OA1A2A3$ in figure 3.3. Similarly, if we vary the relative price of good 2 continuously, that is the inverse of the relative price of good 1, we can trace out all export supplies by country B of good 2 for imports of good 1. Doing this leads to country B's offer curve, the solid line $OB3B2B1$ in figure 3.3. Note that at the intersection of the two offer curves, that is at prices $\mathbf{p}2$ at offer $A2 = B2$, country A's export supply of good 1 for imports of good 2 is equal to country B's export supply of good 2 for imports of good 1. Thus, at prices $\mathbf{p}2$ the world net demand for both good 1 and good 2 is zero, so that $\mathbf{p}2$ is the world's general equilibrium price.

The previous subsection identified the relationship between uncompensated and compensated export supply; see equation (3.19) on the dual Slutsky equation. In particular, after normalizing $E^J_u = 1$ for $J = A, B$,

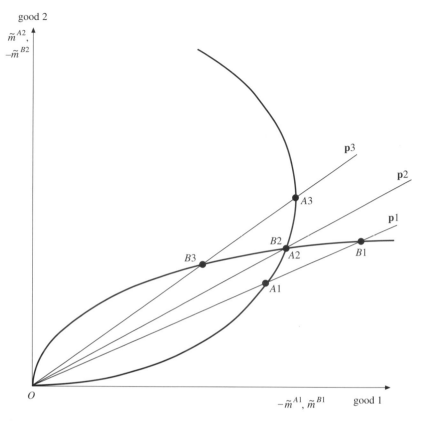

good 2

$\tilde{m}^{A2},$
$-\tilde{m}^{B2}$

p3

p2

A3

B2

p1

B3

A2

B1

A1

O

$-\tilde{m}^{A1}, \tilde{m}^{B1}$ good 1

Figure 3.3   *Market stability and the offer curve*

country A's reaction in terms of a change of exports of good 1 in response to an increase in the price of its export good, that is price p^1, equals

$$-\left(\tilde{m}_{p^1}^{A1}\right) = -\left(m_{p^1}^{A1} - m^{A1}m_u^{A1}\right) \tag{3.20}$$

Similarly, country B's reaction in terms of a change of exports of good 2 in response to an increase in the price of its export good, that is price p^2, equals

$$-\left(\tilde{m}_{p^2}^{B2}\right) = -\left(m_{p^2}^{B2} - m^{B2}m_u^{B2}\right) \tag{3.21}$$

A country's export supply is said to be elastic if an increase of the price of its export good leads to an increase in the supply of its exports. For country A, this would imply $\left(\tilde{m}_{p^1}^{A1}\right) = \left(m_{p^1}^{A1} - m^{A1}m_u^{A1}\right) < 0$; see equation (3.20). Country A's offer curve $OA1A2A3$ in figure 3.3 illustrates that this condition holds, thus country A's supply of export good 1 is elastic as the price of good 1 increases, up to the point $A3$, and inelastic thereafter.

The main text usually chooses a numéraire good and we may wonder what the effect of the choice of numéraire might be. Two results are of importance in this respect. First, note that

$$\tilde{m}_{p^1}^{A1} = m_{p^1}^{A1} \quad m^{A1}m_u^{A1} = -\left(\frac{p^2}{p^1}\right)m_{p^2}^{A1} - m^{A1}m_u^{A1}$$

$$= -\left(\frac{p^2}{p^1}\right)\left(m_{p^2}^{A1} - m^{A2}m_u^{A1}\right) = -\left(\frac{p^2}{p^1}\right)\tilde{m}_{p^2}^{A1}$$

where the first equality follows from the dual Slutsky equation (3.19), the second equality from price homogeneity (see equation [3.15]), the third equality from the budget constraint (see equation [3.14]), and the last equality again from the dual Slutsky equation (3.19). To summarize, it follows that

$$\tilde{m}_{p^1}^{A1} = -\left(\frac{p^2}{p^1}\right)\tilde{m}_{p^2}^{A1} \tag{3.22}$$

Therefore the uncompensated cross-derivative of net demand is always of *opposite* sign to the own (uncompensated) price derivative in a two-good context.

Second, combining the price homogeneity equations (3.15) and (3.16) with the symmetry equation (3.17), it follows that

$$m_{p^1}^{A1} = \left(\frac{p^2}{p^1}\right)^2 m_{p^2}^{A2} \tag{3.23}$$

Similarly, combining the budget constraint, equation (3.14), with the marginal propensity to consume, equation (3.18), gives

$$m^{A1}m_u^{A1} = -\left(1 - p^2 m_u^{A2}\right)\frac{p^2 m^{A2}}{\left(p^1\right)^2} \tag{3.24}$$

Combining this and other information reveals that

$$\widetilde{m}_{p^1}^{A1} = m_{p^1}^{A1} - m^{A1}m_u^{A1} = \left(\frac{p^2}{p^1}\right)^2 m_{p^2}^{A2} + (1 - p^2 m_u^{A2})\frac{p^2 m^{A2}}{(p^1)^2}$$

$$= \left(\frac{p^2}{p^1}\right)^2 \left(m_{p^2}^{A2} - m^{A2}m_u^{A2}\right) + \frac{p^2 m^{A2}}{(p^1)^2} = \left(\frac{p^2}{p^1}\right)^2 \widetilde{m}_{p^2}^{A2} - \frac{m^{A1}}{p^1}$$

where the first equality follows from the dual Slutsky equation (3.19), the second equality from substituting equations (3.23) and (3.24), the third equality from rearranging, the fourth equality from the budget constraint, equation (3.14), and the dual Slutsky equation (3.19). To summarize:

$$\left(p^2\right)^2 \widetilde{m}_{p^2}^{A2} = \left(p^1\right)^2 \widetilde{m}_{p^1}^{A1} + p^1 m^{A1} \tag{3.25}$$

We assumed above that country A exports good 1. Suppose that the export supply is inelastic, that is we are above price $\mathbf{p}3$ in figure 3.3, and $\widetilde{m}_{p^1}^{A1} > 0$, such that country A's (uncompensated) export of good 1 falls if the price of good 1 rises, or equivalently that the (uncompensated) net demand for good 1 rises if the price of good 1 rises. Can we conclude from these presumptions that the (uncompensated) net demand for good 2 rises if the price of good 2 rises? Equation (3.25) shows that we *cannot* draw this conclusion if there is a net trading position. Thus, we have to be careful when switching from one good to another in drawing conclusions from price changes for uncompensated demand. A related issue is the question of Walrasian stability for the world economy equilibrium. In this book we (almost) always take one of the goods as a numéraire. Does the choice matter for Walrasian stability? It does not, because it follows easily that

$$\left(p^2\right)^2 \left(\widetilde{m}_{p^2}^{A2} + \widetilde{m}_{p^2}^{B2}\right) = \left(p^1\right)^2 \left(\widetilde{m}_{p^1}^{A1} + \widetilde{m}_{p^1}^{B1}\right) + p^1 \left(m^{A1} + m^{B1}\right)$$

$$= \left(p^1\right)^2 \left(\widetilde{m}_{p^1}^{A1} + \widetilde{m}_{p^1}^{B1}\right)$$

The first equality follows from equation (3.25), while the second equality follows from the market-clearing condition for good 1 in the world economy equilibrium, that is, world net demand for good 1 is zero: $m^{A1} + m^{B1} = 0$. Therefore, if the world is Walrasian-stable with respect to price p^2 for good 2 (that is, $\widetilde{m}_{p^2}^{A2} + \widetilde{m}_{p^2}^{B2} < 0$) it is also Walrasian-stable with respect to price p^1 for good 1 (that is, $\widetilde{m}_{p^1}^{A1} + \widetilde{m}_{p^1}^{B1} < 0$).[9]

The offer curve, as introduced here, and its properties will be useful in

[9] The cross-effects follow from equation (3.22).

understanding some of the later results. Thus, we will make ample use of it, for example, in chapter 5. To illustrate, consider Samuelson's theorem as derived in section 3.4, in particular the donor's welfare change, equation (3.7):

$$\frac{du^A}{dT} = M_p\Delta = -\frac{m_p^A + m_p^B}{\widetilde{m}_p^A + \widetilde{m}_p^B}$$

Since the net substitution term $m_p^A + m_p^B$ is necessarily non-positive, the donor can only gain if the denominator is positive. From the discussion above, this implies that countries would have a backward bending at least one of the two offer curve, which violates Walrasian stability (see section 3.4).

4   Generalizations of Samuelson's theorem

4.1 Introduction

Chapter 3 analyzed the welfare effects and terms-of-trade effects of an international transfer in a two-good, two-country and Walrasian-stable general equilibrium framework of perfect competition. The model is attractive because its elegant simplicity allows us to derive strong analytic results regarding the terms-of-trade effect and Samuelson's theorem. At the same time, one might argue that the model's simplicity is also its limitation because it does not enable us to analyze some issues of interest in the real world. In his debate with Ohlin, reviewed in chapter 2, Keynes emphasized the importance of a shift of resources from one sector to another as a result of an international transfer. One may wonder, therefore, whether or not such a shift in resources between different sectors can be strong enough in principle to upset Samuelson's theorem under specific circumstances. A few examples may clarify the issue.

First, consider the presence of public goods, that is goods produced and provided by the government after taxing the private sector. Suppose the government of the country receiving the transfer greatly increases the production of public goods as a result of the transfer. Since such an increase draws resources away from the private sector into the public sector, resulting in a decrease in private sector production, can we be sure that the transfer will be beneficial to the recipient as Samuelson's theorem would lead us to believe?

Second, chapter 3 analyzed shifts between traded goods only, but both Keynes and Ohlin stressed the importance of non-traded goods sectors. Keynes claimed that the presence of a non-traded goods sector would shift resources away from the non-traded goods sector into the export industry to exacerbate further the donor's terms-of-trade deterioration expected by Keynes as a result of the transfer. Ohlin, on the other hand, saw no particular reason to expect a shift in the terms of trade in either direction but only opposing changes in the prices of traded goods relative to those of non-traded goods for donor and recipient. Keynes and Ohlin agree, therefore, on the fact that there will be a shift of resources between the traded and non-traded goods sectors. We investigate not only whether either Keynes's or Ohlin's intuition is correct regarding the terms-of-trade effect but also whether or not the shift of resources between the traded and non-traded goods sectors can be large enough to cause transfer paradoxes (see also Jones [1970, 1975]).

Third, chapter 3 analyzed a model with only two traded goods to demonstrate that differences in marginal propensities to consume these goods are the cause of price changes. What if there is a larger number of traded goods and donor and recipient have different marginal propensities to consume this large variety of goods? If we number these traded goods and the recipient has a higher marginal propensity to consume good number 10 than the donor can we conclude that the price of good number 10 will rise? If so, do the prices of complements of good number 10 also rise and those of substitutes fall? Does the potentially complicated interaction between price changes, complements and substitutes in a many-good world allow for transfer paradoxes?

The analysis in this chapter will extend the simple general equilibrium model of chapter 3 in a variety of ways to answer these and related questions. The focus of attention will always be whether or not Samuelson's theorem still holds in the more complicated extended model. As an important bonus the reader will become more familiar during the course of this chapter with the analytical apparatus developed so far, which will enable her to construct and solve her own problems involving international transfers in the future.

4.2 Public goods

Samuelson's theorem is based on the analysis of private goods. A substantial proportion of goods and services are, however, in one way or another publicly provided. The analysis in chapter 3 therefore abstracted from the dual role of the government, as a redistributor of income generated in the private sector and as a provider of public goods. This section investigates this dual role of the government in more detail. The structure of the model is based on Abe (1992). We assume that public goods are both non-excludable, that is particular groups of people cannot be prevented from consuming the good, and non-rival, that is if you consume some of the public good this does not mean that I must consume less of it; we thus investigate pure public goods. Note, however, that few public goods are pure.

As a first example, suppose the government levies taxes to build and operate a museum of fine arts. This is an excludable and rival public good. It is excludable because the government may put conditions on entering the museum; say, you have to buy a ticket or you have to be a member of the museum. It is a rival public good because if all the other 100,000 members of the museum are there it will be hard for you to see the paintings.

As a second example, suppose the government levies taxes to promote clean air. This is a non-excludable and almost non-rival public good. It is non-excludable because the government cannot force you not to breathe. It is an almost non-rival public good because your consumption of clean air will in general have minuscule effects on my consumption of clean air, although these effects may be substantial if you are a chemical company or if you represent the other 20 million breathing people in Mexico City.

As a third and final example, suppose the government levies taxes to promote new knowledge. This is an excludable (e.g. through patents) and non-rival public good. It is non-rival because the design of a computer chip, for example, can be used indefinitely.

4.2.1 The modeling of public goods

We do not use country indices in this subsection, but the same relations apply in both countries, A and B. Throughout this subsection the p's and v's, and thus the w's, may be interpreted as vectors. There are no distortions and it is always assumed that the factors of production are fully occupied. The full employment condition requires that total factors of production v are employed either in the private sector, v^{pr} say, or in the public sector, v^g say:

$$v^{pr} + v^g = v \tag{4.1}$$

This equation implies that the division of the factors of production between the two sectors is endogenously determined by the model. Define the revenue function for the private sector as $\check{R}(p, v^{pr}) = \max_y \{py \mid y \in \check{F}(v^{pr})\}$, where $\check{F}(v^{pr})$ is the production possibility set. For expository convenience we use the following assumption, as in Abe (1992):

Assumption (Abe). $\check{R}_{vv} = 0$

That is, factor prices are not affected by the change in the factor endowments available for the private sector. In the conventional

Heckscher–Ohlin framework this is known as factor price equalization. The conclusions on international transfers derived below do not depend on this simplifying assumption; see Kemp and Abe (1994).

Introducing the unit cost function, $C^g(w)$ say, for public goods, which are produced under constant returns to scale, implies that total employment of factors of production for public goods is equal to per unit employment of factors of production for public goods, equal to C_w^g from the properties of the unit cost function, times the number of public goods g produced in the economy:

$$v^g = C_w^g(w) g$$

We also know from the properties of revenue functions that $\check{R}_v = w$, so we can rewrite the full employment condition (4.1) as:

$$v^{pr} + C_w^g(\check{R}_v(p, v^{pr}))g = v \tag{4.2}$$

Equation (4.2) can in principle be solved for v^{pr} as a function of p, g and v. Since we assume that v is constant this argument will be suppressed:

$$v^{pr} = v^{pr}(p, g) \tag{4.3}$$

Totally differentiating equation (4.2) gives

$$dv^{pr} + C_{ww}^g \check{R}_{vv} g\, dv^{pr} + C_{ww}^g \check{R}_{vp} g\, dp + C_w^g\, dg = 0 \tag{4.4}$$

So that using Abe's assumption ($\check{R}_{vv} = 0$) it follows that

$$v_p^{pr} = -C_{ww}^g \check{R}_{vp} g \quad \text{and} \quad v_g^{pr} = -C_w^g \tag{4.5}$$

Turning attention again to the private sector's revenue function we can now use equation (4.3) to define

$$R(p, g) \equiv \check{R}(p, v^{pr}(p, g)) \tag{4.6}$$

In a sense this is a restricted revenue function for the private sector, since it denotes the private revenue for a given number of public goods g produced by the government. The properties of this function are extensively discussed in Abe (1992). For our purposes it suffices to note that (using equation [4.5], $\check{R}_v = w$ and linear homogeneity of $C^g(w)$ such that $wC_w^g = C^g(w)$ and $wC_{ww}^g = 0$):

$$R_p = \check{R}_p + \check{R}_v v_p^{pr} = \check{R}_p - wC_{ww}^g \check{R}_{vp} g = \check{R}_p \tag{4.7}$$

$$R_g = -\check{R}_v v_g^{pr} = -wC_w^g = -C^g(w) \tag{4.8}$$

Equation (4.8) simply indicates that increasing the production of public goods g by one unit reduces private revenue by the per unit cost of public goods C_g. Differentiating equation (4.8), using $w = \check{R}_v(p, g)$, gives

$$R_{gg} = -C_w^g \check{R}_{vv} v_g^{pr} = 0 \tag{4.9}$$

Suppose there are two tradable private goods x and y, where good x is the numéraire and p is the relative price of good y, and a country-specific public good g, that is residents of one country cannot enjoy the consumption of a public good provided in another country. Let $E(p, g, u)$ be the private sector's expenditure function, that is the minimum expenditure necessary to achieve utility level u given relative price p and the level g of public goods provided by the government. Since the consumer derives utility from the provision of public goods it follows that, other things being equal, the greater the provision of public goods the less the required private expenditures to reach the same utility level, that is E_g is negative. In fact, $-E_g$ is known as the marginal willingness to pay for the provision of public goods in the public choice literature. Before analyzing the consequences of international transfers we must note that efficient provision of public goods requires that the total marginal willingness to pay for the provision of public goods is equal to the marginal cost of providing public goods, that is

$$E_g(p, g, u) = R_g(p, g) \tag{4.10}$$

One way in which to ensure this efficiency criterion is reached is by using a tax system of personalized prices for the public good, known as Lindahl prices, in which each consumer is taxed according to his or her marginal willingness to pay; see, for example, Varian (1992). Suppose that the marginal willingness to pay $-E_g$ falls as the level of provision of public goods rises, that is $-E_{gg} < 0$ or $E_{gg} > 0$. We can then use equation (4.10) to solve for the efficiently produced level of public goods g as a function of price p and welfare u, with the properties as in equation (4.12):[1]

$$g = g(p, u) \quad \text{with} \tag{4.11}$$

---

[1] Under Abe's assumption above, it follows that $E_{gg} - R_{gg} = E_{gg} > 0$ (see equation [4.9]), if the marginal willingness to pay declines as the number of public goods rises. However, as argued by Kemp and Abe (1994), under more general circumstances a strict local optimal level of provision of public goods requires $E_{gg} - R_{gg} > 0$, which is why we have not simplified equation (4.12).

$$g_p = -\frac{(E_{gp} - R_{gp})}{(E_{gg} - R_{gg})} \quad \text{and} \quad g_u = -\frac{E_{gu}}{(E_{gg} - R_{gg})} \tag{4.12}$$

4.2.2 Public goods and transfers

As in the previous subsection we analyze international transfers in the context of public goods where there are two countries, A and B, two private goods, good y with price p and numéraire good x, and a country-specific public good which is provided efficiently (see also Kemp [1984] and Hatzipanayotou and Michael [1995]). Let E^J denote country J's expenditure function, R^J country J's restricted revenue function, g^J the level of public good provided in country J and T the size of the transfer country A gives to country B. Let m^J denote country J's net demand for good y, that is $m^J \equiv E_p^J - R_p^J$. The equilibrium of the world economy is then described by the system of equations:

$$E^A(p, g^A, u^A) = R^A(p, g^A) - T \tag{4.13}$$

$$E_g^A(p, g, u^A) = R_g^A(p, g^A) \tag{4.14}$$

$$E^B(p, g^B, u^B) - R^B(p, g^B) + T \tag{4.15}$$

$$E_g^B(p, g, u^B) = R_g^B(p, g^B) \tag{4.16}$$

$$m^A(p, g^A, u^A) + m^B(p, g^B, u^B) = 0 \tag{4.17}$$

Equation (4.13) is the donor's budget constraint, equation (4.14) is the donor's efficient provision of public goods, equation (4.15) is the recipient's budget constraint, equation (4.16) is the recipient's efficient provision of public goods and equation (4.17) is the market-clearing condition for good y. Note that it is essential that the public goods are provided efficiently. We can now use the methodology of the previous subsection to define

$$g^J = g^J(p, u) \quad \text{for } J = A, B \quad \text{with} \tag{4.18}$$

$$g_p^J - \frac{(E_{gp}^J - R_{gp}^J)}{(E_{gg}^J - R_{gg}^J)} \quad \text{and} \quad g_u^J = -\frac{E_{gu}^J}{(E_{gg}^J - R_{gg}^J)} \tag{4.19}$$

If we substitute equations (4.18) in equations (4.13), (4.15) and (4.17), this simplifies the model to

$$E^A(p, g^A(p, u^A), u^A) = R^A(p, g^A(p, u^A)) - T \tag{4.20}$$

$$E^B(p, g^B(p, u^B), u^B) = R^B(p, g^B(p, u^B)) + T \tag{4.21}$$

$$m^A(p, g^A(p, u^A), u^A) + m^B(p, g^B(p, u^B), u^B) = 0 \tag{4.22}$$

Normalize such that $E_u^J = 1$ and define $\Omega \equiv \sum_J \left(m_p^J + m_g^J g_p^J \right)$ and $F^J \equiv m_u^J + m_g^J g_u^J$ for $J = A, B$ for convenience. Then, differentiating system (4.20)–(4.22) with respect to p, u^A, u^B and T and using equations (4.14) and (4.16), that is the condition for efficient provision of public goods, gives

$$
\begin{bmatrix} m^A & 1 & 0 \\ m^B & 0 & 1 \\ M_p & F^A & F^B \end{bmatrix} \begin{bmatrix} dp \\ du^A \\ du^B \end{bmatrix} = \begin{bmatrix} -1 \\ 1 \\ 0 \end{bmatrix} dT
$$

It is now straightforward to find expressions for the effects of an international transfer T in the presence of public goods by applying Cramer's rule to the system above:

$$
\det = \left(\Omega - m^A F^A - m^B F^B \right) \equiv -\frac{1}{\Delta} < 0 \tag{4.23}
$$

$$
\frac{dp}{dT} = \left(F^B - F^A \right) \Delta \tag{4.24}
$$

$$
\frac{du^A}{dT} = \Omega \Delta \tag{4.25}
$$

$$
\frac{du^B}{dT} = -\Omega \Delta \tag{4.26}
$$

$$
\frac{du^A}{dT} + \frac{du^B}{dT} = 0 \tag{4.27}
$$

The inequality for the determinant in equation (4.23), which can be written as $\det = \sum_J \left[(m_p^J - m^J m_u^J) + m_g^J (g_p^J - m^J g_u^J) \right]$ and is an extended version of chapter 3's determinant, denotes Walrasian stability. Equation (4.24) can be written as

$$
\frac{dp}{dT} = \left[(m_u^B - m_u^A) + (m_g^B g_u^B - m_g^A g_u^A) \right] \Delta
$$

The first term on the right-hand side is then the familiar term involving differences in marginal propensity to consume good y, that is the price of good y increases if the recipient has a higher marginal propensity to consume good y than the donor. The second term on the right-hand side is more difficult to interpret, but it involves the difference between recipient and donor of the cross-effect on the consumption of good y as a result of a change in consumption of public goods (m_g^J) as a consequence of a change in income as measured by welfare (g_u^J; which, from equation [4.19], will be negative if the marginal propensity to consume the public good E_{gu}^J is positive). We cannot draw general conclusions on the size of these effects and thus cannot be very specific regarding the sign of the terms-of-trade effect. Consequently, we also do not know what will happen to the level of the public good produced after the transfer, that is the sign of

$$\frac{dg}{dT} = g_u \frac{du}{dT} + g_p \frac{dp}{dT}$$

cannot be determined.

In contrast, the sign of the welfare terms for both donor and recipient can be determined if we can determine the sign of Ω. If we use equation (4.19) and $m^J \equiv E_p^J - R_p^J$, this term can be written as

$$\Omega \equiv \sum_J \left(m_p^J + m_g^J g_p^J \right) = \sum_J \left(m_p^J - \frac{(E_{gp}^J - R_{gp}^J)^2}{(E_{gg}^J - R_{gg}^J)} \right) < 0$$

where the inequality follows from the fact that the compensated own-price effect m_p^J is non-positive (strictly negative if there is any substitution at all) and from the fact that $(E_{gg}^J - R_{gg}^J) > 0$; see the previous subsection. Therefore, the recipient gains and the donor loses from the transfer; see equations (4.25) and (4.26).

> **Proposition 3:** (Kemp and Abe) Samuelson's theorem, which states that the donor loses and the recipient gains from an international transfer in a perfectly competitive, two-good, two-country and Walrasian-stable world, also holds if there is a country-specific public consumption good which is provided efficiently.

Although we have limited ourselves in this section to what we think is the most interesting case of country-specific public consumption goods, Kemp and Abe also show that Samuelson's theorem holds if there are country-specific public intermediate goods (such that the analysis simplifies in equations [4.14] and [4.16] to $R_g^J = 0$) and if there are pure international public goods.

4.3 Non-traded goods

Samuelson's theorem is based on the analysis of two tradable goods. In contrast, the discussion between Keynes and Ohlin, summarized in chapter 2, in part emphasizes the importance of non-tradable goods. As Keynes expected a terms-of-trade deterioration, that is a fall in the price of export goods, the "necessary" changeover in the character of production, from the non-tradable sector to the export sector (with falling prices), would be very difficult indeed, thereby, in Keynes's view, aggravating the transfer problem. We now investigate what happens if there is a non-tradable good in both countries; see McDougall (1965), Chipman (1974) and Jones (1975). At this point it may not be clear to the reader that there is an analytical similarity between the public goods discussed in the previous section and the non-traded goods discussed in this section. It will become apparent as we continue, however, that the formal model and the solution procedure are the same, although the economic reasoning underlying the model and the derivation of analytic results is quite different.

The discussion between Keynes and Ohlin was partially confused as a result of the inclusion of non-traded goods, where Keynes argued fervently that the transfer would lead to a deterioration of the donor's terms of trade. In contrast, this section demonstrates that the existence of non-traded goods itself does not lead to a presumption of a change in the terms of trade in either direction for the donor, but tends to lead to a rise of the price of non-traded goods relative to traded goods for the recipient and to a fall of the price of non-traded goods relative to traded goods for the donor. This is in exact agreement with Ohlin's view as expressed in chapter 2.

We analyze international transfers in the context of non-traded goods with the assumptions that there are two countries, A and B, two traded goods, good y with price p and numéraire good x, and a non-traded good that has to be locally provided in each country with a relative price of the non-traded good q^J for country $J = A, B$.[2] Let E^J denote country J's expenditure function, R^J country J's revenue function, T the transfer of good x given by country A to country B, and m^J country J's net demand for good y, that is $m^J \equiv E_p^J - R_p^J$. The equilibrium of the world economy is then described by the system of equations.

$$E^A(p, q^A, u^A) = R^A(p, q^A) - T \tag{4.28}$$

$$E_q^A(p, q^A, u^A) = R_q^A(p, q^A) \tag{4.29}$$

$$E^B(p, q^B, u^B) = R^B(p, q^B) + T \tag{4.30}$$

$$E_q^B(p, q^B, u^B) = R_q^B(p, q^B) \tag{4.31}$$

$$m^A(p, q^A, u^A) + m^B(p, q^B, u^B) = 0 \tag{4.32}$$

Equation (4.28) is the donor's budget constraint. Similarly, equation (4.30) is the recipient's budget constraint. Since the non-traded good has

[2] One could argue that the costs of transportation of non-traded goods are infinite.

to be produced domestically for both donor and recipient, domestic demand E_q^J must be equal to domestic supply R_q^J for non-traded goods, as indicated in equations (4.29) and (4.31), respectively. Finally, equation (4.32) is the market-clearing condition for good y.

Note that the analytic structure of the non-traded goods system (4.28) (4.32) in this section is identical to the analytic structure of the public goods system (4.13) (4.17) in the previous section, with the q^J terms in the former substituting for the g^J terms in the latter. However, q^J in the former is the price of the non-traded good in country J, such that, for example, E_q^J denotes the level of consumption of the non-traded good in country J, while g^J in the latter is the quantity of public goods provided in country J, such that, for example, E_g^J is the reduction in private expenditure to achieve a certain welfare level following an increase in the level of public goods provided in country J (equal to minus the marginal willingness to pay). Thus, to continue this example, while in this section $E_{qq}^J \leq 0$ because the expenditure function is concave in prices, in the previous section $E_{gg}^J > 0$ because the marginal willingness to pay falls as the level of public goods provided rises. We cannot, therefore, draw automatic conclusions for international transfers where there are non-traded goods simply because the analytic structure is the same as for public goods.

To analyze the consequences of international transfers in this setting it is of course possible to totally differentiate equations (4.28)–(4.32) and solve, but it is rather cumbersome to invert a five-dimensional matrix. It is simpler to reduce the model from five equations to three equations, as in the previous section. This can be done rather easily since equations (4.29) and (4.31) can be used to solve for the price of non-traded goods for recipient and donor as a function of domestic welfare and the relative price of good y. For country J this implies

$$q^J = q^J(p, u^J) \quad \text{for } J = A, B \quad \text{with} \tag{4.33}$$

$$q_p = -\frac{(E_{qp}^J - R_{qp}^J)}{(E_{qq}^J - R_{qq}^J)} \quad \text{and} \quad q_u = -\frac{E_{qu}^J}{(E_{qq}^J - R_{qq}^J)} \tag{4.34}$$

Note that if there is any substitution at all in either production or consumption of the non-traded good in country J, then equation (4.33) is well-defined because that implies $E_{qq}^J - R_{qq}^J < 0$. Furthermore, note that if the traded good y and the non-traded good are net substitutes (that is, $E_{qp}^J - R_{qp}^J > 0$) then q_p^J is positive, while if the non-traded good is a normal good (that is, $E_{qu}^J > 0$) then q_u^J is also positive; see equation (4.34). Substituting equations (4.33) into equations (4.28), (4.30) and (4.32) leads to the system

$$E^A(p, q^A(p, u^A), u^A) = R^A(p, q^A(p, u^A)) - T \tag{4.35}$$

$$E^B(p, q^B(p, u^B), u^B) = R^B(p, q^B(p, u^B)) + T \tag{4.36}$$

$$m^A(p, q^A(p, u^A), u^A) + m^B(p, q^B(p, u^B), u^B) = 0 \tag{4.37}$$

Normalize such that $E_u^J = 1$ and define $\Omega \equiv \sum_J \left(m_p^J + m_q^J q_p^J \right)$ and $F^J \equiv m_u^J + m_q^J q_u^J$ for $J = A, B$ for convenience. Then, differentiating system (4.35)–(4.37) with respect to p, u^A, u^B and T and using equations (4.29) and (4.31), that is the market-clearing conditions for non-traded goods, gives

$$\begin{bmatrix} m^A & 1 & 0 \\ m^B & 0 & 1 \\ \Omega & F^A & F^B \end{bmatrix} \begin{bmatrix} dp \\ du^A \\ du^B \end{bmatrix} = \begin{bmatrix} -1 \\ 1 \\ 0 \end{bmatrix} dT \tag{4.38}$$

Solving equation (4.38) and using (4.37):

$$\det = \Omega - m^A F^A - m^B F^B \equiv \frac{-1}{\Delta} < 0 \tag{4.39}$$

$$\frac{dp}{dT} = \left(F^B - F^A \right) \Delta \tag{4.40}$$

$$\frac{du^A}{dT} = \Omega \Delta \tag{4.41}$$

$$\frac{du^B}{dT} = -\Omega \Delta \tag{4.42}$$

$$\frac{du^A}{dT} + \frac{du^B}{dT} = 0 \tag{4.43}$$

If we can unambiguously sign the variable Ω, we can derive unambiguous welfare effects as well. Fortunately, it follows from the definition of Ω and equation (4.34) that

$$\Omega \equiv \sum_J \left(m_p^J - \frac{(m_q^J)^2}{(E_{qq}^J - R_{qq}^J)} \right) \tag{4.44}$$

Thus, using the definition of $m^J \equiv E_p^J - R_p^J$, a sufficient condition for Ω to be negative is that each term in the summation is negative, that is

$$(E_{pp}^J - R_{pp}^J) - \frac{(E_{pq}^J - R_{pq}^J)^2}{(E_{qq}^J - R_{qq}^J)} < 0, \quad \text{for } J = A, B \tag{4.45}$$

Since the net expenditure function $E^J - R^J$ is concave in prices, both conditions in equation (4.45) are satisfied (the matrix of second-order price derivatives is negative semi-definite, such that $(E_{pp}^J - R_{pp}^J)$ $(E_{qq}^J - R_{qq}^J) - (E_{pq}^J - R_{pq}^J)^2 > 0)$. Therefore, Ω is negative and the equations (4.41) and (4.42) imply that the donor loses from the transfer and the recipient gains.

> **Proposition 4:** Samuelson's theorem, which states that the donor loses and the recipient gains from an international transfer in a perfectly competitive, two-good, two-country and Walrasian-stable world, also holds if there is a country-specific non-traded good in each country.

The change in the terms of trade is not as easy to derive. From equation (4.40) it follows that the price of traded good y rises relative to traded numéraire good x if, and only if, $F^B - F^A$ is positive. Using the definitions of F^J and equation (4.34) it follows that:

$$F^B - F^A = (m_u^B - m_u^A) - \left(\frac{m_q^B E_{qu}^B}{(E_{qq}^B - R_{qq}^B)} - \frac{m_q^A E_{qu}^A}{(E_{qq}^A - R_{qq}^A)} \right) \qquad (4.46)$$

The first term on the right-hand side of equation (4.46) is the standard effect that the price of good y will rise as a result of the transfer relative to the price of good x if the recipient's marginal propensity to spend on good y is larger than the donor's marginal propensity to spend on good y. The second term on the right-hand side of equation (4.46) demonstrates that the interactive effect of non-traded goods is also important in determining the terms-of-trade effect. Suppose, for the sake of argument, that traded good y and the non-traded good are net substitutes (m_q^J is positive for both countries). Then, other things being equal (that is, assume $m_u^B - m_u^A$, $m_q^B = m_q^A$ and $E_{qq}^B - R_{qq}^B = E_{qq}^A - R_{qq}^A$), if the recipient's marginal propensity to consume non-traded goods is higher than the donor's marginal propensity to consume non-traded goods ($E_{qu}^B > E_{qu}^A$) this will lead to a fall in the demand for traded good x, and hence a rise in the relative price of traded good y. In general, we agree with Ohlin's assertion that there is no presumption for the terms of trade to move in either direction as a result of an international transfer.

Suppose, then, that there is an international transfer in this model with non-traded goods between two identical countries. Since $F^B = F^A$ there is no change in the terms of trade; see equation (4.40). How about the price of non-traded goods? It follows from equation (4.33) that

$$\frac{dq^J}{dT} = q_u^J \frac{du^J}{dT} + q_p^J \frac{dp}{dT} \qquad (4.47)$$

For a transfer between two identical countries $dp/dT = 0$. Since du^B/dT is always positive, it follows from equation (4.47) that under such circumstances the sign of dq^B/dT is the same as the sign of q_u^B, which in turn is the same as the sign of E_{qu}^B. In short, the recipient's price of non-traded goods rises if, and only if, the marginal propensity to consume non-traded goods is positive. Similar reasoning with the opposite effect holds for the donor of the transfer.

> **Proposition 5:** (Ohlin's presumption) If an international transfer between two countries in the presence of non-traded goods does not affect the terms of trade, then the transfer raises (lowers) the price of non-traded goods relative to traded goods for the recipient (donor) if, and only if, the marginal propensity to consume non-traded goods is positive for the recipient (donor).

4.4   Endogenous transfers I

Samuelson's theorem is based on the analysis of strictly autonomous transfers. Analytically this means that transfers are treated parametrically by donors and recipients. In practice, however, many donors relate the amount of aid to be given to the welfare level of the recipient. The richer a developing country is, the less aid it usually receives from donors. Moreover, donors give more the richer they are. The positive relation with respect to the donor's income has even been formalized in United Nations Resolution No. 2626, obliging wealthy nations to give at least 0.7 percent of GNP for development assistance.[3] This suggests that the size of a transfer partially depends on the income or expenditure level of donor or recipient. This dependence is analyzed by Brakman and Van Marrewijk (1991a), who label the phenomenon "endogenization." One might expect at the outset that paradoxes are possible, because the richer the recipient becomes the less aid it will receive, and the poorer the donor becomes the less aid it will give. This section briefly investigates the consequences of such "endogenization"; see also chapter 6 for a more complete analysis.

We analyze international transfers in the context of endogenization with the assumptions that there are two countries, A and B, and two traded goods, good y with price p and numéraire good x. Let E^J denote country J's expenditure function, R^J country J's revenue function and m^J country J's net demand for good y, that is $m^J \equiv E_p^J - R_p^J$. The total transfer of good x given by country A to country B now consists of an endogenous part $T(E^A)$ and an autonomous part Ta. The endogenous

---

[3] Only a few countries comply with this resolution; see chapter 1.

part of the transfer increases if the donor's wealth, as measured by its expenditure level, increases, that is $T_{E^A} > 0$. The equilibrium of the world economy is then described by the system of equations.

$$E^A(p, u^A) = R^A(p) - T(E^A(p, u^A)) - Ta \qquad (4.48)$$

$$E^B(p, u^B) - R^B(p) + T(E^A(p, u^A)) + Ta \qquad (4.49)$$

$$m^A(p, u^A) + m^B(p, u^B) = 0 \qquad (4.50)$$

Normalize such that $E_u^J = 1$ and define $M_p \equiv \sum_J m_p^J$ for $J = A, B$. Then, differentiating system (4.48)–(4.50) with respect to p, u^A, u^B and Ta gives

$$\begin{bmatrix} m^A + E_p^A T_{E^A} & 1 + T_{E^A} & 0 \\ m^B - E_p^A T_{E^A} & -T_{E^A} & 1 \\ M_p & m_u^A & m_u^B \end{bmatrix} \begin{bmatrix} dp \\ du^A \\ du^B \end{bmatrix} = \begin{bmatrix} -1 \\ 1 \\ 0 \end{bmatrix} dTa$$

Solving gives

$$\det = (1 + T_{E^A})\left(\sum_J m_p^J - m^J m_u^J \right) + T_{E^A} R_p^A (m_u^B - m_u^A) \equiv \frac{-1}{\bar{\Delta}} < 0 \quad (4.51)$$

$$\frac{dp}{dTa} = (m_u^B - m_u^A)\bar{\Delta} > 0 \quad \text{iff} \quad m_u^B > m_u^A \qquad (4.52)$$

$$\frac{du^A}{dTa} = M_p \bar{\Delta} \le 0 \qquad (4.53)$$

$$\frac{du^B}{dTa} = -M_p \bar{\Delta} > 0 \qquad (4.54)$$

The inequality in equation (4.51) follows from Walrasian stability applied to the system of equations (4.48)–(4.50) and is a slightly extended version of equation (3.5) in chapter 3. It is apparent from equations (4.52)–(4.54) that endogenization of the transfer has not caused any qualitative changes in the conclusions relating to an autonomous change in the size of international transfers. That is, the donor's terms of trade still only improve if the recipient's marginal propensity to consume the donor's export good is larger than the donor's marginal propensity to consume this good, while the donor always loses and the recipient always gains from the transfer. Chapter 6 discusses these results further and demonstrates that they also apply for other types of endogenization, in which the size of the transfer is related to the donor's revenue and/or the recipient's expenditure or revenue level.

Proposition 6: Samuelson's theorem, which states that the donor loses and the recipient gains from an international transfer in a perfectly competitive, two-good, two-country and Walrasian-stable world, generalizes to endogenous transfers in which the size of the transfer is related to the donor's and/or recipient's expenditure and/or welfare level.

4.5   Many goods

Samuelson's theorem is based on the analysis of just two tradable goods. The introduction of many goods complicates the analysis considerably. Since we are dealing with a multitude of exported and imported goods, the terms-of-trade concept is not easily defined. Furthermore, taking the recipient as an example, is it possible that a fall in the price of all its export goods dominates the income effect, thus leading to recipient-impoverishment? We now analyze what happens if we have an arbitrary, but finite, number of tradable goods. There are again two countries, denoted A and B. Country A makes a transfer to country B. Both countries may produce and consume $n + 1$ final goods, indexed by i for $i = 1, ..., n + 1$. Good $n + 1$ is the numéraire, while p^i is the relative price of good i for $i = 1, ..., n$. The function E^J is the minimum expenditure necessary to achieve utility u^J at relative price $\mathbf{p} = (p^1, ..., p^n)'$ in country J, while R^J is the maximum revenue obtainable using current technology and inputs at price $\mathbf{p}$ in country $J = A, B$. We suppress throughout the remainder of this book the dependence of the revenue function on the available inputs if they remain fixed. Only if the (vector of) available inputs is affected do we explicitly use these as arguments in the revenue function. As in the previous chapter we denote imports for good i, or the net demand for good i, in country J by the variable m^{iJ} and denote $\mathbf{m}^J = (m^{1J}, ..., m^{nJ})'$, such that $\mathbf{m}^J \equiv E_{\mathbf{p}}^J - R_{\mathbf{p}}^J$. The central equations are:

$$E^A(\mathbf{p}, u^A) = R^A(\mathbf{p}) - T \tag{4.55}$$

$$E^B(\mathbf{p}, u^B) = R^B(\mathbf{p}) + T \tag{4.56}$$

$$\mathbf{m}^A(\mathbf{p}, u^A) + \mathbf{m}^B(\mathbf{p}, u^B) = 0 \tag{4.57}$$

Equation (4.55) indicates that total expenditure E^A for the donor of the transfer is equal to the total revenue from production R^A minus the outlays for the transfer abroad T. The latter is assumed to be raised from the inhabitants of the donating country through lump-sum taxes. Similarly, equation (4.56) indicates that total expenditure E^B for the recipient of the transfer is equal to the total revenue from production R^B plus the receipts of the transfer from abroad T. The latter is assumed to be distributed among the inhabitants of the receiving country in a lump-sum fashion. Equation (4.57) gives the n market-clearing conditions for goods $i = 1, .., n$ and thus, by Walras's law, for good $n + 1$. Define the world net substitution matrix $\mathbf{M}_p = \sum_J \mathbf{m}_p^J$. The effect of an international transfer from country A to country B can be derived by totally differentiating system (4.55)–(4.57):

$$
\begin{bmatrix} \mathbf{m}^{A'} & 1 & 0 \\ \mathbf{m}^{B'} & 0 & 1 \\ \mathbf{M}_p & \mathbf{m}_u^A & \mathbf{m}_u^B \end{bmatrix} \begin{bmatrix} d\mathbf{p} \\ du^A \\ du^B \end{bmatrix} = \begin{bmatrix} -1 \\ 1 \\ 0 \end{bmatrix} dT \tag{4.58}
$$

Although the total effect on the prices of the various goods is not transparent (and analytically not very informative) the sign of the welfare effect for donor and recipient is remarkably easy to determine. Thus, if we want to determine the welfare effect of the transfer for the donor we must investigate the determinant of the coefficient matrix on the left-hand side of (4.58) with the column vector on the right-hand side of (4.58) substituted at column $n + 1$:

$$
\begin{vmatrix} \mathbf{m}^{A'} & -1 & 0 \\ \mathbf{m}^{B'} & 1 & 1 \\ \mathbf{M}_p & 0 & \mathbf{m}_u^B \end{vmatrix} = (-1)^{n+3} \begin{vmatrix} \mathbf{m}^{B'} & 1 \\ \mathbf{M}_p & \mathbf{m}_u^B \end{vmatrix} + (-1)^{n+3} \begin{vmatrix} \mathbf{m}^{A'} & 0 \\ \mathbf{M}_p & \mathbf{m}_u^B \end{vmatrix}
$$

$$
= (-1)^{2(n+1)+1} |\mathbf{M}_p| - |\mathbf{M}_p| \tag{4.59}
$$

The first equality in equation (4.59) follows from expansion of the determinant with respect to column $n + 1$. The second equality in equation (4.59) follows from expansion of the two sub-determinants with respect to the first row, using $m^{iA} + m^{iB} = 0$ for the first n terms of expansion. The third equality in (4.59) follows from the fact that $2(n + 1) + 1$ is odd. Thus, using Cramer's rule the recipient's welfare change (which is equal to minus the donor's welfare change, as the reader may verify) is given by:

$$
\frac{du^B}{dT} = -\frac{du^A}{dT} = \frac{|\mathbf{M}_p|}{\begin{vmatrix} \mathbf{m}^{A'} & 1 & 0 \\ \mathbf{m}^{B'} & 0 & 1 \\ \mathbf{M}_p & \mathbf{m}_u^A & \mathbf{m}_u^B \end{vmatrix}} \geq 0 \tag{4.60}
$$

The inequality in (4.60) follows from Walrasian stability, implying that the signs of numerator and denominator are both equal to $(-1)^n$. As pointed out by Kemp (1995, p. 352) the above result that transfer paradoxes are ruled out in a perfectly competitive Walrasian-stable world with many traded goods and just two countries "seems to be missing from the literature." Safra (1983), however, provides an unpublished, somewhat more complicated proof.

> **Proposition 7:** (Safra) Samuelson's theorem, which states that the donor loses and the recipient gains from an international transfer in a perfectly competitive, two-good, two-country and Walrasian-stable world, generalizes to an arbitrary, but finite, number of traded goods.

4.6   Conclusion

The preceding chapter introduced the bare structural essentials for giving a complete analytic description of international transfers in a general equilibrium framework. That is, chapter 3 only analyzed autonomous transfers where there are two traded private goods and two countries in a perfectly competitive Walrasian-stable world. That structure allowed us to draw a sharp conclusion which we labeled Samuelson's theorem: the recipient gains and the donor loses as a result of the transfer.

This chapter has built on the results of chapter 3 by extending the basic model in various ways to analyze several issues which seem to be important in the real world. Some people might argue that such extensions make the model "less abstract." However, something is either abstract or real. Any model is abstract, otherwise it would not be a model. It is therefore better, although less attractive, to say that such extensions make the model "more complicated." In any case, section 4.2 analyzed public goods, while section 4.3 investigated non-traded goods using a structurally identical model. Section 4.4 discussed "endogenous" transfers in which the size of the transfer depended on a nation's level of wealth. Section 4.5, finally, introduced an arbitrary, but finite, number of traded goods. In all extensions considered, Samuelson's theorem still holds. We may therefore conclude that Samuelson's basic theorem is fairly robust with respect to a number of interesting extensions. On the other hand, however, the remainder of this book will demonstrate that this chapter has stretched Samuelson's result close to its limits.

5   Clouds on the horizon 1: distortions

The previous chapter analyzed several generalizations of the simple two-good, two-country, distortion-free Samuelson model introduced in chapter 3. Samuelson's theorem, that the recipient gains and the donor loses as a result of an international transfer, was shown to hold for all generalizations considered in chapter 4, in particular for public goods, non-traded goods and an arbitrary number of traded goods. Chapter 4 did not, however, analyze a variety of interesting phenomena which seem to be important in the real world, such as tariffs, rent-seeking, cost of administration, unemployment, etc. These phenomena fall under the heading "distortions," that is deviations from the standard neoclassical assumptions which lead to Pareto-optimal outcomes. The concept of non-Pareto optimality with respect to distortions says that as a result of a distortion *some* countries' welfare (utility) can be increased without decreasing any other countries' welfare. For example, if for some reason a country levies a tariff on its import good, the resulting world economy equilibrium will in general not be Pareto-optimal; the abolishment of tariffs raises the welfare for some or all concerned.[1] This chapter analyzes a number of such distortions. Naturally, we could investigate several different distortions at the same time in one model.[2] The problem with such an approach is that it is in principle difficult to associate any particular analytical result to a specific distortion. It is therefore both simpler and possibly better to analyze one distortion at a time. We confine ourselves in this chapter to a number of important distortions that have attracted attention in the empirical literature; see Jepma (1991) for a survey.

As we shall see in this chapter, under some circumstances transfer paradoxes may arise as a result of distortions (Polemarchakis [1983];

---

[1] In order to improve actual welfare for everybody it might be necessary to redistribute income in such a way that indeed everybody is at least as well of as before.

[2] See, for example, Lahiri and Raimondos (1995) or Michael and Van Marrewijk (1998).

Safra [1984]; Jones [1985]; Bhagwati *et al.* [1985]). This immediately raises the question why a recipient would accept such a welfare-reducing transfer in the first place. The answer is clear. First, prices are treated parametrically, that is taken as given, by all agents in the economy. Second, decision-making is decentralized and the interaction of these decisions determines prices at the macro-level. It is important to keep in mind that for any *given* price level, receiving a transfer will always improve welfare for the recipient. The fact that a transfer can lead to price *changes* is essential for understanding transfer paradoxes.

5.1   Immiserizing growth and the administration of foreign aid

There is a close, but not very obvious, link between the costs of administration of foreign aid and the concept of immiserizing growth. These costs can range from the costs of administrative procedures to transportation costs, spoilage, rent-seeking, etc. "Immiserizing growth" is the phenomenon of a country experiencing a decline in welfare despite the fact that it has increased its productive capacity, such that it is able to produce more goods. This section first analyzes immiserizing growth and then turns to the costs of administration of foreign aid. The reader should keep in mind that the next subsection on immiserizing growth does not involve international transfers. The link between the immiserizing growth literature and the international transfer literature will become clear when we subsequently discuss the cost of administration of foreign aid.

5.1.1   Immiserizing growth or advantageous destruction

It has been known for a long time in the international trade literature, at least since the seminal article of Jagdish Bhagwati (1958), that an economic expansion may harm the growing country itself (see also Bhagwati [1969]; Brecher and Bhagwati [1982]; Srinivasan and Bhagwati [1983a, 1983b, 1984]; and Bhagwati *et al.* [1984]).[3] To reverse the logic of the "immiserizing growth" argument: it may be beneficial to throw away some produced goods, as we will now show. This is called "advantageous destruction." There are two countries, A and B, and two goods, good y with relative price p and numéraire good x. Let E^J denote country J's expenditure function, R^J its revenue function, u^J its welfare level and m^J

---

[3] Bhagwati gives due credit to Harry Johnson in his 1958 contribution. See Bhagwati (1968) for a further analysis of immiserizing growth. Here we have simplified his analysis somewhat by directly throwing away a produced good rather than a factor of production; see, however, section 5.3.

its net demand for good y, that is $m^J \equiv E_p^J - R_p^J$. The perfectly competitive, two-good, two-country destruction model is then given by equations (5.1)–(5.3):

$$E^A(p, u^A) = R^A(p) - D \tag{5.1}$$

$$E^B(p, u^B) = R^B(p) \tag{5.2}$$

$$m^A(p, u^A) + m^B(p, u^B) = 0 \tag{5.3}$$

Equation (5.1) denotes the budget constraint of country A which throws some of its produced goods x away, where D is the number of destroyed numéraire goods. It is thus implicitly assumed that there are no costs involved in the destruction of the produced goods. Equation (5.2) denotes the budget constraint of the outside country, not involved in the destruction of goods. Equation (5.3) is the market-clearing condition for good y, and thus by Walras's law for good x.

Totally differentiate equations (5.1)–(5.3), normalize $E_u^J = 1$, evaluate at $D = 0$ and define $M_p = \sum_J m_p^J$ and $\Delta^{-1} = -\sum_J (m_p^J - m^J m_u^J)$ for $J = A, B$ to obtain equation (5.4).

$$\begin{bmatrix} m^A & 1 & 0 \\ m^B & 0 & 1 \\ M_p & m_u^A & m_u^B \end{bmatrix} \begin{bmatrix} dp \\ du^A \\ du^B \end{bmatrix} = \begin{bmatrix} -1 \\ 0 \\ 0 \end{bmatrix} dD \tag{5.4}$$

Solving equation (5.4) gives

$$\det = \sum_J (m_p^J - m^J m_u^J) \equiv \frac{-1}{\Delta} < 0 \tag{5.5}$$

$$\frac{dp}{dD} = -m_u^A \Delta \tag{5.6}$$

$$\frac{du^A}{dD} = (M_p - m^B m_u^B) \Delta \tag{5.7}$$

$$\frac{du^B}{dD} = m^B m_u^A \Delta \tag{5.8}$$

$$\frac{du^A}{dD} + \frac{du^B}{dD} = (M_p - m^B m_u^B + m^B m_u^A) \Delta = \det \Delta = -1 < 0 \tag{5.9}$$

The inequality in equation (5.5) indicates Walrasian stability. Equation (5.6) shows that the relative price of good y, that is of the good that is *not* thrown away, falls as a result of the destruction, provided the destroyer's marginal propensity to consume good y is positive. Equation (5.8) shows that in that case the non-destroying country loses if, and only if, it is a net demander of the destroyed good. Equation (5.7) demonstrates that the country which destroys some of the goods it produces will gain from this action if, and only if, the following condition holds:

$$M_p - m^B m_u^B > 0 \qquad (5.10)$$

Since M_p is non-positive, a necessary, but not sufficient, condition for the destroyer to gain is $-m^B m_u^B > 0$, which, if the non-destroying country's marginal propensity to consume good y is positive ($m_u^B > 0$), requires that it is a net supplier of good y (that is $-m^B > 0$), such that the destroyer has a net demand for good y (that is $m^A = -m^B > 0$) and a net supply of the good x, which is thrown away. This demonstrates that it may be advantageous to limit the supply of your export good, that is to exercise your monopoly power on the world market, in order to improve your terms of trade to such an extent that your welfare improves (see also Choi and Yu [1987]). Equation (5.9), finally, demonstrates that world welfare declines as a result of country A's action, which obviously is not Pareto-optimal.

To be somewhat more precise on the extent of the monopoly power of country A, let $\tilde{m}^B$ denote the non-destroying country's *un*compensated import demand curve for good y. Recall the net Slutsky equation (see the appendix to chapter 3), decomposing the uncompensated price change into the substitution effect and the income effects:

$$\tilde{m}_p^B = m_p^B - m^B m_u^B \qquad (5.11)$$

Substituting equation (5.11) into condition (5.10), and recalling $M_p \equiv m_p^A + m_p^B$, demonstrates that the country which destroys some of the goods it produces will gain from this action if, and only if, the following alternative condition holds:

$$\tilde{m}_p^B + m_p^A > 0 \qquad (5.12)$$

Since m_p^A, the compensated price effect, is non-positive, this demonstrates that the destroying country will gain (or immiserizing growth may occur) only if $\tilde{m}_p^B$ is positive, that is only if the non-destroying country's offer curve is inelastic (thus its import demand rises if the price of country A's export good increases). Remember, that a backward-bending offer curve for the non-destroying country ($\tilde{m}_p^B > 0$) is only compatible with Walrasian stability if country A's uncompensated price effect is sufficiently negative that the stability condition $\tilde{m}_p^B + \tilde{m}_p^A < 0$ holds; see the appendix to chapter 3.

> **Proposition 8:** (Bhagwati) In a two-good, Walrasian-stable, two-country world of perfect competition it may be advantageous for one country to throw away a small portion of a good under the necessary, but not sufficient, condition that the offer curve of the other country is backward-bending.

5.1.2   The costs of administration

Murray Kemp and Kar-yiu Wong (1993) investigate a perfectly competitive two-good, two-country model in which the administration of foreign aid is costly. For simplicity, these costs of administration are borne by the recipient only and modeled analogously to Samuelson's "iceberg" costs of transportation; see Samuelson (1952, 1954). Thus, it is assumed that if T^c units of aid are transferred from the donor to the recipient, where the superscript c is a reminder of the costs of administration, only ωT^c units arrive, where $0 \leq \omega \leq 1$. The *higher* the parameter ω, the larger the fraction of aid that arrives, and hence the *lower* the costs of administration. As the costs of administration diminish the income effect for the recipient, one might expect that adverse terms-of-trade effects could dominate the income effect.

There are two countries, donor A and recipient B, and two goods, good y with relative price p and numéraire good x. Let E^J denote country J's expenditure function, R^J its revenue function, u^J its welfare level and m^J its net demand for good y, that is $m^J \equiv E_p^J - R_p^J$. The cost-of-administration model is then given by equations (5.13)–(5.15):

$$E^A(p, u^A) = R^A(p) - T^c \tag{5.13}$$

$$E^B(p, u^B) = R^B(p) + \omega T^c \tag{5.14}$$

$$m^B(p, u^B) + m^A(p, u^A) = 0 \tag{5.15}$$

Equation (5.13) denotes the donor's budget constraint, taking the transfer of T^c units of good x into consideration. Equation (5.14) denotes the recipient's budget constraint, where ω is the fraction of aid that arrives or is not wasted, such that ωT^c is available. Equation (5.15) is the market-clearing condition for good y. Totally differentiating equations (5.13)–(5.15), normalizing $E_u^J = 1$ and defining $M_p = \sum_J m_p^J$ and $\Delta^{-1} = -\sum_J \left(m_p^J - m^J m_u^J \right)$ for $J = A, B$ gives:

$$\begin{bmatrix} m^A & 1 & 0 \\ m^B & 0 & 1 \\ M_p & m_u^A & m_u^B \end{bmatrix} \begin{bmatrix} dp \\ du^A \\ du^B \end{bmatrix} = \begin{bmatrix} -1 \\ \omega \\ 0 \end{bmatrix} dT^c \qquad (5.16)$$

Solving equation (5.16):

$$\det = \sum_J \left(m_p^J - m^J m_u^J \right) \equiv \frac{-1}{\Delta} < 0 \qquad (5.17)$$

$$\frac{dp}{dT^c} = \left(\omega m_u^B - m_u^A \right) \Delta \qquad (5.18)$$

$$\frac{du^A}{dT^c} = \left[M_p - (1 - \omega) m^B m_u^B \right] \Delta \qquad (5.19)$$

$$\frac{du^B}{dT^c} = \left[(1 - \omega) m^B m_u^A - \omega M_p \right] \Delta \qquad (5.20)$$

$$\frac{du^A}{dT^c} + \frac{du^B}{dT^c} = -(1 - \omega) \qquad (5.21)$$

It is important to note that from a world welfare point of view, the costs of administration of foreign aid are a pure waste; see equation (5.21). The higher the costs of administration, the greater the decrease in world welfare. Both the standard two-country model of international transfers discussed in chapter 3 (see equations [3.1]–[3.3] in section 3.4), and the destruction model discussed in the previous subsection (see equations [5.1]–[5.3]) are special cases of this subsection's cost-of-administration model (5.13)–(5.15). If there are no costs of administration ($\omega = 1$), the standard model results. We know from Samuelson's theorem that transfers cannot lead to paradoxes in that context. For ease of reference we restate section 3.4's standard results here:

$$\frac{dp}{dT} = \left(m_u^B - m_u^A \right) \Delta \qquad (5.22)$$

$$\frac{du^A}{dT} = M_p \Delta \qquad (5.23)$$

$$\frac{du^B}{dT} = -M_p \Delta \qquad (5.24)$$

If the costs of administration are equal to the transfer itself and no aid at all arrives ($\omega = 0$), the destruction model results. We have seen that this may lead to a paradoxical gain for the destroying country and it may also lead to a loss for the outside world if its terms of trade are negatively affected; see equation (5.7). Since the standard model and the destruction model are extreme cases of the cost-of-administration model, it is not surprising that the results of the cost-of-administration model can be written as the weighted average of the two extreme cases, with the fraction of aid that arrives as the weight.[4] That is, it follows from equations (5.6)–(5.8) and (5.22)–(5.24) that equations (5.18)–(5.20) can be written as

$$\frac{dp}{dT^c} = (1 - \omega)\frac{dp}{dD} + \omega\frac{dp}{dT} \tag{5.25}$$

$$\frac{du^A}{dT^c} = (1 - \omega)\frac{du^A}{dD} + \omega\frac{du^A}{dT} \tag{5.26}$$

$$\frac{du^B}{dT^c} = (1 - \omega)\frac{du^B}{dD} + \omega\frac{du^B}{dT} \tag{5.27}$$

We know from Samuelson's theorem that under standard conditions the donor is worse off as a result of the transfer, that is $du^A/dT < 0$. Now suppose that the donor would gain if it destroyed some of the numéraire goods, that is assume $du^A/dD > 0$. It was discussed in the previous subsection under what conditions this is possible. It then follows from equation (5.26) that there is a critical value for the costs of administration of foreign aid such that if these costs exceed that critical value, the donor gains, rather than loses, as a result of the transfer. Moreover, under these circumstances there is the striking observation that the donor's gain is increasing with the costs of administration. Note, however, that in the case of optimal destruction, that is $du^A/dD = 0$, it follows from (5.26) that Samuelson's theorem still applies for the donor.

Similarly, to give another possibility, we know from Samuelson's theorem that under standard conditions the recipient gains from a transfer, that is $du^B/dT > 0$. Now suppose that the recipient loses if the donor destroyed some of good x, that is assume $du^B/dD < 0$. It then follows from equation (5.27) that there is a concomitant critical value for the costs of administration of foreign aid such that if these costs exceed that critical value the recipient loses, rather than gains, as a result of the transfer. Moreover, under those circumstances the recipient's loss is increasing with the costs of administration.

Proposition 9: (Kemp and Wong) Transfer paradoxes are possible in a perfectly competitive two-good, two-country world if

---

[4] This was not explictly noted by Kemp and Wong (1993).

the administration of international transfers is costly. Moreover, such potential paradoxes, which can only arise if the recipient's offer curve is backward-bending, are more pronounced the higher the costs of administration.

5.2   Unemployment

In the Keynes–Ohlin debate, reviewed in chapter 2, Keynes argued that international transfers will shift resources from one sector to another. Potential difficulties in the economic reasoning underlying Samuelson's theorem may arise, therefore, if resources are shifted into or out of the unproductive "unemployment" sector (Bhaduri and Skarstein 1996). Needless to say, Germany was plagued by massive unemployment during the time of the Keynes–Ohlin debate. Indeed, Keynes emphasized in his rejoinder (1929b) that the terms-of-trade deterioration, that he thought necessary to pay for the transfer, would enable German manufacturers to absorb workers who were then unemployed into the production of exports. Two stylized representations of unemployment will be considered in this section: first, sticky wage unemployment for the donor (see also Berthélemy [1988] and Beladi [1990]); and second, Harris–Todaro-type unemployment for the recipient. In this section and the next two sections, (changes in) factors of production become important, which implies that the method of analysis could also be cast in terms of the profit function (see Varian [1992]).

5.2.1   Sticky wage unemployment

There are two countries, donor A and recipient B, and two goods, numéraire good x and good y with relative price p. Let E^J denote country J's expenditure function, R^J its revenue function, u^J its welfare level and m^J its net demand for good y, that is $m^J \equiv E_p^J - R_p^J$. We investigate the effects of a sticky real wage w in terms of numéraire good x for the donor A. Extension of the analysis to a sticky real wage for the recipient (reverse the transfer below) or for both donor and recipient is straightforward. The present setting may be regarded as a stylized representation of a transfer given by a European country (where a number of economists claim unemployment arises from too high real wages). If donor A's sticky real wage w^A is a binding restriction, as we will assume throughout this subsection, actual employment v^A is endogenously (demand) determined; see equation (5.29). The sticky real wage transfer problem is summarized in equations (5.28)–(5.31):

$$E^A(p, u^A) = R^A(p, v^A) - T \tag{5.28}$$

$$R_v^A(p, v^A) = w^A \tag{5.29}$$

$$E^B(p, u^B) = R^B(p) + T \tag{5.30}$$

$$m^A(p, u^A, v^A) + m^B(p, u^B) = 0 \tag{5.31}$$

Equation (5.28) is the donor's budget constraint, taking the transfer T into consideration. Note, in particular, that the donor's revenue function R^A depends on actual employment v^A. Equation (5.29) determines donor A's employment level v^A, given the relative price p for good y and real wage w^A. Equation (5.30) is the recipient's budget constraint. Equation (5.31), finally, determines market equilibrium for good y. Equations (5.28)–(5.31) are four equations in the four unknowns p, u^A, u^B and v^A. Totally differentiating (5.28)–(5.31), normalizing the derivative of expenditure with respect to utility to unity at the initial equilibrium ($E_u^J = 1$), defining $M_p \equiv \sum_J m_p^J$ and recalling $dw^A = 0$ gives:

$$\begin{bmatrix} m^A & 1 & 0 & -w^A \\ R_{vp}^A & 0 & 0 & R_{vv}^A \\ m^B & 0 & 1 & 0 \\ M_p & m_u^A & m_u^B & -R_{pv}^A \end{bmatrix} \begin{bmatrix} dp \\ du^A \\ du^B \\ dv^A \end{bmatrix} = \begin{bmatrix} -1 \\ 0 \\ 1 \\ 0 \end{bmatrix} dT \tag{5.32}$$

Define country A's Stolper–Samuelson factor price elasticity, ε^A, for good y as

$$\varepsilon^A \equiv \frac{\partial w^A}{\partial p} \frac{p}{w^A} = R_{pv}^A \frac{p}{R_v^A}$$

Thus, in a standard Heckscher–Ohlin model ε^A will be larger than 1 if good y uses factor v (labor in this case) intensively and negative if good x uses factor v intensively. Alternatively, ε^A will be positive but smaller than 1 in a Ricardo–Viner model; see, for example, Dixit and Norman (1980). Let μ^A denote the marginal propensity to consume good y in country A, such that $\mu^A = pm_u^A$. Then solving (5.32) gives equations (5.33) and (5.34), while equations (5.35) and (5.36) follow directly from differentiating equations (5.28) and (5.30). Equation (5.37) follows from equations (5.35) and (5.36).

$$\det = R_{vv}^A \left[\sum_J \left(m_p^J - m^J m_u^J \right) \right] + \left(\frac{w^A}{p} \right)^2 \varepsilon^A \left(\varepsilon^A - \mu^A \right) \equiv \frac{1}{\Delta} > 0 \quad (5.33)$$

$$\frac{dp}{dT} = \left(-R_{vv}^A \right) \left(m_u^B - m_u^A \right) \Delta > 0 \qquad \text{iff} \quad m_u^B > m_u^A \qquad (5.34)$$

$$\frac{du^A}{dT} = -1 - m^A \frac{dp}{dT} + w^A \frac{dv^A}{dT} = -1 - m^A \frac{dp}{dT} + \frac{\varepsilon^A \left(w^A \right)^2}{-pR_{vv}^A} \frac{dp}{dT} \qquad (5.35)$$

$$\frac{du^B}{dT} = 1 - m^B \frac{dp}{dT} \qquad (5.36)$$

$$\frac{du^A}{dT} + \frac{du^B}{dT} = \frac{\varepsilon^A \left(w^A \right)^2}{-pR_{vv}^A} \frac{dp}{dT} \qquad (5.37)$$

The inequality in equation (5.33) ensures Walrasian stability. The price of good y rises if, and only if, the recipient's marginal propensity to consume good y exceeds the donor's marginal propensity to consume this good; see (5.34) and recall that $R_{vv}^A \leq 0$. Investigating the donor's welfare change, equation (5.35), we see that there are three rather than two welfare effects: the direct income effect (-1), the terms-of-trade effect $(-m^A[dp/dT])$ and a value-of-employment effect $(w^A[dv^A/dT])$. Using equation (5.29) we see that the employment effect is equal to

$$\frac{dv^A}{dT} = \frac{\varepsilon^A w^A}{-pR_{vv}^A} \frac{dp}{dT}$$

The transfer paradox of donor-enrichment can arise from this third welfare effect. Suppose, for example, that factor v is used intensively by good y in a Heckscher–Ohlin framework, such that $\varepsilon^A > 1$. Then a large rise in the price of good y can lead to such a large gain in employment and income for the donor that its welfare actually rises, rather than falls. This does not necessarily mean that recipient B loses from the transfer because Pareto improvements (in which both countries gain simultaneously) are possible. This depends on the employment effect, as follows from equation (5.37):

$$\frac{du^A}{dT} + \frac{du^B}{dT} = \frac{\varepsilon^A \left(w^A \right)^2}{-pR_{vv}^A} \frac{dp}{dT} = w^A \frac{dv^A}{dT}$$

Proposition 10: In a two-good, two-country world in which the donor of an international transfer is plagued by sticky wage unemployment, as described above, the price of good y rises if, and only if, the recipient's marginal propensity to consume good y is higher than the donor's marginal propensity to consume good y. World welfare rises if, and only if, unemployment is reduced.

5.2.2 Harris–Todaro unemployment

The Harris–Todaro (1970) model of the developing economy distinguishes between a rural sector, producing "basic" products (good x, the numéraire), and an urban sector, producing "manufactures" (good y, with price p).[5] Production in both sectors is perfectly competitive, and uses capital K and labor L. The payment to an input is equal to its marginal revenue product. Workers are attracted from the rural area into the city because of higher real wages there. The fundamental equation underlying the Harris–Todaro model (equation [5.38]) is the combination of a high fixed wage in the manufacturing sector y and the equalization of the expected wage income in the basic sector and the manufacturing sector by laborers. This results in unemployment equal to the fixed supply of labor L minus employment in sectors x and y, L^x and L^y respectively. Throughout the analysis in this subsection we assume that the fixed wage in the manufacturing sector is high enough to result in unemployment in the developing economy.

$$w^x = \frac{L^y}{(L - L^x)} \bar{w}^y \equiv \gamma \bar{w}^y \tag{5.38}$$

The economics underlying the Harris–Todaro model is well known, so we restrict ourselves to simply listing the most important results as summarized in tables 5.1 and 5.2.

If capital is sector-specific (see Khan [1982] and table 5.1), an increase of sector-specific capital at constant prices increases employment in that sector, reduces or keeps constant employment in the other sector, and increases w^x. An increase of the price of manufactures at constant levels of sector-specific capital increases employment in the y sector, reduces employment in the x sector and also drives up w^x.

If capital is intersectorally mobile, the rental rates are the same in the two sectors and internal stability is ensured if, and only if, $\gamma(K^y/L^y) > K^x/L^x$, that is the urban sector is relatively capital-intensive, as we henceforth assume; see Neary (1981). Under this condition, an

---

[5] This subsection builds on Michael and Van Marrewijk (1998).

Table 5.1. *Sector-specific capital*

	w^x	L^x	L^y
K^x	+	+	0
K^y	+	−	+
p	+	−	+

Table 5.2. *Mobile capital*

	w^x	L^x	L^y
K	0	−	+
p	−	−	+

increase in capital, at constant prices, increases employment in the capital-intensive y industry, reduces employment in the labor-intensive x industry (Rybczynski effect) and does not affect w^x; see table 5.2. An increase in the price of manufactures, at constant capital stock, leads to similar employment effects, but reduces w^x (Stolper–Samuelson effect).

Consider now an international transfer T in a world economy in which the above Harris–Todaro model for the developing economy is embedded, characterized by equations (5.39)–(5.41) below. There are two countries, donor A and recipient B, and two goods, manufactures y with relative price p and numéraire good x. Let E^J denote country J's expenditure function, R^J its revenue function, u^J its welfare level and m^J its net demand for good y, that is $m^J \equiv E^J_p - R^J_p$.

$$E^A(p, u^A) = R^A(p) - T \tag{5.39}$$

$$E^B(p, u^B) = R^B(p, L^x(K^x, K^y, p), L^y(K^x, K^y, p)) + T \tag{5.40}$$

$$m^A(p, u^A) + m^B(p, u^B, L^x(K^x, K^y, p), L^y(K^x, K^y, p)) = 0 \tag{5.41}$$

Equation (5.39) is the donor's budget constraint. Similarly, equation (5.40) is the recipient's budget constraint. Its Harris–Todaro-type economic structure results in the indirect dependence of sectoral employment on the level of (sector-specific or mobile) capital and the price of manufactures y, as in equation (5.40). Equation (5.41) gives the market-clearing condition for manufactures y. For convenience, define the terms λ_p and η_p as $\lambda_p \equiv \sum_{i=x,y} w^i L^i_p = (L - L^x) w^x_p$ and $\eta_p \equiv R_{pL^y} L^y_p > 0$. Therefore, using equation (5.38), the sign of λ_p (respectively η_p) is the same as the sign of w^x_p (respectively L^y_p) and represents an increase in labor income (indirect supply effect) as a result of a change in the price of manufactures y. Note from tables 5.1 and 5.2 that η_p is always positive, but λ_p is negative if capital is mobile between sectors and positive if capital is sector-specific. If we now totally differentiate equations (5.39)–(5.41), normalize $E_u^J = 1$ for $J = A, B$ and define, in addition, $M_p = \sum_J m_p^J$ we obtain equation (5.42):

$$\begin{bmatrix} m^A & 1 & 0 \\ m^B - \lambda_p & 0 & 1 \\ M_p - \eta_p & m_u^A & m_u^B \end{bmatrix} \begin{bmatrix} dp \\ du^A \\ du^B \end{bmatrix} = \begin{bmatrix} -1 \\ 1 \\ 0 \end{bmatrix} dT \tag{5.42}$$

Note that if we put λ_p and η_p equal to 0 in equation (5.42), this model reduces to the full employment model of chapter 3. Solving equation (5.42) gives equations (5.43)–(5.47):

$$\det = \left[\sum_J \left(m_p^J - m^J m_u^J \right) \right] - \eta_p + \lambda_p m_u^B \equiv \frac{-1}{\Delta} < 0 \tag{5.43}$$

$$\frac{dp}{dT} = \left(m_u^B - m_u^A \right) \Delta > 0 \qquad \text{iff} \quad m_u^B > m_u^A \tag{5.44}$$

$$\frac{du^A}{dT} = \left(M_p - \eta_p + \lambda_p m_u^B \right) \Delta \tag{5.45}$$

$$\frac{du^B}{dT} = \left(-M_p + \eta_p - \lambda_p m_u^A \right) \Delta \tag{5.46}$$

$$\frac{du^A}{dT} + \frac{du^B}{dT} = \lambda_p \left(m_u^B - m_u^A \right) \Delta = \lambda_p \frac{dp}{dT} \tag{5.47}$$

The inequality in equation (5.43) denotes Walrasian stability. From equation (5.47) it is clear that world welfare increases if the price change as a result of the international transfer has a beneficial effect on the employment level in the developing country. This is evident from the recipient's welfare change in equation (5.46), which can be rewritten as $du^B/dT = 1 - \left(m^B - \lambda_p \right)(dp/dT)$ (rather than chapter 3's standard $du^B/dT = 1 - m^B(dp/dT)$). The basic influence of Harris–Todaro-type unemployment for the recipient's welfare change resulting from an international transfer is thus through the additional effect of a change in the terms of trade on labor income. We can consider two cases.

Case 1: mobile capital ("long-run"; λ_p is negative). If capital is intersectorally mobile, an increase in the price p of manufactures y decreases labor income due to a Stolper–Samuelson effect. From equations (5.45) and (5.46) it follows that the donor's welfare falls and the recipient's welfare rises if the demand for manufactures y is a normal good for the recipient, and respectively for the donor. World welfare rises if, and only if, the price p of manufactures y falls, that is if the donor's marginal propensity to consume manufactures is higher than the recipient's marginal propensity to consume manufactures.

Case 2: sector-specific capital ("short run"; λ_p is positive). If capital is sector-specific, an increase in the price p of manufactures y draws laborers out of the basic sector x into the manufacturing sector y. Equations (5.45) and (5.46) indicate that no conclusions concerning welfare changes for recipient or donor can be drawn if manufactures y are a normal good. However, the donor's welfare falls and the recipient's welfare rises if the demand for manufactures y is an inferior good for the recipient, and respectively for the donor. World welfare falls if, and only if, the price p of manufactures y falls, that is if the donor's marginal propensity to consume manufactures is higher than the recipient's marginal propensity to consume manufactures. Under such circumstances world welfare falls in the short run (sector-specific capital), but rises in the long run (mobile capital).

> **Proposition 11**: In a two-good, two-country world of perfect competition in which the recipient of an international transfer is plagued by Harris–Todaro-type unemployment, as described above, the price of manufactures falls if, and only if, the donor's marginal propensity to consume manufactures is higher than the recipient's marginal propensity to consume manufactures. Such a price fall is beneficial for world welfare (through a positive labor income effect for the recipient) if capital is intersectorally mobile, but detrimental (through a negative labor income effect for the recipient) if capital is sector-specific. Transfer paradoxes may arise in general, but donor welfare falls and recipient welfare rises if manufactures are a normal good in both countries and capital is intersectorally mobile.

5.3   Transfer of factors of production

Up to now we have discussed the transfer of final products. It is also possible to use our framework to analyze the transfer of production factors. For some applications this might be more relevant, for example in the cases of technical assistance, migration issues or a transfer of machines or know-how in order to stimulate growth in the developing world. To make the analysis tractable, we assume that production factors, once transferred from donor to recipient, can readily be used by the recipient, that such factors remain in the receiving country, and that the income generated by such factors of production is spent by the recipient. Furthermore, we only analyze the transfer of a single factor of production. Accordingly, if $\bar{v}^B$ and $\bar{v}^A$ represent the initial endowments of this production factor for recipient and donor and τ is the amount transferred, then $v^B = \bar{v}^B + \tau$ is the amount available for the recipient after the transfer and $v^A = \bar{v}^A - \tau$ is the amount available for the donor after the transfer; see equations (5.48) and (5.49).

Consider then an international transfer τ of a factor of production if there are two countries, donor A and recipient B, and two goods, good y with relative price p and numéraire good x. Let E^J denote country J's expenditure function, R^J its revenue function, u^J its welfare level and m^J its net demand for good y, that is $m^J \equiv E_p^J - R_p^J$. We do not a priori assume factor price equalization. Let w^J denote the remuneration for the transferred factor of production in country J, that is $R_v^J = w^J$. The model is given by equations (5.48)–(5.50).

$$E^A(p, u^A) - R^A(p, \bar{v}^A - \tau) \tag{5.48}$$

$$E^B(p, u^B) = R^B(p, \bar{v}^B + \tau) \tag{5.49}$$

$$m^A(p, u^A, \bar{v}^A - \tau) + m^B(p, u^B, \bar{v}^B + \tau) = 0 \tag{5.50}$$

Equation (5.48) is country A's budget constraint, taking into consideration the transfer of τ units of the factor of production to country B. Similarly, equation (5.49) is country B's budget constraint, taking into consideration the transfer from country A. Equation (5.50) is the market-clearing condition for good y. Normalizing the derivative of expenditure with respect to utility to unity at the initial equilibrium ($E_u^J = 1$), defining $M_p \equiv \sum_J m_p^J$, differentiating equations (5.48)–(5.50) and assuming $\tau = 0$ initially gives:

$$\begin{bmatrix} m^A & 1 & 0 \\ m^B & 0 & 1 \\ M_p & m_u^A & m_u^B \end{bmatrix} \begin{bmatrix} dp \\ du^A \\ du^B \end{bmatrix} = \begin{bmatrix} -w^A \\ w^B \\ R_{pv}^B - R_{pv}^A \end{bmatrix} d\tau \tag{5.51}$$

As in the previous section, define country A's Stolper–Samuelson factor price elasticity ε^A for good y as

$$\varepsilon^A \equiv \frac{\partial w^A}{\partial p} \frac{p}{w^A} = R_{pv}^A \frac{p}{R_v^A}$$

Thus, in a standard Heckscher–Ohlin model, ε^A will be larger than 1 if good y uses factor v (labor in this case) intensively and negative if good x uses factor v intensively. Alternatively, ε^A will be positive but smaller than 1 in a Ricardo–Viner model; see, for example, Dixit and Norman (1980). Let μ^J denote the marginal propensity to consume good y in country J, such that $\mu^J = pm_u^J$. Solving equation (5.51) gives:

$$\det = \sum_J (m_p^J - m^J m_u^J) \equiv \frac{-1}{\Delta} < 0 \tag{5.52}$$

$$\frac{dp}{d\tau} = \left[\left(w^B \mu^B - w^A \mu^A \right) - \left(w^B \varepsilon^B - w^A \varepsilon^A \right) \right] \frac{\Delta}{p} \tag{5.53}$$

$$\frac{du^A}{d\tau} = \left\{ w^A M_p - \frac{m^A}{p} \left[\left(w^B - w^A \right) \mu^B - \left(w^B \varepsilon^B - w^A \varepsilon^A \right) \right] \right\} \Delta \tag{5.54}$$

$$\frac{du^B}{d\tau} = \left\{ -w^B M_p - \frac{m^B}{p} \left[\left(w^B - w^A \right) \mu^A - \left(w^B \varepsilon^B - w^A \varepsilon^A \right) \right] \right\} \Delta \tag{5.55}$$

$$\frac{du^A}{d\tau} + \frac{du^B}{d\tau} = w^B - w^A \tag{5.56}$$

A transfer of a factor of production has, in principle, two effects: an income effect, which in different variants has been extensively discussed in previous sections and chapters, and a supply effect due to changes in production capacity. Both effects together influence the terms of trade; see equation (5.53). The first part of equation (5.53), the term $\left(w^B \mu^B - w^A \mu^A \right)$, is the familiar influence of the income effect through the marginal propensities to consume on the price of good y, where we obviously have to weigh the effect in country J by the value of marginal product, w^J, in that country. The second part of equation (5.53), the term $-\left(w^B \varepsilon^B - w^A \varepsilon^A \right)$, is the supply effect of a transfer of a factor of production through country J's Stolper–Samuelson factor price elasticity ε^J for good y. If, other things being equal, the transferred input is more effective in the production of good y for the recipient than for the donor this will cause the price of good y to fall. As is clear from equations (5.54) and (5.55) the potential difference in supply effects for donor and recipient, that is a difference in productivity and/or elasticity of the transferred factor of production, plays a prominent role in the welfare effects for the two countries. Transfer paradoxes are thus, in general, quite possible. Indeed, as is clear from equation (5.56), the world as a whole (and therefore in principle both donor and recipient) may benefit from the transferred factor of production if, and only if, this factor is more productive for the recipient than for the donor, that is if $w^B > w^A$.

The discussion above assumes that factors of production are not traded, perhaps because this is illegal (as is usually the case for most types of labor) or because there are other barriers (for example, capital controls) to such trade. However, if a factor of production can be transferred from one country to another, it can, in principle, also be traded. In the absence of barriers to such trade, factor price equalization should result, that is $w^B = w^A = w$. Alternatively, trade in final goods in a standard Heckscher–Ohlin framework also leads to factor price equalization. If, in addition, the Stolper–Samuelson factor price elasticities are the same (for example, on account of identical technologies), that is $\varepsilon^B = \varepsilon^A$, the outcome of the above model greatly simplifies to: $dp/d\tau = (\mu^B - \mu^A)(w/p)\Delta$; $du^A/d\tau = wM_p\Delta < 0$ and $du^B/d\tau = -wM_p\Delta > 0$; the standard Samuelson effects of chapter 3 multiplied by w, the size of the income generated by the transfer of τ (measured in terms of numéraire good x).

> **Proposition 12**: In a two-good, two-country world of perfect competition in which a factor of production is transferred from one country to another the price of good y falls if, other things being equal, (i) the donor's marginal propensity to consume good y is higher than the recipient's marginal propensity to consume good y (that is $\mu^A > \mu^B$) or (ii) the transferred input is more effective in the production of good y for the recipient than for the donor (that is $\varepsilon^B > \varepsilon^A$). World welfare rises if, and only if, the transferred factor of production is more productive for the recipient than for the donor, that is if $w^B > w^A$. Transfer paradoxes are possible in general, but if there are no supply effects, that is if the remuneration for the transferred factor of production and the Stolper–Samuelson factor price elasticities are the same in the two countries ($w^B = w^A$ and $\varepsilon^B = \varepsilon^A$), then the recipient gains and the donor loses from the transfer.

5.4 Lobbying and rent-seeking

Jagdish Bhagwati (1982) introduces and characterizes "directly unproductive profit-seeking" (DUP) activities. In this section we analyze DUP activities for the recipient of an international transfer. The recipient B spends resources v_t^B on lobbying activities to increase the size of the transfer given to country B by country A. We assume that only one factor of production is used for such activities. The size of the transfer from A to B is therefore endogenous: $T = T(v_t^B)$, with $T_v(v_t^B) > 0$. Obviously, resources spent on DUP activities cannot be used elsewhere, so that only $\bar{v}^B - v_t^B$ of the recipient's endowment of the lobbying factor of production is available for the production of goods.

Consider the effect of an increase in the recipient's lobbying efforts to increase the international transfer T given by donor A to recipient B in a two-country, perfectly competitive world with two goods, good y with relative price p and numéraire good x. Let E^J denote country J's, expenditure function, R^J its revenue function, u^J its welfare level, m^J its net demand for good y, that is $m^J \equiv E_p^J - R_p^J$, and w^J the remuneration for the lobbying activity, that is $R_v^J = w^J$. The model is given by equations (5.57)–(5.59):

$$E^A(p, u^A) = R^A(p) - T(v_t^B) \tag{5.57}$$

$$E^B(p, u^B) = R^B(p, \bar{v}^B - v_t^B) + T(v_t^B) \tag{5.58}$$

$$m^A(p, u^A) + m^B(p, u^B, \bar{v}^B - v_t^B) = 0 \tag{5.59}$$

Denoting country J's Stolper–Samuelson factor price elasticity ε^J for good y as

$$\varepsilon^J \equiv \frac{\partial w^J}{\partial p} \frac{p}{w^J} = R_{pv}^J \frac{p}{R_v^J}$$

then in a standard Heckscher–Ohlin model ε^J will be larger than 1 if good y uses factor v (the factor used for lobbying) intensively and negative if good x uses factor v intensively. Alternatively, ε^A will be positive but smaller than 1 in a Ricardo–Viner model; see, for example, Dixit and Norman (1980). Let $\mu^J = pm_u^J$ denote the marginal propensity to consume good y in country J. Normalize such that $E_u^J = 1$, and define $M_p \equiv \sum_J m_p^J$ and $\sum_J (m_p^J - m^J m_u^J) \equiv -\mathbf{\Delta}^{-1}$. Totally differentiating equations (5.57)–(5.59) gives:

$$\begin{bmatrix} m^A & 1 & 0 \\ m^B & 0 & 1 \\ M_p & m_u^A & m_u^B \end{bmatrix} \begin{bmatrix} dp \\ du^A \\ du^B \end{bmatrix} = \begin{bmatrix} -T_v \\ T_v - w^B \\ -R_{pv}^B \end{bmatrix} dv_t^B \tag{5.60}$$

Solving equation (5.60), rearranging and using the above definitions gives:

$$\det = \sum_J (m_p^J - m^J m_u^J) \equiv \frac{-1}{\mathbf{\Delta}} < 0 \tag{5.61}$$

$$\frac{dp}{dv_t^B} = \left[T_v \left(\mu^B - \mu^A \right) - w^B \left(\mu^B - \varepsilon^B \right) \right] \frac{\Delta}{p} \tag{5.62}$$

$$\frac{du^A}{dv_t^B} = \left[T_v M_p + m^A \frac{w^B}{p} \left(\mu^B - \varepsilon^B \right) \right] \Delta \tag{5.63}$$

$$\frac{du^B}{dv_t^B} = \left[-\left(T_v - w^B \right) M_p + m^B \frac{w^B}{p} \left(\mu^B - \varepsilon^B \right) \right] \Delta \tag{5.64}$$

$$\frac{du^A}{dv_t^B} + \frac{du^B}{dv_t^B} = -w^B < 0 \tag{5.65}$$

An increase of lobbying activities by country B to increase the international transfer from country A to country B has two effects: a standard income effect, and a destruction effect due to the wasteful DUP activities. Both effects together influence the terms of trade; see equation (5.62). The first part of equation (5.62), the term $T_v \left(\mu^B - \mu^A \right)$, is the familiar influence of the income effect through the differences in marginal propensities to consume on the price of good y, where we obviously have to multiply by T_v, the effectiveness of lobbying activities in increasing the size of the transfer. The second part of equation (5.62), the term $-w^B \left(\mu^B - \varepsilon^B \right)$, is the destruction effect on *net* demand for good y as a result of wasting resources on lobbying activities in country B, represented by the marginal propensity to consume μ^B on the demand side and the Stolper–Samuelson factor price elasticity ε^B on the supply side.[6] As is clear from equations (5.63) and (5.64) the destruction effect plays a prominent role in the welfare effects for the two countries. Transfer paradoxes are thus, in general, quite possible, but as is clear from equation (5.65) the world as a whole loses from the lobbying activities as these resources are directly wasted for productive activities, that is

$$\frac{du^A}{dv_t^B} + \frac{du^B}{dv_t^B} = -w^B < 0$$

Note, in particular, that if the recipient lobbies "optimally," such that $du^B/dv_t^B = 0$, this implies that the donor loses for sure.

If there is no destruction effect on the net demand for good y, that is if $\mu^B = \varepsilon^B$, the outcome of the above model simplifies to: $dp/dv_t^B = \left(\mu^B - \mu^A \right)(T_v/p)\Delta$; $du^A/dv_t^B = T_v M_p \Delta < 0$ and $du^B/dv_t^B = -\left(T_v - w^B \right) M_p \Delta > 0$ if and only if $T_v > w^B$.

[6] Note that in subsection 5.1.1 a final good is thrown away, whereas here a factor of production is wasted. For that reason the term ε^B, which may be either positive or negative, appears in this section but not in subsection 5.1.1.

Proposition 13: In a two-good, two-country world of perfect competition in which the recipient of an international transfer spends resources on lobbying activities to increase this transfer, an increase in such lobbying activities causes the price of good y to fall if, other things being equal, (i) the donor's marginal propensity to consume good y is higher than the recipient's marginal propensity to consume good y (that is $\mu^A > \mu^B$) or (ii) the resources used for lobbying activities reduce the net supply of good y (that is $\varepsilon^B < \mu^B$). World welfare falls by the value of productive resources w^B wasted on lobbying activities. Transfer paradoxes are possible in general, but if there is no net destruction effect on the supply of good y (that is if $\varepsilon^B = \mu^B$) the donor loses from the transfer, while the recipient gains if, and only if, the marginal benefits of lobbying are higher than those of production from the recipient's point of view (that is if, and only if, $T_v > w^B$).

5.5   Trade policy

Trade policies, like tariffs or quotas, may influence the outcome of a transfer process, because they affect the terms of trade. The "optimum tariff" argument, for instance, is based on the fact that welfare can be influenced (maximized) by changing the terms of trade in one's favor. In principle, transfer paradoxes may therefore arise, as investigated by Ohyama (1974). First, we analyze the effects of transfers in the context of tariffs imposed by the recipient. Second, we investigate transfers where the donor imposes a tariff, and we consider a variant of the "trade or aid?" discussion.

5.5.1   Tariff imposed by the recipient

Consider the effect of an international transfer T from country A to country B in a two-country, perfectly competitive world with two goods, good y with relative price p and numéraire good x, where the recipient imposes a tariff on the good it imports. Let E^J denote country J's expenditure function, R^J its revenue function, u^J its welfare level, and m^J its net demand for good y, that is $m^J \equiv E_p^J - R_p^J$. Without loss of generality, the recipient B imports good y, such that $m^B > 0$, and imposes a tariff on these imports. The tariff revenue tm^B, like the transfer, is distributed to the consumers in a non-distortionary lump-sum fashion, which implies that the recipient's private budget constraint consists of the sum of the value of production, the tariff revenue and the transfer. The price of good y in country B is equal to import price p plus the (specific) tariff t, that is $p + t$. The model consists of equations (5.66)–(5.68).

$$E^A(p, u^A) = R^A(p) - T \tag{5.66}$$

$$E^B(p + t, u^B) = R^B(p + t) + tm^B + T \tag{5.67}$$

$$m^A(p, u^A) + m^B(p + t, u^B) = 0 \tag{5.68}$$

Equation (5.66) is the donor's budget constraint, equation (5.67) is the recipient's budget constraint and equation (5.68) is the market-clearing condition for good y. Differentiating equations (5.66)–(5.68), normalizing such that $E_u^J = 1$ and defining $M_p = \sum_J m_p^J$ gives:

$$\begin{bmatrix} m^A & 1 & 0 \\ \left(m^B - tm_p^B\right) & 0 & 1 - tm_u^B \\ M_p & m_u^A & m_u^B \end{bmatrix} \begin{bmatrix} dp \\ du^A \\ du^B \end{bmatrix} = \begin{bmatrix} 1 \\ -1 \\ 0 \end{bmatrix} dT \tag{5.69}$$

Solving equation (5.69) gives:

$$\det = \left(1 - tm_u^B\right)\left(m_p^A - m^A m_u^A\right) + \left(m_p^B - m^B m_u^B\right) \equiv \frac{-1}{\Delta} < 0 \tag{5.70}$$

$$\frac{dp}{dT} = \left[m_u^B - \left(1 - tm_u^B\right)m_u^A\right]\Delta \tag{5.71}$$

$$\frac{du^A}{dT} = \left[\left(1 - tm_u^B\right)M_p + tm_u^B m_p^B\right]\Delta \tag{5.72}$$

$$\frac{du^B}{dT} = -\left(M_p + tm_p^B m_u^A\right)\Delta \tag{5.73}$$

$$\frac{du^A}{dT} + \frac{du^B}{dT} = t\left(m_p^B m_u^A + m_p^A m_u^B\right)\Delta \tag{5.74}$$

The inequality in equation (5.70) indicates Walrasian stability. The price of good y rises if, and only if, the recipient's marginal propensity to consume good y is larger than the donor's marginal propensity to consume good y, after correction for the impact of the tariff revenue; see equation (5.71). That is, other things being equal, the imposition of a tariff by the recipient of a transfer makes it more likely that the terms of trade will change in the donor's favor. If both goods are normal goods in both countries, that is if $0 \le tm_u^B \le 1$ and $m_u^A \ge 0$, then equations (5.72)–(5.74) show that the donor's welfare falls, $du^A/dT \le 0$ and the recipient's welfare rises, $du^B/dT \geq 0$. This was demonstrated for the first time by Ohyama (1974). Otherwise, transfer paradoxes are possible.[7]

> **Proposition 14**: (Ohyama) In a two-good, two-country, Walrasian-stable world of perfect competition in which the recipient of an international transfer levies a tariff on its import good, transfer paradoxes are possible in principle, but the recipient gains and the donor loses if both goods are normal goods in both countries.

5.5.2   Tariff imposed by the donor: trade or aid?

An interesting, and frequently posed, question which can be answered within this framework, is whether a country benefits more from aid or from trade: the so-called "trade versus aid" discussion (Kemp and Shimomura [1991]; Lahiri and Raimondos [1995]). To analyze this problem we assume that the donor is a protectionist and that the recipient adheres to free trade. The recipient now faces the problem of how to choose between a tariff reduction and a lump-sum transfer. If one option is better than the other, it might try to negotiate its preferred way of help. In this subsection the donor imports good y, that is $m^A > 0$. The price of good y in country A is equal to the import price p plus the specific tariff t, that is $p + t$. The basic model is given in equations (5.75)–(5.77).

$$E^A(p+t, u^A) = R^A(p+t) + t m^A - T \tag{5.75}$$

$$E^B(p, u^B) = R^B(p) + T \tag{5.76}$$

$$m^A(p+t, u^A) + m^B(p, u^B) = 0 \tag{5.77}$$

Equation (5.75) is the donor's budget constraint, equation (5.76) is the recipient's budget constraint and equation (5.77) is the market-clearing condition for good y. Differentiating equations (5.75)–(5.77), normalizing $E_u^J = 1$, assuming that $t = 0$ initially and defining $M_p = \sum_J m_p^J$ gives:

$$\begin{bmatrix} m^A & 1 & 0 \\ m^B & 0 & 1 \\ M_p & m_u^A & m_u^B \end{bmatrix} \begin{bmatrix} dp \\ du^A \\ du^B \end{bmatrix} = \begin{bmatrix} -1 \\ 1 \\ 0 \end{bmatrix} dT + \begin{bmatrix} 0 \\ 0 \\ -m_p^A \end{bmatrix} dt \tag{5.78}$$

---

[7] Note that this analysis includes the special case of an "optimal" tariff imposed by the recipient. From equation (5.67) it follows that this tariff equals $t_{opt} = m^B/m_p^B$.

This system allows us to analyze differences between the effects of a change in the transfer and those of a change in the tariff imposed by the donor. The solutions to equation (5.78) are given in the pairs of equations (5.79)–(5.81).

$$\frac{dp}{dT}\Big|_{t=0}= (m_u^B - m_u^A)\Delta; \qquad \frac{dp}{dt}\Big|_{t=0}= m_p^A \Delta \leq 0 \qquad (5.79)$$

$$\frac{du^A}{dT}\Big|_{t=0}= M_p\Delta \leq 0; \qquad \frac{du^A}{dt}\Big|_{t=0}= -m^A m_p^A \Delta \geq 0 \qquad (5.80)$$

$$\frac{du^B}{dT}\Big|_{t=0}= -M_p\Delta \geq 0; \qquad \frac{du^B}{dt}\Big|_{t=0}= m^A m_p^A \Delta \leq 0 \qquad (5.81)$$

The results on the left of the pairs of equations (5.79)–(5.81) are the standard results of an increase in the transfer, where the recipient benefits and the donor loses. The results on the right of the pairs of equations are the standard results of the imposition of a small tariff, where the country that imposes the tariff (country A) benefits and the other (country B) loses. Thus, if there is a small tariff imposed by country A, then country B would benefit either from a reduction in that tariff or from an increase in the transfer given from country A to country B. Which effect is more important? Or, to turn the question around, which country would benefit if country A imposed a tariff, thus in general improving its terms of trade (see the right-hand equation of the pair [5.79]), and simultaneously transferred the proceeds of this tariff imposition to country B, thereby improving its terms of trade only if the recipient has a lower marginal propensity to consume good y (see the left-hand equation of the pair [5.79])? To answer this question we substitute equation (5.82) below into equations (5.75) and (5.76) and differentiate with respect to p, u^A, u^B and t to get equation (5.83). Solving equation (5.83) gives equations (5.84)–(5.86).

$$T = tm^A \qquad (5.82)$$

$$\begin{bmatrix} m^A & 1 & 0 \\ m^B & 0 & 1 \\ M_p & m_u^A & m_u^B \end{bmatrix} \begin{bmatrix} dp \\ du^A \\ du^B \end{bmatrix} = \begin{bmatrix} -m^A \\ m^A \\ -m_p^A \end{bmatrix} dt \qquad (5.83)$$

$$\frac{dp}{dt}\Big|_{T=tm^A; t=0}= \left[m^A (m_u^B - m_u^A) + m_p^A\right]\Delta \qquad (5.84)$$

$$\frac{du^A}{dt}\Big|_{T=tm^A; t=0}= m^A m_p^B \Delta \leq 0 \qquad (5.85)$$

$$\frac{du^B}{dt}\Big|_{T=tm^A;\, t=0} = -m^A m_p^B \Delta \geq 0 \tag{5.86}$$

$$\text{note}: \quad \frac{dz}{dt}\Big|_{T=tm^A;\, t=0} = m^A \frac{dz}{dT}\Big|_{t=0} + \frac{dz}{dt}\Big|_{t=0} \quad \text{for } z = p, u^A, u^B$$

Equations (5.84)–(5.86) demonstrate that although the terms-of-trade effect of the tariff-cum-transfer policy is indeterminate (see equation [5.84]), the donor of the transfer unambiguously loses (see equation [5.85]), while the recipient of the transfer unambiguously gains (see equation [5.86]). In this sense the "aid" effect dominates the "trade" effect, at least when starting from a situation where all the benefits of trade have already been reaped (that is, evaluated at $t = 0$). The direct income effect of the transfer dominates the indirect terms-of-trade effect. This is also clear from equations (5.80) and (5.81), where the welfare effects for a change in the transfer involve the world net substitution $m_p^A + m_p^B$ (in the left-hand equations), while the welfare effects for a change in country A's tariff only involve country A's net substitution m_p^A (in the right-hand equations).

Of course, the reader may wonder whether, and to what extent, these results generalize to changes in the tariff (or transfer) if an arbitrarily large tariff t is imposed by donor country A. As the reader may wish to verify, the answer is given in equations (5.87)–(5.89) below, which obviously reduce to equations (5.84)–(5.86) above when evaluated at $t = 0$.

$$\frac{dp}{dt}\Big|_{T=tm^A} = \left\{ m^A \left[(1 - tm_u^A) m_u^B - m_u^A \right] + m_p^A \right\} \Delta \tag{5.87}$$

$$\frac{du^A}{dt}\Big|_{T=tm^A} = m^A \left(m_p^B + tm_p^A m_u^B \right) \Delta \tag{5.88}$$

$$\frac{du^B}{dt}\Big|_{T=tm^A} = -\left[\left(m^A m_u^A - m_p^A \right) tm_p^A + m^A \left(1 - tm_u^A \right) m_p^B \right] \Delta \tag{5.89}$$

Equation (5.87) demonstrates that the total effect on the change in the terms of trade is indeterminate as it is the combined effect of imposing a tariff, the term m_p^A, and of transferring the proceeds of the revenue to the other country, the term $m^A \left[(1 - tm_u^A) m_u^B - m_u^A \right]$. Moreover, equations (5.88) and (5.89) demonstrate that the "aid effect" still dominates the "trade effect," provided both goods are normal goods in both countries, that is if $m_u^B \geq 0$ and $0 \leq tm_u^A \leq 1$.

Proposition 15: In a two-good, two-country, Walrasian-stable world of perfect competition in which the donor of an international transfer levies a tariff on its import good to finance the transfer, the recipient of the transfer gains and the donor loses if (i) both goods are normal goods in both countries or (ii) the tariff (and therefore the transfer) is sufficiently small. In this sense "aid" is preferred to "trade."

5.6   Conclusion

Chapter 3 introduced Samuelson's theorem in a Walrasian-stable, two-good, two-country, perfectly competitive world: the recipient of an international transfer gains, while the donor loses. Chapter 4 generalized Samuelson's theorem in several important ways, introducing, for example, public goods, non-traded goods or an arbitrary number of traded goods. This chapter investigates the first clouds on the horizon for Samuelson's theorem: distortions. We have analyzed a variety of such distortions, in particular the cost of administration, unemployment for donor or recipient, a transfer of productive resources if there is a difference in technology, lobbying and trade policy, to demonstrate that Samuelson's theorem does not hold in general if there are distortions present in the equilibrium of the world economy. Fortunately, the horizon is not so cloudy as to preclude us from drawing interesting or reassuring analytic conclusions from our models, albeit by imposing somewhat more stringent conditions, such as normality, than before. For example, we show that the recipient prefers "aid" to "trade" in the sense that the recipient's welfare improves if a donor imposes a tariff and transfers the proceeds of the tariff to the recipient.

6   Clouds on the horizon 2: third parties

6.1   From two to three: a trivial extension?

The analysis in chapters 3 and 4 investigated international transfers from one country to another in a two-country world. There is a donor and a recipient, but there are no other countries. Are these other countries, which do not participate in the transfer, of any importance to the results derived in chapters 3 and 4? One might think not, and in one respect this assertion is true. In his analysis, Pigou (1932), following up on the Keynes–Ohlin controversy, treats all countries which neither pay nor receive payments as though they were part of the receiving country. This procedure is criticized by Elliot (1938), who goes on to argue that it is equally inappropriate to treat the non-participating countries as though they were part of the paying country; instead, they should be treated separately. After some verbal argumentation, building on Pigou's (1932) analysis and concentrating on the terms-of-trade effect, Elliot concludes, however: "It follows from these cases that the introduction of a neutral country does not alter the probability that a series of unilateral payments will tend to turn the terms of trade against the paying as compared with the receiving country." (p. 489)

As we shall see later in this chapter, Elliot's conclusion that the presence of non-participating countries has no effect on the direction of the *terms-of-trade* effect of a transfer is correct. Unfortunately, following this conclusion, and despite many analyses of different aspects of the transfer problem by leading economic experts, it seems as if it was implicitly assumed that the presence of non-participating countries has no influence on the *welfare* effects of the transfer either. Recall that in a two-country world, transfer paradoxes are not possible if the economy is Walrasian-stable (see chapter 3) and free from distortions (see chapter 5). It was the important contribution of David Gale (1974), many years later, to demonstrate that this is not true in the presence of bystanders.

Gale gives an example to show that it is not inevitable that the donor gains and the recipient loses from a transfer – even if the world economy is Walrasian-stable and free of distortions. Gale's work on the import- ance of bystanders in the transfer literature was extended and popular- ized by Graciela Chichilnisky (1980), Avinash Dixit (1983) and Jagdish Bhagwati, Richard Brecher and Tatsuo Hatta (1983). The crucial insight that it is always the difference between the economic (demand) structure of the *other* two countries that is important for *your* welfare, and not the difference in demand structure between you and either one or the other country, is most clearly understood using the Bhagwati *et al.* (1983) welfare decomposition. After reading this chapter it should be absolutely clear that the correct answer to the question posed in the title of this section is: the extension of the transfer problem from two to three countries is not at all trivial!

6.2   The transfer paradox: Gale's example

Chapter 3 described how Wasily Leontief presented an example in 1936 in which an international transfer from one country to another in a two- country world increases the donor's welfare and reduces the recipient's welfare. For almost four decades this example was treated as an anomaly because Paul Samuelson pointed out shortly afterwards that the Leontief example analyzes an unstable world economy and argued that in a stable two-country world the paradoxes of donor-enrichment and recipient- impoverishment are not possible. Interest in the problem was rekindled in 1974 when David Gale gave a second famous example, involving international transfers in which three countries play a role. This section describes a rewritten version of Gale's (1974) example.

Consider a world economy consisting of three countries, A, B and C. Each country J has a direct utility function u^J, depending on the levels of consumption of the two goods, grapes (G) and lemons (L), of the fixed proportions (or Leontief) type:

$$u^A(G, L) = \min\{4G, L\} \tag{6.1}$$
$$u^B(G, L) = \min\{G, 4L\} \tag{6.2}$$
$$u^C(G, L) = \min\{G, L\} \tag{6.3}$$

This preference relation and the optimal consumption points for countries A, B and C are illustrated in figure 6.1 under the assumption that the price of grapes relative to the price of lemons equals one and the income level for each country is 15. Under these conditions, as indicated

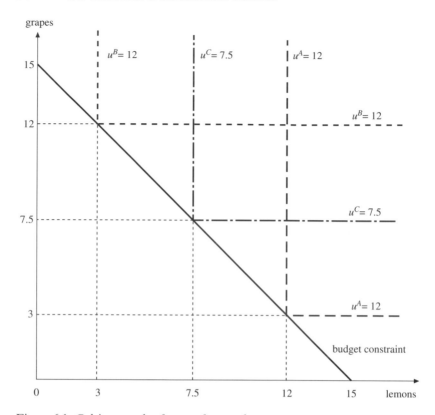

Figure 6.1. *Gale's example of a transfer paradox*

in figure 6.1, country A consumes 12 lemons and 3 grapes, country C consumes 7.5 lemons and 7.5 grapes, while country B consumes 3 lemons and 12 grapes. Thus, country A has a high preference for lemons, while country B has a high preference for grapes. Let grapes G be the numéraire and let p be the relative price of lemons. It is straightforward, using the illustration in figure 6.1, to derive the expenditure functions for the three countries, that is the minimum expenditure E^J to obtain utility u^J at relative price p:

$$E^A(p, u^A) = (p + \frac{1}{4})u^A \tag{6.4}$$

$$E^B(p, u^B) = (1 + \frac{p}{4})u^B \tag{6.5}$$

$$E^C(p, u^C) = (1 + p)u^C \tag{6.6}$$

Now suppose that there is no production of goods, but that countries A and B have endowments of one unit of grapes and country C has an endowment of three units of lemons. Alternatively, one unit of grapes is produced in countries A and B, which both completely specialize in the production of grapes, and three units of lemons are produced in country C, which completely specializes in the production of lemons.[1] Under these circumstances the revenue functions R^J, the maximum revenue in terms of grapes for country J at a given price p for lemons, are simply:

$$R^A(p) = 1 \tag{6.7}$$

$$R^B(p) = 1 \tag{6.8}$$

$$R^C(p) = 3p \tag{6.9}$$

Consider now the effects of transferring T units of grapes from country A to country B. Then, in line with section 3.4, the world economy equilibrium can be written as:[2]

$$E^A(p, u^A) = R^A(p) - T \tag{6.10}$$

$$E^B(p, u^B) = R^B(p) + T \tag{6.11}$$

$$E^C(p, u^C) = R^C(p) \tag{6.12}$$

$$m^A(p, u^A) + m^B(p, u^B) + m^C(p, u^C) = 0 \tag{6.13}$$

where, as before, $m^J \equiv E^J_p - R^J_p$ for country $J = A, B, C$, such that m^J represents country J's excess demand for lemons. These four equations can be simplified, with the aid of the above information, to

$$(p + \tfrac{1}{4})u^A = 1 - T \tag{6.14}$$

$$(1 + \tfrac{p}{4})u^B = 1 + T \tag{6.15}$$

$$(1 + p)u^C = 3p \tag{6.16}$$

$$u^A + \frac{u^B}{4} + u^C - 3 = 0 \tag{6.17}$$

---

[1] That is, Pigou's assumption of complete specialization of production mentioned in chapter 2 is equivalent to investigating an exchange economy in which each country is endowed with only one good, as analyzed by Gale.

[2] It should be noted that the example in this section, unlike those in the remainder of this book, does not normalize the derivative of expenditure with respect to utility to unity at the initial equilibrium.

Thus, country A imports u^A units of lemons, country B imports $u^B/4$ units of lemons and country C exports $3 - u^C$ units of lemons. We are interested in the effect of a small transfer T from A to B on the welfare levels of all three countries, that is evaluated at $T = 0$. To do this, we can totally differentiate equations (6.14)–(6.17), solve and then evaluate at the initial equilibrium $T = 0$. First, however, we have to find the initial equilibrium. The easiest way to do this is to substitute equations (6.14)–(6.16) in equation (6.17) to obtain

$$\frac{4(1 - T)}{4p + 1} + \frac{1 + T}{4 + p} + \frac{3p}{1 + p} - 3 = 0$$

or $4p^2 + (26 + 5T)p - (5 - 15T) = 0$ (6.18)

For small T the unique equilibrium price $\bar{p}$ of lemons, that is the positive solution to equation (6.18), is given by

$$\bar{p} = \frac{-(26 + 5T) + \sqrt{(26 + 5T)^2 + 14(5 - 15T)}}{8}$$ (6.19)

Denote the equilibrium values of utility and price at $T = 0$ with $\tilde{\ }$, then substituting $\tilde{p}$ from equation (6.19) in equations (6.14)–(6.16) gives

$$\tilde{p} \approx 0.187 \qquad \tilde{u}^A \approx 2.288$$
$$\tilde{u}^B \approx 0.955 \qquad \tilde{u}^C \approx 0.473$$

Now, totally differentiating equations (6.14)–(6.17) gives

$$\begin{bmatrix} \left(p + \frac{1}{4}\right) & 0 & 0 & u^A \\ 0 & \left(1 + \frac{p}{4}\right) & 0 & u^B \\ 0 & 0 & (1 + p) & (u^C - 3) \\ 1 & \frac{1}{4} & 1 & 0 \end{bmatrix} \begin{bmatrix} du^A \\ du^B \\ du^C \\ dp \end{bmatrix} = \begin{bmatrix} -1 \\ 1 \\ 0 \\ 0 \end{bmatrix} dT$$ (6.20)

The solution and subsequent evaluation of equation (6.20) at $T = 0$ gives

$$\det = -\left[\left(p + \frac{1}{4}\right)\left(1 + \frac{p}{4}\right)(u^C - 3) + \left(p + \frac{1}{4}\right)(1 + p)u^B/16\right.$$

$$\left. +(1 + p)\left(1 + \frac{p}{4}\right)u^A\right] + (1 + p)\left(1 + \frac{p}{4}\right)u^A \equiv \frac{-1}{\Delta} \approx -1.718 < 0$$

$$\frac{du^A}{dT} = -\left[\left(1+\frac{p}{4}\right)\left(u^C - 3\right) + (1+p)\left(\frac{u^B}{16}+\frac{u^A}{4}\right)\right]\Delta \approx 1.103 > 0$$

$$\frac{du^B}{dT} = \left[\left(p+\frac{1}{4}\right)\left(u^C - 3\right) + (1+p)\left(u^A+\frac{u^B}{4}\right)\right]\Delta \approx 0.773 > 0$$

$$\frac{du^C}{dT} = (u^C - 3)\left[\left(1+\frac{p}{4}\right) - \left(p+\frac{1}{4}\right)\frac{1}{4}\right]\Delta \approx -1.379 < 0$$

$$\frac{dp}{dT} - \left[(1+p)\left(p+\frac{1}{4}\right)\frac{1}{4} - (1+p)\left(1+\frac{p}{4}\right)\right]\Delta \approx -0.715 < 0$$

Several important observations arise from Gale's example. First, the unique equilibrium is Walrasian-stable at $T = 0$ since the determinant of the coefficient matrix on the left-hand side of equation (6.20) is negative.

Second, the donor of the transfer, country A, *gains* from this transfer, as does the recipient, country B. This is in strong contrast to Samuelson's theorem derived in chapter 3 and further elaborated in chapter 4, where the donor's welfare always falls as a result of a transfer when the world economy is stable.

Third, and somewhat obviously given the Pareto-optimal initial equilibrium in this distortion-free world, donor and recipient gain from the transfer at the expense of the non-participating country C, which loses. The economics behind the example is quite simple. Country A has a high preference for lemons, which it imports. By transferring part of its endowment (in terms of grapes) to country B, which has a low preference for lemons, the price of lemons (which country A must import) drops by so much that the donating country A gains in real terms despite its lower initial wealth (in terms of grapes).

Fourth, by reversing the transfer, that is if country B donates T units of grapes to country A, it is clear that both the donor and recipient can *lose* from the transfer, while the non-participating country can gain. To summarize.

Example 2 (Gale) In a two-good, Walrasian-stable endowment economy with fixed proportion preferences and three, rather than two, countries, an international transfer from one country to another may benefit both donor and recipient at the expense of the non-participating country.

6.3   More examples

6.3.1 Strong paradox

Gale's 1974 example, in the previous section, of what can be viewed as a transfer paradox, was a succinct (four pages) contribution to the mathematical economics literature, focusing on the technical possibilities of what is called an "advantageous reallocation." Initial attention to the example was given by fellow mathematical economists; see Aumann and Peleg (1974), Guesnerie and Laffont (1978), Léonard and Manning (1983) and subsection 6.3.2 below. The importance of bystanders for the economic consequences of international transfers was not fully realized or analyzed in the transfer literature until the discussion in the *Journal of Development Economics* following Graciela Chichilnisky's (1980) seminal contribution in that journal. Building upon a variation of Gale's example using fixed proportion preferences, Chichilnisky distinguishes between two different income groups in the North and one income group in the South. She analyzes the effects of a transfer from the rich income group in the North to the South. Obviously, this is analytically equivalent to distinguishing between three different countries in which the poor income group in the North is the bystander. In Gale's example the donor and recipient of the transfer both gain as a result of the transfer, at the expense of the bystander country.[3] Chichilnisky analyzes conditions under which the donor (that is, the rich income group in the North) gains and the recipient loses as a result of the transfer.[4] Furthermore, she identifies economic conditions under which the recipient gains from the transfer of goods from the rich income group in the North if, and only if, the poor income group in the North (the bystander) suffers from this transfer. Under such circumstances there is thus an interesting trade-off between more equality between the North and the South and more equality within the North.

> **Example 3** (Chichilnisky) In a two-good, Walrasian-stable endowment economy with fixed proportion preferences and three, rather than two, countries an international transfer from one country to another may benefit the donor and hurt the recipient.

The economics underlying Chichilnisky's analysis, the analysis itself and the possibility of an equality trade-off inspired so many prominent economists to investigate this question that in 1983 the *Journal of*

---

[3] If the transfer is reversed in Gale's example, donor and recipient both lose, and the bystander gains.

[4] A general analysis of such conditions will be discussed later in this chapter.

Development Economics published a special edition to address the issues raised by Chichilnisky.

Many authors have pointed out small mistakes or omissions in Chichilnisky's analysis. It will be shown in section 6.4, and more extensively discussed in section 6.5, that the net trading position of the bystander country (the variable λ for the low income group in the North in Chichilnisky's analysis; m^C for country C in our analysis below) is of crucial importance in deriving transfer paradoxes. Unfortunately, Chichilnisky used a condition on λ in the proof of her theorem 1 which was not stated in the theorem itself. This was implicitly or explicitly stated and discussed to various degrees by Gunning (1983a), Ravallion (1983), Saghafi and Nugent (1983), Srinivasan and Bhagwati (1983a) and Geanakoplos and Heal (1983). In addition, Chichilnisky puts a lot of emphasis on the type of good ("basic goods" or "luxury goods" in her terminology) that is being transferred. Both Gunning and Geanakoplos and Heal point out that the results are independent of the type of good that is being transferred, as has already been discussed in chapter 3.

Most of the discussion in the special edition of the *Journal of Development Economics* is within the fixed proportion preferences cum endowment framework of Gale and Chichilnisky. In contrast, Ravallion analyzes the transfer problem for more general preferences within an endowment framework, very much in the spirit of the next section, but without production. He also discusses the plausibility of Chichilnisky's result and gives a diagrammatic demonstration. Geanakoplos and Heal give a more extensive geometric analysis. In her reply Chichilnisky (1983) emphasizes the fact that the economy in her 1980 example is Walrasian-stable. This also holds for Gale's 1974 example, as was demonstrated in section 6.2, but it was not emphasized or even pointed out by him.[5]

6.3.2   Smooth preferences

Gale's example, discussed in section 6.2, uses an endowment economy and fixed proportion preferences. Thus Gale, in evaluating his own work

---

[5] Instead of welcoming the attention and the additional analysis of the possibility and plausibility of transfer paradoxes, and simply admitting her small mistakes and omissions, Chichilnisky dismisses the latter as typos and gives a rather contrived interpretation of some loose terminology in her earlier paper. This entices Gunning (1983b) and Srinivasan and Bhagwati (1983b) to respond again. These responses are rather impassioned. For example, Gunning starts as follows: "I made three points ... Chichilnisky admits all of that, but in the least graceful way imaginable," while Srinivasan and Bhagwati start with: "Footnotes 5, 8 and 11 of Chichilnisky's response to our Comment are gross distortions" and end with: "This only goes to show the naivete of drawing major policy conclusions from simple models without caution."

and referring to two more examples involving non-smooth preferences, one by McFadden and the other by Dréze and Gabszewicz, comments (1974, p. 64):

I should point out however, that my example is one with non-smooth preferences, and several attempts to construct examples involving smooth preferences have been unsuccessful, so that for the present the question of existence of smooth examples of this phenomenon remains open.

In response to Gale's challenge, Aumann and Peleg (1974) give an example of smooth preferences involving two agents in which it is advantageous for one agent to throw away some of its endowments. That example is thus not directly related to the transfer problem, but to the immiserizing growth literature, as discussed in chapter 5. Roger Guesnerie and Jean-Jacques Laffont (1978) demonstrate that it is in principle possible in an endowment economy to generalize Gale's example for many goods and many countries, such that an arbitrary collection of sufficiently different countries is able to engage in advantageous reallocations of their initial endowments. Finally, Léonard and Manning (1983) demonstrate how one can construct whole families of two-commodity examples of transfer paradoxes in a three-country setting with smooth preferences and market stability.

> **Example 4** (Guesnerie and Laffont; Léonard and Manning) Gale's example on transfer paradoxes in a setting of three agents can be generalized to smooth preferences involving at least three countries and an arbitrary number of goods.

Léonard and Manning's procedure is as follows. In the spirit of Gale's example, they give the donor and recipient endowments of commodity 1 only, while the bystander country is exclusively endowed with commodity 2. Donor and recipient are given different Cobb–Douglas preferences, which allows Léonard and Manning to derive net demand schedules for donor and recipient as a result of a transfer of, say, 4 units. They then demonstrate that both donor and recipient will gain if the relative price of good 1 before the transfer is 1 and after the transfer is 3. This determines, in principle, the required net demand in order to clear the world market at those prices for the bystander country, whose preferences have not yet been specified. By specifying a smooth class of preferences for the bystander country depending on two parameters, solving for the bystander's net demand (as a function of the relative price of good 1 and of the two parameters) and equating this with the required net demand to clear the world market at relative prices of 1 and 3,

Léonard and Manning are able to find values for the two parameters such that a transfer paradox occurs. It remains to show that Walrasian stability prevails. Since this is basically a technical matter we refer the interested reader to Léonard and Manning's analysis for further details.

6.4   The model

Although the various examples discussed in the preceding two sections are very instructive in determining what is and is not possible as a result of a transfer in a three-country setting, such examples do not lead to analytic insight into the reasons and circumstances under which a transfer paradox might occur. It is time, therefore, to turn to a formal analysis of the conditions under which gains and losses in the presence of bystanders may arise.

There are three countries, donor A, recipient B and bystander C, and two goods, numéraire good x and good y with price p. The two private goods are tradable, taxes and benefits are collected and distributed in a lump-sum fashion, there are no distortions and perfect competition prevails. Analogously to equations (6.10)–(6.13), the general transfer problem can then be written as

$$E^A(p, u^A) = R^A(p) - T \tag{6.21}$$

$$E^B(p, u^B) = R^B(p) + T \tag{6.22}$$

$$E^C(p, u^C) = R^C(p) \tag{6.23}$$

$$m^A(p, u^A) + m^B(p, u^B) + m^C(p, u^C) = 0 \tag{6.24}$$

That is, expenditure equals revenue for all countries, taking into consideration that country A transfers T units of the numéraire good to country B. The last equation ensures that net world demand for the non-numéraire good is zero in equilibrium. As before, we normalize the derivative of expenditure with respect to utility to unity for all countries, $E^J_u = 1$ for $J = A, B, C$, and define $M_p \equiv \sum_J m^J_p \leq 0$ and $\Delta^{-1} \equiv -\sum_J \left(m^J_p - m^J m^J_u \right)$. Total differentiation of equations (6.21)–(6.24) gives

$$
\begin{bmatrix}
1 & 0 & 0 & m^A \\
0 & 1 & 0 & m^B \\
0 & 0 & 1 & m^C \\
m^A_u & m^B_u & m^C_u & M_p
\end{bmatrix}
\begin{bmatrix}
du^A \\
du^B \\
du^C \\
dp
\end{bmatrix}
=
\begin{bmatrix}
-1 \\
1 \\
0 \\
0
\end{bmatrix}
dT
\tag{6.25}
$$

Solving (6.25) reveals

$$\det = \sum_J \left(m_p^J - m^J m_u^J \right) \equiv \frac{-1}{\Delta} < 0$$

$$\frac{dp}{dT} = \left(m_u^B - m_u^A \right) \Delta > 0 \quad \text{iff} \quad m_u^B > m_u^A \tag{6.26}$$

$$\frac{du^A}{dT} = \left[M_p - m^C \left(m_u^C - m_u^B \right) \right] \Delta \tag{6.27}$$

$$\frac{du^B}{dT} = \left[-M_p + m^C \left(m_u^C - m_u^A \right) \right] \Delta \tag{6.28}$$

$$\frac{du^C}{dT} = -m^C \frac{dp}{dT} = -m^C \left(m_u^B - m_u^A \right) \Delta \tag{6.29}$$

$$\sum_J \frac{du^J}{dT} = 0 \tag{6.30}$$

As before, the relative price p rises if, and only if, the recipient has a higher marginal propensity to consume y than the donor; see equation (6.26). Thus, Elliot's (1938) claim, quoted in section 6.1, that the introduction of neutral (non-participating) countries has no material influence on the terms-of-trade change analysis of an international transfer is correct. As before, the sum of the welfare changes equals zero, indicating that the transfer moves the world economy from one Pareto-optimal allocation to another; see equation (6.30). Now note from the right-hand side of equations (6.27)–(6.29) that they contain the marginal propensity to consume terms $(m_u^J, J = A, B, C)$ for all countries involved *except* for the country whose welfare change is stated by the equation in question. Why this peculiar fact holds is analyzed in section 6.5.

From equation (6.28) it is clear that the recipient B gains from the transfer if, and only if, the following condition holds (see also Ravallion [1983], p. 208):

$$m^C \left(m_u^C - m_u^A \right) \geq M_p \tag{6.31}$$

It is immediately clear that the bystander (the non-participating country C) *must* be a net trader of goods for the recipient to lose rather than gain from the transfer, because condition (6.31) trivially holds if $m^C = 0$. This is obviously just another way of saying that in a two-country world, the Samuelson theorem holds (see also Yano [1983]).

Let us now take a look at Gale's example. Gale uses an endowment economy and fixed proportion preferences for all countries involved, which implies that grapes and lemons are complements and $M_p = 0$. From condition (6.31) it then follows that the recipient gains if, and only if, $m^C (m_u^C - m_u^A) \geq 0$. By construction, country C is a net supplier of lemons (there is no endowment or production of grapes in country C), that is $m^C < 0$. Thus, the recipient gains in Gale's example if, and only if, donor A's marginal propensity to consume lemons exceeds bystander C's marginal propensity to consume lemons, as Gale assumed.

Turning to an investigation of the welfare effects for the donor, it is apparent from equation (6.27) that the donor (strictly) gains from a transfer if, and only if, the following condition holds:

$$m^C (m_u^B - m_u^C) > -M_p \tag{6.32}$$

It is immediately clear that the bystander (the non-participating country C) *must* be a net trader of goods for the donor A to gain rather than lose from the transfer, because condition (6.32) cannot hold if $m^C = 0$.

Gale uses an endowment economy and fixed proportion preferences for all countries involved ($M_p = 0$); it then follows from equation (6.32) that the donor gains if, and only if, $m^C (m_u^B - m_u^C) > 0$. Since country C is a net supplier of lemons ($m^C < 0$) the donor gains in Gale's example if, and only if, bystander country C's marginal propensity to consume lemons exceeds recipient country B's marginal propensity to consume lemons, as Gale assumed.

Finally, from equation (6.29) it is clear that the bystander country C gains from the transfer if, and only if, the following condition holds:

$$- m^C (m_u^B - m_u^A) > 0 \tag{6.33}$$

The bystander country C is not directly involved in the transfer and therefore can only gain or lose as a result of a change in its terms of trade. As should be obvious by now, the change in the terms of trade is determined exclusively by the difference in marginal propensity to consume between recipient and donor and is not affected by the bystander's marginal propensity to consume.

In Gale's example the bystander country C is a net supplier of lemons ($m^C < 0$). Thus, bystander country C loses in Gale's example if, and only if, recipient B's marginal propensity to consume lemons is smaller than donor A's marginal propensity to consume lemons, again as Gale assumed.

6.5   A decomposition of welfare effects

The welfare effects for the three countries given in equations (6.27)–(6.29) can, analogously to chapter 3, also be written as $du^A/dT = -1 - m^A(dp/dT)$; $du^B/dT = 1 - m^B(dp/dT)$; $du^C/dT = -m^C(dp/dT)$. Thus, the bystander is affected only by the terms-of-trade effect, while the donor and recipient are affected also by an income effect. The disadvantage of this straightforward decomposition is that it does not shed light on the intricate relationships between the countries which make paradoxes possible if there are more than two countries, as demonstrated by Gale.

It was noted in section 6.4 above that in a multilateral world the welfare change of any country as a result of an international transfer contains the marginal propensity to consume terms m_u^J ($J = A, B, C$) for all countries involved *except* the country whose welfare change is stated by the equation in question; see equations (6.27)–(6.29). This may seem puzzling. Keep in mind, however, that this peculiar fact is readily understood for the bystander C since its welfare is affected only through a change in its terms of trade, which in turn is determined by the difference in the marginal propensities to consume of the other two countries (that is, donor and recipient). To help with the understanding of this fact for donor and recipient as well, it is illuminating to follow the Bhagwati *et al.* (1983) welfare decomposition which demonstrates that any paradoxical results for donor and recipient arise from a "bystander effect."

6.5.1   Donor welfare decomposition

Suppose we conceptually decompose the transfer of T units from country A to country B into two stages. At the *first* stage, country A gives transfers to both country B and country C in proportion to their initial import demand for lemons. At the *second* stage, country C gives to country B what it received from country A in the first stage. The final situation is therefore equivalent to the actual transfer going exclusively from country A to country B. Let us summarize and make precise this conceptual decomposition.

- First stage: country B receives $[m^B/(m^B + m^C)]T$ units from country A and country C receives $[m^C/(m^B + m^C)]T$ units from country A.
- Second stage: country B receives the $[m^C/(m^B + m^C)]T$ units from country C that were first given to country C by country A.

Note that if the two ratios mentioned in the first stage of this decomposition are positive, both country B and country C receive positive transfers from country A. However, if for example,

$m^C/(m^B + m^C)$ is negative, this implies that country C receives a negative transfer, that is it gives a positive transfer to country A at the first stage which it then gets back at the second stage.

What is the welfare effect of the first stage for donor country A? This can be readily determined by exploiting the essence of the result in equation (6.27), which gives country A's welfare effect as a result of a transfer to country B, and is restated here as

$$\frac{du^A}{dT_{AB}} = \left[M_p - m^C \left(m_u^C - m_u^B \right) \right] \Delta \tag{6.34}$$

where T_{AB} indicates that the transfer is from country A to country B. By interchanging the roles of countries B and C in equation (6.34) we can determine the effect on country A's welfare as a result of a transfer from country A to country C as:

$$\frac{du^A}{dT_{AC}} = \left[M_p - m^B \left(m_u^B - m_u^C \right) \right] \Delta \tag{6.35}$$

where T_{AC} indicates that the transfer is from country A to country C. To determine donor A's welfare change as a result of the first stage of the transfer decomposition we have to weight equations (6.34) and (6.35) with the appropriate transfer shares from country A to countries B and C, respectively, and add:

$$\left. \frac{du^A}{dT} \right|_{1st\ stage} = \left(\frac{m^B}{m^B + m^C} \right) \left[M_p - m^C \left(m_u^C - m_u^B \right) \right] \Delta$$

$$+ \left(\frac{m^C}{m^B + m^C} \right) \left[M_p - m^B \left(m_u^B - m_u^C \right) \right] \Delta \quad \text{or}$$

$$\left. \frac{du^A}{dT} \right|_{1st\ stage} = M_p \Delta \leq 0 \tag{6.36}$$

Equation (6.36) demonstrates that the structure of the change in the donor's welfare as a result of the first stage of our decomposition is exactly the same as the welfare change derived for the donor for a transfer in the two-country world of chapter 3 (compare equation [6.36] above with equation [3.7]). Giving transfers to every other country in a multilateral world in proportion to its initial import demand is therefore the same as making a transfer to another country in a two-country context. From Samuelson's theorem, this gives rise to a welfare decline for the donor, such that the paradox of donor-enrichment cannot come from this first stage. However, the welfare change for country A from the second stage of the process is very easy to understand: country A acts as a bystander in that stage and is only affected through the change in its terms of trade resulting from the second-stage transfer from country C to country B. Appropriately rewriting the result in equation (6.29) and weighting by the size of the transfer gives

$$\left.\frac{du^A}{dT}\right|_{2nd\ stage} = \left(\frac{m^C}{m^B + m^C}\right)\frac{du^A}{dT_{CB}} = \left(\frac{m^C}{m^B + m^C}\right)(-m^A)\left(m_u^B - m_u^C\right)\Delta \quad \text{or}$$

$$\left.\frac{du^A}{dT}\right|_{2nd\ stage} = \left(\frac{m^C}{-m^A}\right)(-m^A)\left(m_u^B - m_u^C\right)\Delta = -m^C\left(m_u^C - m_u^B\right)\Delta \quad (6.37)$$

The term T_{CB} above refers to a transfer from country C to country B. We have now decomposed donor country A's welfare effect of a transfer to country B, that is equation (6.27), into two parts given by equations (6.36) and (6.37):

$$\frac{du^A}{dT} = (M_p\Delta) + \left(-m^C\left(m_u^C - m_u^B\right)\Delta\right) = \left.\frac{du^A}{dT}\right|_{1st\ stage} + \left.\frac{du^A}{dT}\right|_{2nd\ stage}$$

Thus, if the total effect from the two stages (that is, a direct transfer from country A to country B) results in a paradoxical donor-enrichment this is caused exclusively, and understandably, by the second-stage bystander effect of country A's welfare change.

6.5.2   Recipient welfare decomposition

We can make a similar welfare decomposition for the recipient country B if we conceptually decompose the transfer of T units from country A to country B into two stages. At the *first* stage, both of countries A and C give transfers to country B in proportion to their initial import demand for lemons. At the *second* stage, country A gives to country C what it should have given to country B in the first stage. The final situation is therefore equivalent to the actual transfer going exclusively from country A to country B. Let us summarize and make precise this conceptual decomposition.

- First stage: country B receives $[m^A/(m^A + m^C)]T$ units from country A and $[m^C/(m^A + m^C)]T$ units from country C.
- Second stage: country C receives $[m^C/(m^A + m^C)]T$ units from

country A; that is, it receives from country A what it gave away to country B in the first stage.

Following the same procedure as in the previous subsection for the donor country A, it is possible to demonstrate that the structure of the change in the recipient's welfare as a result of the first stage of the decomposition is exactly the same as the welfare change for the recipient of a transfer in the two-country world of chapter 3. Receiving transfers from every other country in a multilateral world in proportion to its initial import demand is therefore the same as receiving a transfer from another country in a two-country context. From Samuelson's theorem, this gives rise to a welfare increase for the recipient, such that the paradox of recipient-impoverishment cannot come from this first stage. At the second stage of the decomposition, country B is a bystander and is affected by the transfer from country A to country C only through the impact on its terms of trade.

> **Proposition 16:** (Bhagwati, Brecher and Hatta) The welfare changes for donor and recipient resulting from an international transfer in a three-country setting can be decomposed into two stages to demonstrate that any transfer paradoxes result from the second-stage "bystander effect."

6.5.3   Alternative conditions for paradoxes

To derive alternative conditions for welfare paradoxes which might shed some light on the likelihood of their occurrence we let $\tilde{m}^C$ denote country C's uncompensated import demand curve for lemons. Recall the Slutsky equation, the well-known decomposition into substitution and income effects; see the mathematical appendix or the appendix to chapter 3:

$$\tilde{m}_p^C = m_p^C - m^C m_u^C \tag{6.38}$$

Applying equation (6.38) to donor country A's welfare change (equation [6.27]), and recalling $M_p \equiv m_p^A + m_p^B + m_p^C$ gives:

$$\frac{du^A}{dT} = \Delta\left(m_p^A + m_p^B + \tilde{m}_p^C + m^C m_u^B\right) \tag{6.39}$$

Assume throughout the rest of this section, and without loss of generality, that bystander country C exports lemons ($m^C < 0$). Since

$\Delta > 0$, $m_p^A \leq 0$ and $m_p^B \leq 0$ it then follows from (6.39) that donor country A can gain from the transfer only if either (i) $\tilde{m}_p^C > 0$, or (ii) $m_u^B < 0$, or both. Condition (i) ($\tilde{m}_p^C > 0$) implies that bystander country C's offer curve is inelastic, so that country C's export supply of lemons falls if the relative price of lemons rises. Condition (ii) ($m_u^B < 0$) implies that lemons are an inferior good to recipient country B. Thus, donor country A can only gain from making a transfer if either the bystander's offer curve is inelastic, or the bystander's export good is an inferior good to the recipient, or both.

Similarly, substituting equation (6.38) into the recipient's welfare change, equation (6.28), gives:

$$\frac{du^B}{dT} = \Delta\left(m_p^A + m_p^B + \tilde{m}_p^C + m^C m_u^A\right) \tag{6.40}$$

From equation (6.40) it then follows that immiserization occurs for the recipient only if either (i) $\tilde{m}_p^C > 0$, or (ii) $m_u^A < 0$, or both. That is, recipient country B may lose from the transfer if either the bystander's offer curve is inelastic, or the bystander's export good is an inferior good to the donor, or both.[6]

> **Proposition 17:** (Bhagwati, Brecher and Hatta) In a Walrasian-stable, perfectly competitive, two-good world with three countries, the donor can only gain from giving a transfer if (i) the bystander's offer curve is inelastic (that is, backward-bending), or (ii) the bystander's export good is an inferior good to the recipient, or both. Similarly, the recipient may lose from the

---

[6] In their analysis, Bhagwati et al. (1983) also argue that any transfer paradoxes in a three-country setting arise from a "foreign distortion." This "distortion" is the failure of the countries involved in the transfer to exploit their monopoly power relative to the outside world. Thus, if countries A and B are involved in a transfer they should first levy an "optimal tariff" against country C. If they do, no transfer paradoxes will occur. There are, we think, several drawbacks to this argument. First, the "optimal tariff" argument itself has many weaknesses if retaliation is taken into account, as it usually makes the "optimal tariff" not optimal for anyone involved. Second, in a multi-country world many different and potentially conflicting "optimal tariffs" are involved. For example, if the United States gave a transfer to both China and India it would have to collaborate on an "optimal tariff" with China relative to its outside world (which includes India), but at the same time it would have to collaborate with India on an "optimal tariff" relative to its outside world (which includes China). Third, the procedure of first identifying three independent separate countries and then showing that something cannot occur if we take away the independence of two of the countries involved is not very satisfying. Fourth, there may not be much incentive for a donor who gains from a transfer in the absence of tariffs to impose a tariff which ensures that it will lose from the transfer. A further discussion of this issue is in Kemp and Wong (1993, section 3, especially note 2).

transfer if either (i) the bystander's offer curve is inelastic, or (ii) the bystander's export good is an inferior good to the donor, or both.

6.6   Endogenous transfers II

In this section, which is based on Brakman and Van Marrewijk (1991a) we want to point out the remarkable robustness of transfer paradoxes with respect to "endogenization" of transfers. We use this term to reflect the empirical observation that transfers are given from *rich* countries to *poor* countries and that the size of the transfer is positively related to the donor's income and negatively related to the recipient's income. The positive relation with respect to the donor's income has been formalized, for example, by United Nations Resolution No. 2626, which states that at least 0.7 percent of a rich country's GNP should be used for development assistance. The negative relation with respect to the recipient's income can be illustrated by the recent proposal of the IGGI countries[7] to decrease (in real terms) the development assistance given to Indonesia because of its recently flourishing economy. Relations like this make transfers partly endogenous. This section investigates the main consequences of this type of endogenization. Section 7.4 below analyzes altruism more explicitly.

6.6.1   The model

Consider a perfectly competitive world with two goods, numéraire good x and good y, produced and consumed in three countries, A, B and C.[8] Tariffs, quotas, transport costs and other barriers to trade are absent from the model. The relative price of good y is therefore equal in the three countries. It should be noted that the model can also be applied to represent a transfer from one agent to another within a country.

We will model endogenization as follows. The total transfer given from country A to country B consists of two parts: an autonomous part denoted by Ta, which represents discretionary policy, and an endogenous part. The latter depends on the expenditure level of the donor and is represented by $T\left(E^A(p, u^A)\right)$, where E^J is country J's expenditure

---

[7] The InterGovernmental Group on Indonesia (IGGI) is a group of donor countries that collaborate on development issues with respect to Indonesia.

[8] Extension to an arbitrary number of countries is straightforward, see Brakman and Van Marrewijk (1993).

function, p is the relative price of good y and u^J is country J's utility level.[9] It is assumed that $T(.)$ is a smooth and monotonically increasing function; that is, the richer the donor gets, the larger the transfer it gives. Let R^J be country J's revenue function and let m^J denote country J's net demand for good y, that is $m^J \equiv E_p^J - R_p^J$ for $J = A, B, C$. Then the endogenous transfer model is summarized in equations (6.41)–(6.44):

$$E^A(p, u^A) = R^A(p) - T(E^A(p, u^A)) - Ta \qquad (6.41)$$
$$E^B(p, u^B) = R^B(p) + T(E^A(p, u^A)) + Ta \qquad (6.42)$$
$$E^C(p, u^C) = R^C(p) \qquad (6.43)$$
$$m^A(p, u^A) + m^B(p, u^B) + m^C(p, u^C) = 0 \qquad (6.44)$$

That is, expenditure equals revenue for all countries, taking into consideration that country A transfers $T(.) + Ta$ units of the numéraire good x to country B. The last equation ensures that net world demand for good y is zero in equilibrium. As before, we normalize the derivative of expenditure with respect to utility to unity for all countries, $E_u^J = 1$ for $J = A, B, C$, and define $M_p \equiv \sum_J m_p^J \leq 0$ and $\Delta^{-1} \equiv -\sum_J \left(m_p^J - m^J m_u^J \right)$. In addition, we define

$$\Lambda^{-1} \equiv \left[(1 + T_{E^A}) - R_p^A T_{E^A} \frac{dp}{dT} \bigg|_{ex} \right] \Delta^{-1}$$

where the notation $|_{ex}$ denotes "exogenous" and is used to refer to the general results derived for exogenous transfers in section 6.4, see equations (6.26)–(6.29). Total differentiation of equations (6.41)-(6.44) gives:

$$\begin{bmatrix} 1 + T_{E^A} & 0 & 0 & m^A + E_p^A T_{E^A} \\ -T_{E^A} & 1 & 0 & m^B - E_p^A T_{E^A} \\ 0 & 0 & 1 & m^C \\ m_u^A & m_u^B & m_u^C & M_p \end{bmatrix} \begin{bmatrix} du^A \\ du^B \\ du^C \\ dp \end{bmatrix} = \begin{bmatrix} -1 \\ 1 \\ 0 \\ 0 \end{bmatrix} dTa \qquad (6.45)$$

Solving (6.45) and using the results in equations (6.26)–(6.29) reveals that

$$\det = \frac{-1}{\Lambda} < 0 \qquad (6.46)$$

[9] For a more general description of endogenization, see the next subsection.

$$\frac{dp}{dTa} = \frac{\Lambda}{\Delta}\frac{dp}{dT}\bigg|_{ex} \tag{6.47}$$

$$\frac{du^J}{dTa} = \frac{\Lambda}{\Delta}\frac{du^J}{dT}\bigg|_{ex} \quad J = A, B, C \tag{6.48}$$

The inequality in equation (6.46) reflects the condition of Walrasian stability for the endogenous transfer problem. It follows from equations (6.47) and (6.48) that all multipliers in the endogenous transfer case are a positive scalar multiple, namely Λ/Δ, of the multipliers in the exogenous case. We conclude, therefore, that

> **Proposition 18:** Transfer paradoxes (donor-enrichment and/or recipient-impoverishment) occur in the case of endogenous transfers if, and only if, they occur in the case of exogenous transfers. Furthermore, the price of good y rises in the case of endogenous transfers if, and only if, it rises in the case of exogenous transfers.

The model displays a remarkable robustness with respect to this type of endogenization. Donor-enrichment and recipient-impoverishment can still occur, but only if they already occur in the exogenous case. Even though there is no particular relation between income levels and income derivatives of consumption, which implies that transfer paradoxes cannot be ruled out *a priori*, one would at least expect a change in the conditions under which transfer paradoxes do arise because the welfare and price effects are influenced (that is, mitigated – see the next proposition) by the endogenous transfer. A possible explanation is given in Bhagwati *et al.* (1983) who argue that (exogenous-type) transfer paradoxes in the three-country setting used here are caused by a "foreign" distortion; see section 6.5. By this they mean that the countries involved in the transfer (the donor and the recipient) are not using an optimal tariff (are not exploiting their joint monopoly power) *vis-à-vis* the non-participant. As the distortion is still present, the transfer paradox should also still occur, as indeed it does.

For obvious reasons we will call the term Λ/Δ the "multiplier" and say that "dampening" occurs if this multiplier is smaller than 1. This allows us to formulate the following proposition:

> **Proposition 19:** Endogenization of transfers causes a dampening effect, that is $\Lambda/\Delta < 1$, if, and only if, the following condition holds:

$$\frac{dR^A(p)}{dT}\bigg|_{ex} < 1 \tag{6.49}$$

A sufficient condition for dampening is the absence of price effects, that is if the marginal propensity to consume good y is the same for donor and recipient.

The condition in equation (6.49) is easy to understand and straightforward to derive. Suppose it does not hold, then transferring one unit of purchasing power results in a revenue increase of more than one unit and thus increases the endogenous transfer.

In the absence of price effects, that is if the marginal propensity to consume good y is the same for donor and recipient, condition (6.49) will hold. In that case the multiplier is simply $\Lambda/\Delta = 1/(1 + T_{E^A}) < 1$. This effect is not hard to understand either. Suppose country A gives one extra unit of (autonomous) aid. Its expenditure will have to be reduced by one unit while, at the same time, country B's expenditure can increase by one unit. But then the (endogenous) aid will decrease by T_{E^A} units. Country A's expenditure will then increase by this amount. Endogenous aid will increase by $(T_{E^A})^2$ units, etc. Adding up all these transfer changes leads to: $1 - (T_{E^A}) + (T_{E^A})^2 - (T_{E^A})^3 + (T_{E^A})^4 - ... = 1/(1 + T_{E^A})$.

6.6.2   Sensitivity

We saw in the previous subsection that in a competitive and Walrasian-stable world with two goods, transfer paradoxes are robust with respect to endogenization and that endogenization tends to cause a dampening effect (smaller price and welfare changes), provided a revenue condition is satisfied. In that subsection we assumed that the endogenous transfers are only related to the donor's expenditure level. It is equally plausible, however, as argued in the introduction to this section, to relate the transfers to the recipient's expenditure level, or to the revenue levels of either country. We now demonstrate that the results above are very robust with respect to the type of endogenization. To this end, let us analyze the most general formulation, in which the endogenous part of the transfer is given by

$$T\left(E^A(p, u^A), R^A(p), E^B(p, u^B), R^B(p)\right) \tag{6.50}$$

Assume that $T(.)$ is smooth, rising in E^A and R^A (the richer the donor becomes, the more it gives), decreasing in E^B and R^B (the richer the recipient becomes, the less it receives from the donor), and that country A will not give away all of its extra earnings or expenditures to country B or reduce the amount of the transfer to country B by more than country B earns or spends additionally, that is $0 \le T_{E^A} < 1$; $0 \le T_{R^A} < 1$; $-1 < T_{E^B} \le 0$; and $-1 < T_{R^B} \le 0$. After making some obvious changes in equations (6.41), (6.42) and (6.45) and after some elementary calculations it can be shown that the results obtained in equations (6.47) and (6.48) still hold, provided we redefine Λ as follows:

$$\Lambda^{-1} \equiv \left\{ (1 + T_{E^A} - T_{E^B}) - \left[\sum_{J=A,B} R_p^J (T_{E^J} + T_{R^J}) \right] \left(\frac{dp}{dT} \bigg|_{ex} \right) \right\} \Delta^{-1} \quad (6.51)$$

This allows us to conclude the following.

Proposition 20: The results obtained in the previous two propositions are independent of the type of endogenization, provided that condition (6.49) for dampening is changed to

$$\sum_{J=A,B} \left[(T_{E^J} + T_{R^J}) \frac{dR^J(p)}{dT} \bigg|_{ex} \right] < (T_{E^A} - T_{E^B}) \quad (6.52)$$

Again, the absence of price effects is sufficient for dampening.[10] In practice, however, the bystander country will be comprised of all countries not engaged in the transfer. This aggregate country (the rest of the world) will be large in comparison to countries A and B, making the occurrence of significant price changes due to the transfer unlikely. Thus, we have a strong case for the mitigating welfare effects due to the endogenization of transfers.

6.7 Conclusion

In this chapter we first demonstrated, by means of Gale's example, that transfer paradoxes, that is donor-enrichment and/or recipient-

---

[10] Equation (6.52) gives the combined condition for four separate cases. If the endogenous transfer is exclusively related to the donor's expenditure we obtain condition (6.49). If it is exclusively related to the donor's revenue we obtain $(dR^A(p))/dT|_{ex} < 0$, if exclusively related to the recipient's expenditure $(dR^B(p))/dT|_{ex} > -1$, and if exclusively related to the recipient's revenue $(dR^B(p))/dT|_{ex} > 0$. These last three cases have similar interpretations to those given for the first case in the previous subsection. Note that dampening condition (6.52) is stronger than the Walrasian-stability condition that equation (6.51) is positive (which can be rewritten in the form of equation [6.52] with an identical left-hand side and "1" added to the right-hand side; that is, the latter becomes $(1 - T_{E^A} - T_{E^B})$).

impoverishment, are possible in a two-good, Walrasian-stable world without distortions, provided there are at least three countries involved: the donor, the recipient and a bystander. Gale's example was extended by several authors (Chichilnisky, Léonard and Manning, and Guesnerie and Laffont) to include different types of paradoxes and smooth preferences. The economic analysis following these examples, which includes production, and builds on Bhagwati *et al.*, demonstrated that potential transfer paradoxes for donor and/or recipient follow from the "bystander effect" of the transfer and that such paradoxes require backward-bending offer curves and/or inferior goods. Finally, if the transfer is partially "endogenous," that is its size may depend on the donor and/or recipient's expenditure and/or revenue level, transfer paradoxes occur if, and only if, they also occur when the transfer is purely exogenous.

7   The economics of multilateral transfers

7.1   Introduction

As we have shown in the previous chapters, transfer paradoxes can arise
in the presence of three participating countries: a donor, a recipient and a
bystander. However, on many occasions aid is given in the form of
multilateral aid or multilateral lending.[1] The reason for multilateral aid is
not as clear as one might expect. Why would a government give aid
through a multilateral agency if it can give aid to a recipient bilaterally?
Three reasons come to the fore. First, information gathering has a
public-good character; for example, the assessment of the political
situation for potential recipients, or the choice of which (environmental)
projects or investment opportunities to support. Multilateral agencies
might be better equipped for this specific informational task at the
international level, just as the government of a country is at the national
level. These agencies, such as the International Monetary Fund (IMF) or
the World Bank, employ many specialists to watch closely the evolution
of the economic situation in the developed and developing world. Of
course, economies of scale may play a role in this process of information
gathering. The task of monitoring the use of aid by a recipient can also
be delegated to a multilateral agency. Second, rent-seeking behavior,
either by the donor or the recipient, or other political problems can
sometimes be prevented or avoided. The international relations between
a donor and a recipient can sometimes become so clouded by political
issues as to prevent a working economic relationship. In the early 1990s,
for example, Indonesia, a former Dutch colony, refused the aid given to
it by the Netherlands because of the associated political irritations, and
subsequently attempted to get more lenient conditions on this bilateral
aid (see Yano [1991]). If the aid had been multilateral this probably

---

[1] If the interest rate on a loan is below the market rate then this loan has a transfer aspect.

would not have happened. Third, multilateral aid can also be conditional. For a private agency, the simple fact that, for instance, the World
Bank is helping a specific country might be a signal of the recipient's
prudent economic policies.

In any case, multilateral aid is important (see also chapter 1) and
deserves separate treatment (Dixit [1983]; Fluckiger [1987]). The questions we will answer are the following. Is it better for a recipient to
receive a transfer multilaterally or unilaterally? If the reasons for the
existence of multilateral agencies mentioned above are valid, one would
expect some welfare gain from multilateral aid. If so, what is the optimal
form of aid? And what are the effects for donors, recipients and
bystanders? Thus, the problem discussed in chapter 6, of who might gain
and lose as a result of a transfer in a three-or-more-country world, is not
addressed in this chapter. Here we are interested in the welfare consequences of one policy option relative to another, not in gains or losses
per se.

7.2   Multilateral transfers

In this section, we distinguish two tradable commodities, good y with
price p and numéraire good x. We identify three groups of countries.[2]
There are n^A donors, identified by an A with a subindex $h = 1, ..., n^A$.
Similarly, there are n^B recipients, identified by a B with a subindex
$i = 1, ..., n^B$, and there are n^C bystanders, identified by a C with a
subindex $j = 1, ..., n^C$. Each country has a well-behaved expenditure
function E and revenue function R. The total transfer collected from all
donors and redistributed to all recipients equals T. The parameter λ^{A_h},
with $0 < \lambda^{A_h} < 1$, denotes the share of the total transfer paid by country
A_h, while the parameter π^{B_i}, with $0 < \pi^{B_i} < 1$, denotes the share of the
total transfer received by country B_i. This formulation, in which aid is
donated to a "pool" from which transfers are then received, is a primitive
description of a multilateral agency. As usual, let m denote the net
demand for good y, that is $m^{D_k} \equiv E_p^{D_k} - R_p^{D_k}$ for $D = A, B, C$ and
$k = 1, .., n^D$. Then the world economy is described by equations (7.1)–
(7.5).

$$E^{A_h}(p, u^{A_h}) = R^{A_h}(p) - \lambda^{A_h} T \quad \text{for } h = 1, .., n^A \tag{7.1}$$

$$E^{B_i}(p, u^{B_i}) = R^{B_i}(p) + \pi^{B_i} T \quad \text{for } i = 1, .., n^B \tag{7.2}$$

$$E^{C_j}(p, u^{C_j}) = R^{C_j}(p) \quad \text{for } j = 1, .., n^C \tag{7.3}$$

---

[2] This section and the next are based on Brakman and Van Marrewijk (1993).

$$\sum_{h=1}^{n^A} m^{A_h}(p, u^{A_h}) + \sum_{i=1}^{n^B} m^{B_i}(p, u^{B_i}) + \sum_{j=1}^{n^C} m^{C_j}(p, u^{C_j}) = 0 \tag{7.4}$$

$$\sum_{h=1}^{n^A} \lambda^{A_h} = \sum_{i=1}^{n^B} \pi^{B_i} = 1 \tag{7.5}$$

Equations (7.1)–(7.3) are the budget restrictions for donors, recipients and bystanders, respectively. Equation (7.4) gives the market-clearing condition for good y. Finally, equation (7.5) indicates that some donor pays for a good in the transfer pool, which is subsequently redistributed to some recipient. Alternatively, it is possible to analyze the efficiency benefits of a multilateral agency relative to bilateral aid, as discussed in the introduction, in this framework by letting $\sum_{i=1}^{n^B} \pi^{B_i} < 1$. The redistributive costs $\left(1 - \sum_{i=1}^{n^B} \pi^{B_i}\right)$ of setting up a multilateral agency would then have to be contrasted with the redistributive costs of bilateral aid. Let $\mathbf{Z}^D \equiv (Z^{D_1}, ..., Z^{D_{n^D}})'$ for $D = A, B, C$ and $Z = E, R, u, m, \lambda, \pi$, if defined, and let $\mathbf{i}_{n^D}$ be an n^D-dimensional unit vector. Then the above equations can be written more succinctly as in (7.6)–(7.10):

$$\mathbf{E}^A(p, \mathbf{u}^A) = \mathbf{R}^A(p) - \lambda T \tag{7.6}$$

$$\mathbf{E}^B(p, \mathbf{u}^B) = \mathbf{R}^B(p) + \pi T \tag{7.7}$$

$$\mathbf{E}^C(p, \mathbf{u}^C) = \mathbf{R}^C(p) \tag{7.8}$$

$$\mathbf{i}'_{n^A}\mathbf{m}^A(p, \mathbf{u}^A) + \mathbf{i}'_{n^B}\mathbf{m}^B(p, \mathbf{u}^B) + \mathbf{i}'_{n^C}\mathbf{m}^C(p, \mathbf{u}^C) = 0 \tag{7.9}$$

$$\mathbf{i}'_{n^A}\lambda - \mathbf{i}'_{n^B}\pi - 1 \tag{7.10}$$

As in the previous chapters, we normalize the derivative of expenditure with respect to utility to unity for all countries and let M_p be the world net substitution of good y (net substitution summed over all countries) and $-\Delta^{-1}$ the world gross substitution of good y (gross substitution summed over all countries, which is negative under Walrasian stability). Moreover, we let $\mathbf{I}_{n^D}$ denote the n^D-dimensional identity matrix. Then, total differentiation of equations (7.6)–(7.9) gives equation (7.11). Solving (7.11) gives (7.12)–(7.16):

$$\begin{bmatrix} \mathbf{I}_{n^A} & 0 & 0 & \mathbf{m}^A \\ 0 & \mathbf{I}_{n^B} & 0 & \mathbf{m}^B \\ 0 & 0 & \mathbf{I}_{n^C} & \mathbf{m}^C \\ \mathbf{m}'_{u^A} & \mathbf{m}'_{u^B} & \mathbf{m}'_{u^C} & M_p \end{bmatrix} \begin{bmatrix} d\mathbf{u}^A \\ d\mathbf{u}^B \\ d\mathbf{u}^C \\ dp \end{bmatrix} = \begin{bmatrix} -\lambda \\ \pi \\ 0 \\ 0 \end{bmatrix} dT \tag{7.11}$$

$$\frac{dp}{dT} = \left(\pi' \mathbf{m}_u^B - \lambda' \mathbf{m}_u^A\right)\Delta > 0 \quad \text{iff} \quad \pi' \mathbf{m}_u^B > \lambda' \mathbf{m}_u^A \tag{7.12}$$

$$\frac{d\mathbf{u}^A}{dT} = -\lambda^A - \mathbf{m}^A \frac{dp}{dT} \tag{7.13}$$

$$\frac{d\mathbf{u}^B}{dT} = \pi^B - \mathbf{m}^B \frac{dp}{dT} \tag{7.14}$$

$$\frac{d\mathbf{u}^C}{dT} = -\mathbf{m}^C \frac{dp}{dT} \tag{7.15}$$

$$\mathbf{i}'_{n^A}\frac{d\mathbf{u}^A}{dT} + \mathbf{i}'_{n^B}\frac{d\mathbf{u}^B}{dT} + \mathbf{i}'_{n^C}\frac{d\mathbf{u}^C}{dT} = 0 \tag{7.16}$$

From equation (7.12) we see that the conclusion on the change in the terms of trade of previous chapters is easily generalized. The price of good y rises if, and only if, the weighted average of the recipients' marginal propensities to consume good y is larger than the donors' weighted average to consume good y. The share of the transfer received or paid, respectively, is the relevant weight, that is the price of good y rises if, and only if, $\sum_i^{n^B}\left(\pi^{B_i} m_u^{B_i}\right) > \sum_h^{n^A}\left(\lambda^{A_h} m_u^{A_h}\right)$. Equation (7.15) shows that nothing has changed for bystanders, that is a bystander gains or loses if its terms of trade improve or deteriorate, respectively. The same terms-of-trade principle also affects the welfare of donors and recipients, as equations (7.13) and (7.14) show. In this case, however, the size of the income effect depends on the share of the transfer paid or received. Since each country in the three groups of countries distinguished here can either import or export good y and may contribute to or receive a different share of the transfer, each group of countries, that is donors, recipients and bystanders, can in principle be subdivided into two subgroups: a subgroup that gains from the transfer and a subgroup that loses from the transfer. In other words, there is no uniformity within groups with respect to the welfare effects of a transfer. Equation (7.16) is a reminder of the Pareto optimality of the initial situation.

7.3   Friend or foe?

The model described in the previous section allows for some interesting observations concerning the desirability of using a multilateral agency for international transfers, either from a donor's or a recipient's point of view. Suppose, for example, that donor A_1 wants to transfer one unit of numéraire good x in aid. There are two options. Country A_1 can choose a recipient, say country B_1, and make a bilateral transfer to this recipient. From chapter 6 we know that the welfare change resulting from this bilateral transfer for country A_1 is given by equation (7.17), where T_{bi} denotes a bilateral transfer. Alternatively, country A_1 can make a multilateral transfer to the World Bank, which then redistributes the transfer to a number of recipients. From the previous section we know that the welfare change of this multilateral transfer for country A_1 is given in equation (7.18), where T_{multi} denotes a multilateral transfer.[3] Assume, without loss of generality, that country A_1 exports good y, that is $m^{A_1} < 0$. Moreover, assume that donor A_1 prefers the multilateral transfer to the bilateral transfer if its welfare loss is smaller (or, possibly, if its welfare gain is larger; see chapter 6), that is if $du^{A_1}/dT_{multi} > du^{A_1}/dT_{bi}$. Comparing equations (7.17) and (7.18), then, shows that the multilateral transfer is preferred if equation (7.19) holds.

$$\frac{du^{A_1}}{dT_{bi}} = -1 - m^{A_1}\left(m_u^{B_1} - m_u^{A_1}\right)\Delta \tag{7.17}$$

$$\frac{du^{A_1}}{dT_{multi}} = -1 - m^{A_1}\left[\sum_{i=1}^{n^B}\left(\pi^{B_i} m_u^{B_i}\right) - m_u^{A_1}\right]\Delta \tag{7.18}$$

$$\sum_{i=1}^{n^B}\left(\pi^{B_i} m_u^{B_i}\right) > m_u^{B_1} \tag{7.19}$$

The intuitively straightforward condition (7.19) indicates that donor A_1 prefers giving multilateral aid rather than bilateral aid to country B_1 if the multilateral average marginal propensity to consume good y, the donor's export good, is higher than country B_1's marginal propensity to consume good y. This is equivalent to a more advantageous terms-of-trade effect for the donor. We can take this logic one step further because condition (7.19) can only hold if there is at least one recipient of the multilateral transfer with a higher marginal propensity to consume good y than country B_1. Indeed, one of the countries receiving the multilateral transfer, say $\bar{B} \in \{B_1, ..., B_{n^B}\}$, must have the highest marginal propensity to consume good y. But then donor A_1 prefers giving bilateral aid to country $\bar{B}$ rather than multilateral aid because it is always true that

$$\sum_{i=1}^{n^B}\left(\pi^{B_i} m_u^{B_i}\right) \leq m_u^{\bar{B}}$$

We have thus established that a donor determined to give a transfer of a certain size has a preference for a bilateral transfer to the recipient with

---

[3] Use equations (7.12) and (7.13) and the fact that the transfer is given exclusively by country A_1.

the highest marginal propensity to consume the donor's export good. Similarly, if recipient B_1 receives a bilateral transfer from donor A_1 its welfare change is given by equation (7.20), whereas if it receives a multilateral transfer its welfare change is given by equation (7.21). Thus, assuming that recipient B_1 exports good y, it prefers the multilateral transfer to the bilateral transfer if equation (7.22) holds.

$$\frac{du^{B_1}}{dT_{bi}} = 1 - m^{B_1}\left(m_u^{B_1} - m_u^{A_1}\right)\Delta \tag{7.20}$$

$$\frac{du^{B_1}}{dT_{multi}} = 1 - m^{B_1}\left[m_u^{B_1} - \sum_{h=1}^{n^A}\left(\lambda^{A_h} m_u^{A_h}\right)\right]\Delta \tag{7.21}$$

$$\sum_{h=1}^{n^A}\left(\lambda^{A_h} m_u^{A_h}\right) < m_u^{A_1} \tag{7.22}$$

Recipient B_1, therefore, prefers receiving multilateral aid rather than bilateral aid from donor A_1 if the multilateral average marginal propensity to consume good y, the recipient's export good, is lower than country A_1's marginal propensity to consume good y. Again, condition (7.22) can only hold if there is at least one donor of the multilateral transfer with a lower marginal propensity to consume good y than donor A_1. Since one of the donors must have the lowest marginal propensity to consume good y, say $\bar{A} \in \{A_1, ..., A_{n^A}\}$, recipient B_1 prefers receiving bilateral aid from country $\bar{A}$ rather than multilateral aid because it is always true that

$$\sum_{h=1}^{n^A}\left(\lambda^{A_h} m_u^{A_h}\right) \geq m_u^{\bar{A}}$$

We have thus established that a recipient receiving a transfer of a certain size has a preference for a bilateral transfer from the donor with the lowest marginal propensity to consume the recipient's export good. To summarize:

> **Proposition 21:** Given the size of the transfer to be given or received, respectively, both donors and recipients prefer bilateral transfers to multilateral transfers. In general, there is a conflict of interest since a donor prefers to give a bilateral transfer to the recipient with the highest marginal propensity to consume the donor's export good, while a recipient prefers to receive a bilateral transfer from the donor with the lowest marginal propensity to consume the recipient's export good.

A brief comment on the conflict of interest alluded to in the above proposition may be in order. Neglecting for the moment the question of how to determine each potential recipient's marginal propensity to consume before the transfer is made (by no means an easy task), the group of donors may be divided into two subgroups: those who export good y and those who import it. The preceding analysis demonstrates that each of these subgroups has a preferred recipient. Following that logic to the extreme, none of the other potential recipients would get any aid.[4] Thus a multilateral agency might serve to circumvent this undesirable outcome.

Advocates of multilateral agencies might not like the above proposition. However, the preference for bilateral transfers is not quite as gloomy a situation for multilateral agencies as might appear at first sight, even if we neglect the returns to scale in distribution and information gathering favoring multilateral agencies, which were mentioned in the introduction to this chapter and the previous section. On many occasions aid is given to fulfill the needs of a specific country, say because of the general poverty level or because it has been struck by a famine, a flood or an earthquake. Given the fact that there is a need to aid a certain country, say recipient B_1, would donor A_1 prefer to coordinate its efforts by trying to convince other donors to assist in aiding country B_1 through a multilateral agency such as the World Bank? If donor A_1 tries to help recipient B_1 individually its welfare change is given by equation (7.23), where T_{bi} denotes an uncoordinated bilateral transfer. On the other hand, working from equation (7.13) (with country B_1 as the only recipient), donor A_1's welfare change resulting from a coordinated effort is given in equation (7.24), where T_{coor} denotes a coordinated transfer. Let $m_u^{A_{notl}}$ be the other donors' weighted average marginal propensity to consume good y, that is $m_u^{A_{notl}} \equiv \sum_{h=2}^{n^A} \left[(\lambda^{A_h}/(1-\lambda^{A_1})) m_u^{A_h} \right]$. Then donor A_1 prefers coordinated aid, that is $du^{A_1}/dT_{coor} > du^{A_1}/dT_{bi}$, if equation (7.25) holds.

$$\frac{du^{A_1}}{dT_{bi}} = -1 - m^{A_1}\left(m_u^{B_1} - m_u^{A_1}\right)\Delta \tag{7.23}$$

$$\frac{du^{A_1}}{dT_{coor}} = -\lambda^{A_1} - m^{A_1}\left[m_u^{B_1} - \sum_{h=1}^{n^A}(\lambda^{A_h} m_u^{A_h}) \right]\Delta \tag{7.24}$$

$$1 > \left(-m^{A_1}\right)\left(m_u^{A_{notl}} - m_u^{A_1}\right)\Delta \tag{7.25}$$

[4] For developments which mitigate the extremity of this position, see below and the next section.

Assuming that donor A_1 exports good y, that is $m^{A_1} < 0$, the right-hand side of condition (7.25) is non-positive if, and only if, the other donors' weighted average marginal propensity to consume good y does not exceed donor A_1's marginal propensity to consume good y, that is if $m_u^{A_{not1}} \leq m_u^{A_1}$. The latter is, therefore, a sufficient condition for country A_1 to prefer coordinated aid. In general, condition (7.25) holds even if the other donors' weighted average marginal propensity to consume good y is larger than donor A_1's marginal propensity to consume good y, that is if $m_u^{A_{not1}} > m_u^{A_1}$, because the right-hand side of condition (7.25) may be positive, but below unity. Only if the other donors' marginal propensity to consume donor A_1's export good is substantially larger than donor A_1's marginal propensity to consume its own export good may the inequality in (7.25) be reversed. If so, country A_1 prefers bilateral, or uncoordinated, aid to coordinated aid because of the large disadvantageous terms-of-trade effect of coordinated aid relative to bilateral aid. The following proposition summarizes the discussion.

> **Proposition 22:** Given the desire of a specific donor, say A_1, to aid a certain recipient, coordinated aid is preferred over bilateral aid by donor A_1 if the potential other donors' weighted average marginal propensity to consume donor A_1's export good does not exceed donor A_1's marginal propensity to consume its own export good. Only if the other donors' marginal propensity to consume donor A_1's export good is substantially larger than donor A_1's marginal propensity to consume its own export good, as given in (7.25), will donor A_1 prefer uncoordinated bilateral aid.

7.4   Transfers, politics and welfare

The discussion of multilateral transfers brings us into the realm of political economy. The coordination issue itself is a political aspect of transfers. Points of discussion in multilateral agencies are, among others, which country should donate how much and in what form, which country will receive how much, over what time period and under what conditions, etc. One important question not addressed in the discussion so far is why voluntary donations are given in the first place, particularly if the donor's welfare falls. This question, in principle, takes us out of economics and into ethics, but a few remarks are in order (see Opeskin [1996]).

The purpose of this chapter, and for that matter of the whole book, is to analyze the welfare consequences of transfers. The fact that a transfer is given is taken for granted; we merely analyze the outcomes of a transfer for the countries involved. Studies in development economics indicate that the most frequent major reason for giving donations, apart from military and political considerations, is genuine concern about the low welfare level of certain countries. The goal of many donors is to improve the predicament of potential recipients. Any decision rule employed by multilateral agencies should take the welfare level of the recipients into consideration.

In practice, donors do not give away their entire income, so simply maximizing the welfare level of the recipients cannot be the only objective of the donors. This indicates that the donor's own welfare level is also important in determining how much aid to give to whom. An easy way out of this difficult question, say for the single donor A, is by positing a "meta" welfare function W for this donor, with donor A's own welfare level and the welfare levels of n potential recipients u_{B_i} as arguments; see equation (7.26). Donor A may then determine the size of the transfer T to give, and the distribution π of the transfer over the potential recipients, where recipient B_i gets share $\pi^{B_i} \in [0, 1]$. As we saw in section 7.2 the donor's and potential recipients' welfare levels will depend in general not only on the size of the transfer T, but also on the distribution of the transfer over the recipients, as in equation (7.27). Naturally, the restrictions in equation (7.28) have to be fulfilled.

$$W = W(u^A, u^{B_1}, ..., u^{B_n}) \tag{7.26}$$

$$u^A = u^A(-T, \pi) ; \qquad u^{B_i} = u^{B_i}(T_i, \pi) , \quad \text{for } i = 1, ..., n \tag{7.27}$$

$$T_i = \pi^{B_i} T ; \quad \sum_{i=1}^{n} \pi^{B_i} = 1 \tag{7.28}$$

To determine the "optimal" transfer donor A can substitute (7.27) in (7.26) and maximize meta welfare W subject to the distribution restriction (7.28). Normalize such that $W_{u^A} = 1$ and let ψ be the Lagrange multiplier of the adding-up constraint, then the efficiency conditions (7.29) and (7.30) have to be satisfied for an internal solution.[5]

$$u_T^A = \sum_{i=1}^{n} \left(W_{u^{B_i}} \pi^{B_i} u_T^{B_i} \right) \tag{7.29}$$

$$\left[u_{\pi^{B_i}}^A + \sum_{j=1}^{n} \left(W_{u^{B_j}} u_{\pi^{B_i}}^{B_j} \right) \right] + \left[\pi^{B_i} W_{u^{B_i}} u_T^{B_i} \right] = \psi , \quad \text{for } i = 1, ..., n \tag{7.30}$$

[5] Otherwise, equation (7.30) only holds for countries actually receiving a transfer, that is if $\pi^{B_i} > 0$.

Equation (7.29) indicates that the marginal cost u_T^A of taking away from the donor has to be equal to the sum of the marginal benefit of transferring to recipient B_i, that is $\pi^{B_i} u_T^{B_i}$, weighted by the meta-welfare impact $W_{u^{B_i}}$. Equation (7.30), on the other hand, balances the marginal contributions across recipients, where the first term in square brackets on the left-hand side is country B_i's impact on redistributive efficiency, a term which disappears if the marginal propensity to consume is the same across all countries, and the second term in square brackets is country B_i's marginal contribution to welfare.

Following this general procedure, the size and distribution of international transfers can be modeled as the outcome of an optimization procedure. The analysis can be complicated by having several players with different objectives interact to produce a game-theoretic equilibrium, say a Nash equilibrium or a Leader–Follower equilibrium. We will limit ourselves to explaining in detail the economic outcome of a similar procedure in a dynamic setting in chapter 10, basing our explanation on the work of Kemp *et al.* (1990).

7.5   Pareto-improving transfers

Arja Turunen-Red and Alan Woodland (1988) analyze international transfers in a quite general setting, allowing not only for an arbitrary number of countries but also for an arbitrary number of tradable goods. Their main concern is to answer the question whether or not strict Pareto-improving international transfers are possible. That is, is it possible to have a scheme of transfers between nations across the world such that at least one country gains and no country loses? If such a scheme exists it also immediately answers the question posed in the previous section of why a nation should engage in transfers. Unfortunately, perhaps, Turunen-Red and Woodland conclude that such a scheme does not exist in general, unless a normality condition is violated.

Suppose there are K countries and N tradable goods in a perfectly competitive economy. Let u^k be country k's welfare level, $\mathbf{p}$ the international price vector of traded goods and $\mathbf{p}^k = \mathbf{p} + \boldsymbol{\tau}^k$ the domestic price vector in country k, where $\boldsymbol{\tau}^k$ denotes the (possibly negative) tariff on net imports. Both $\mathbf{p}$ and $\mathbf{p}^k$ are assumed to be strictly positive. For notational convenience we follow Turunen-Red and Woodland and define the net revenue function S^k as the difference between the revenue function R^k and the expenditure function E^k; see equation (7.31).[6] The net revenue

---

[6] The net revenue function is therefore equal to minus the net expenditure function describing offer curves, as discussed in the appendix to chapter 3.

function S^k inherits its characteristics from the revenue and expenditure functions. Thus, S^k is linearly homogeneous in prices; see equation (7.32). In the first proposition below, however, we fix the price of good 1 such that it is the numéraire. Normalization of $E_u^k = 1$ gives equation (7.33). The latter, together with the requirement that the sum of marginal propensities to consume is unity, gives equation (7.34). Finally, the derivative of S^k with respect to price gives the net supply of goods, which is used in equation (7.35).

$$S^k(\mathbf{p}^k, u^k) \equiv R^k(\mathbf{p}^k) - E^k(\mathbf{p}^k, u^k), \quad \text{for } k = 1, ..., K \tag{7.31}$$

$$\mathbf{p}^{k\prime} S_{\mathbf{pp}}^k(\mathbf{p}^k, u^k) = \mathbf{0}, \quad \text{for } k = 1, ..., K \tag{7.32}$$

$$S_u^k(\mathbf{p}^k, u^k) = -1, \quad \text{for } k = 1, ..., K \tag{7.33}$$

$$\mathbf{p}^{k\prime} S_{\mathbf{p}u}^k(\mathbf{p}^k, u^k) = -1, \quad \text{for } k = 1, ..., K \tag{7.34}$$

The world equilibrium, which we assume to exist, is characterized by equations (7.35)–(7.37) below. Equation (7.35) gives the world market-clearing condition for all tradable goods. Equation (7.36) constrains each nation's balance of trade to be equal to the transfer T^k, which can be either positive or negative. Finally, equation (7.37) ensures that the sum of the transfers, and thus the sum of the balance-of-trade surpluses, is equal to zero (a transfer given by one nation must be received by another nation). Given the vector of transfers $\mathbf{T} \equiv (T^1, ..., T^K)$ and the vector of tariffs $\boldsymbol{\tau} \equiv (\tau^1, ..., \tau^K)$ one may solve for the world price vector $\mathbf{p}$ and the vector of welfare $\mathbf{u} \equiv (u^1, ..., u^K)$. By virtue of the linear homogeneity of the net revenue functions one of the equations is redundant, so that prices are determined up to a proportional factor.

$$\sum_{k=1}^{K} S_{\mathbf{p}}^k(\mathbf{p} + \tau^k, u^k) = \mathbf{0} \tag{7.35}$$

$$\mathbf{p}' S_{\mathbf{p}}^k(\mathbf{p} + \tau^k, u^k) = T^k, \quad \text{for } k = 1, ..., K \tag{7.36}$$

$$\sum_{k=1}^{K} T^k = 0 \tag{7.37}$$

Let $S_{\mathbf{pp}}$ denote the world substitution effects of changes in the international prices $\mathbf{p}$; see equation (7.38). Moreover, let Rev^k denote country k's tariff revenue (see equation [7.40]), and let Rev be the world tariff revenue (see equation [7.41]). It follows from equation (7.36) and this definition that equation (7.39) holds, that is, country k's expenditure level is equal to its revenue from production or tariffs minus the transfer to other countries.

$$S_{pp} \equiv \sum_{k=1}^{K} S_{pp}^k(\mathbf{p} + \tau^k, u^k) \tag{7.38}$$

$$E^k(\mathbf{p}^k, u^k) = R^k(\mathbf{p}^k) - T^k + Rev^k(\mathbf{p}, \tau^k, u^k), \quad \text{for } k = 1, ..., K \tag{7.39}$$

$$Rev^k(\mathbf{p}, \tau^k, u^k) \equiv -\tau^{k\prime} S_p^k(\mathbf{p} + \tau^k, u^k), \quad \text{for } k = 1, ..., K \tag{7.40}$$

$$Rev(\mathbf{p}, \tau, \mathbf{u}) \equiv \sum_{k=1}^{K} Rev^k(\mathbf{p}, \tau^k, u^k) = -\sum_{k=1}^{K} \tau^{k\prime} S_p^k(\mathbf{p} + \tau^k, u^k) \tag{7.41}$$

To understand why Pareto-improving differential international transfers should be possible at all it is most instructive to differentiate the balance-of-trade equation (7.36) using (7.32), which gives (7.42). Before we look at the three terms affecting country k's welfare as given in equation (7.42) we must consider the term $\mathbf{p}' S_{pu}^k(\mathbf{p} + \tau^k, u^k)$ in front of the welfare change du^k. If this term is negative we say that the so-called *Hatta normality condition* is satisfied for country k. Note in particular that this condition is satisfied if (i) country k imposes no tariffs ($\tau^k = \mathbf{0}$), since it follows from (7.34) that then $\mathbf{p}' S_{pu}^k = -1 < 0$, or (ii) all goods are normal goods in country k, since then $S_{pu}^k < \mathbf{0}$ such that $\mathbf{p}' S_{pu}^k < 0$. We assume that the Hatta normality condition is satisfied. Equation (7.42) shows that there are three terms affecting country k's welfare: the direct income effect dT^k, the terms-of-trade effect $-S_p^{k\prime} d\mathbf{p}$ and the tariff revenue effect $\tau^{k\prime} S_{pp}^{k\prime} d\mathbf{p}$. The direct income effect shows that welfare declines if the transfer given to other countries is increased. The terms-of-trade effect shows that welfare increases if the price of export goods increases. The tariff revenue effect shows that welfare increases if the tariff revenue increases as a result of the change in world prices.[7]

$$\mathbf{p}' S_{pu}^k du^k = dT^k - S_p^{k\prime} d\mathbf{p} + \tau^{k\prime} S_{pp}^{k\prime} d\mathbf{p}, \quad \text{for } k = 1, ..., K \tag{7.42}$$

$$\sum_{k=1}^{K} \mathbf{p}' S_{pu}^k du^k = -Rev_p(\mathbf{p}, \tau, \mathbf{u}) d\mathbf{p} = -\mathbf{p}' S_{pp} d\mathbf{p} \tag{7.43}$$

We can also sum the individual welfare changes in equation (7.42) and use the above definitions to obtain equation (7.43). If the Hatta normality condition holds for all countries ($\mathbf{p}' S_{pu}^k < 0$, for all k) and we want a strict Pareto-improving differential international transfer ($du^k \geq 0$ for all k with strict inequality for at least one k), the left-hand side of equation (7.43) is negative. Thus the price vector *must* change for a strict Pareto-improving differential international transfer to be pos-

---

[7] Note that $Rev_p^k(\mathbf{p}, \tau^k, u^k) = -\tau^{k\prime} S_{pp}^k$.

sible. This will not be the case if, for example, the marginal propensity to consume is the same for all goods in all countries. It is also clear from (7.43) that any gains must come from an increase in the world tariff revenue function. If the latter is stationary $(\mathbf{p}'\mathbf{S_{pp}} = \mathbf{0})$ world tariff revenue cannot be increased, so that strict Pareto-improving differential international transfers are not possible if the Hatta normality condition holds in all countries. This explains the second proposition below.

We think that the above discussion makes the next proposition intuitively plausible. Since a formal proof requires the investigation of the system of equations (7.35)–(7.37) after differentiation and uses a methodology not used anywhere else in this book we refer the interested reader to Turunen-Red and Woodland (1988) and the references therein.

> **Proposition 23:** (Turunen-Red and Woodland) Let the world substitution matrix have full rank $(N - 1)$ and fix the price of good 1. In addition, assume that (i) all commodities are normal in every nation $(\mathbf{S}_{pu}^{k} \ll 0$, for $k = 1, ..., K)$ and (ii) all commodities are world net substitutes $(\mathbf{S_{pp}}$ has negative off-diagonal elements) at the initial equilibrium. Then a strict Pareto-improving differential international transfer does not exist.

> **Proposition 24:** (Turunen-Red and Woodland) If the world tariff revenue function $Rev(\mathbf{p}, \tau, \mathbf{u})$ is stationary with respect to the world price vector $\mathbf{p}$ at the initial equilibrium $(\mathbf{Rev_p}(\mathbf{p}, \tau, \mathbf{u}) = \mathbf{p}'\mathbf{S_{pp}} = \mathbf{0})$ and the Hatta normality condition holds in all nations $(\mathbf{p}'\mathbf{S}_{pu}^{k}(\mathbf{p} + \tau^{k}, u^{k}) < 0$ for $k = 1, ..., K$), then a strict Pareto-improving differential international transfer does not exist.

The first result above thus generalizes the conclusions on tariffs and the "trade or aid" discussion in chapter 5.

7.6 Conclusion

We have investigated international bilateral and multilateral transfers in a world with many countries. If the transfers are given by a group of donors to a multilateral agency which then redistributes them to a group of recipients, the terms-of-trade effect of the transfer is determined by the difference between the recipients' weighted average marginal propensity to consume and the donors' weighted average marginal propensity to consume, with the share of the aggregate transfer received or paid, respectively, as the relevant weight. From this observation it follows that a donor whose aim is to give a transfer of a certain size has a preferred bilateral recipient. Analogously, a recipient, given the size of the transfer, has a preferred bilateral donor. This does not mean that multilateral or coordinated transfers are necessarily bad for a donor, since such transfers allow the donor to share the (income) burden of a transfer with other donors. Indeed, we show that given a donor's desire to aid a particular recipient, say to partially overcome the consequences of a famine or flood, it is generally better for that donor to coordinate efforts in a multilateral agency. We are tempted to conclude that this case is relevant in practice, in view of the attention the World Bank, OECD and other multilateral organizations receive compared to the attention given to individual countries. Finally, we point out that in a world with tariffs, many tradable goods and many countries, strict Pareto-improving differential transfers (in which no country loses and at least one country gains) are not possible if all goods are normal goods in all countries and all commodities are world net substitutes.

8   The consequences of tied aid

8.1   Introduction

The term "tied aid" indicates that the recipient is in some way restricted in the allocation of the resources it receives.[1] As already indicated by Bhagwati (1967) these restrictions may take different forms. Aid may be linked to a specific project, to a specific commodity or service, or to procurement in a specific country, in all cases limiting the recipient government's policy options. Even if the donor does not directly oblige the recipient to purchase from the donor, the choice of the sector supported can give a similar result. The most commonly acknowledged way of restricting the allocation of aid is through regional tying. In this respect the OECD's Development Assistance Committee (DAC) distinguishes between untied aid, partially tied aid and tied aid. Procurement for untied aid is obviously unrestricted, while for partially tied aid it is restricted to the donor or any developing country. The remainder of aid is tied aid. Thus, even if, say, Denmark only restricts procurement to any developing country or any country of the European Union, then this is considered tied aid.

Table 8.1 gives an overview of the DAC estimates of untied, partially tied and tied aid over a number of years for ten large donors. A brief look at this table is instructive and allows us to draw some conclusions. First, the extent of tying of aid may vary widely from country to country. In 1989, for example, Australia gave about 10 percent of its aid untied, compared to 75 percent for Switzerland. Second, the extent of tying of aid may vary widely from year to year. Australia, for example, increased the share of untied aid from 10 percent in 1989 to 42 percent in 1993 and Italy from 9 percent to 43 percent in the same period. Third, a substantial

---

[1] The former US president Nixon once said: "remember that the main purpose of American aid is not to help other nations but to help ourselves" (Opeskin 1996, p. 21).

Table 8.1. *Tying of bilateral ODA by DAC members ($ millions)*

	1979			1983[a]			1989			1993		
	Untied	Part. tied	Tied	Untied	Part. tied	Tied	Untied	Part. tied	Tied	Untied	Part. tied	Tied
Australia	299.0	2.5	159.6	329.2		194.5	47.0		406.0	318.0		442.0
Canada	99.9		470.7	132.8		655.6	701.0	73.0	917.0	923.0	75.0	507.0
France	1369.9	283.1	1872.5	1365.0	342.4	2102.1	3330.0	260.0	3378.0	1628.0	753.0	2794.0
Germany	2182.7		637.7	1659.7		704.0	2615.0		2160.0	2736.0		2980.0
Italy	51.0		12.4				202.0		2020.0	686.0		905.0
Japan	602.4	637.7	939.9	1561.4	661.3	586.5	5935.0	296.0	1371.0	12194.0	321.0	2027.0
Netherlands[b]	711.9	283.2	52.8	494.2	196.7	138.4	777.0	686.0	232.0	1212.4	2552.0	3535.0
Switzerland	43.5		67.9	142.3		71.3	372.0		125.0	429.0		40.0
United Kingdom	204.7	153.6	956.0	238.4	5.7	685.0	398.0		1261.0	573.0	1.0	1056.0
United States	1504.0	596.0	2633.0	2210.0	985.0	2509.0	2552.0	1442.0	3316.0	3307.0	1871.0	3670.0

Notes:

Figures relate to gross disbursements and, from 1989 on, to commitments.

Untied aid: Fully and freely available for essentially world-wide procurement.

Partially tied aid: Contributions available for procurement in the donor and developing countries.

Tied aid: Includes aid tied to procurement in donor country only.

[a] Excluding administrative costs.

[b] For 1993, total commitments (including multilateral organizations).

Source: DAC, *Development Co-operation*, various issues.

proportion of aid is either tied or partially tied. In 1993, for example, the average proportion of *un*tied aid for the ten countries in table 8.1 is only 50 percent. Fourth, even though individual members may increase or decrease their share of tied aid, in the aggregate there is only a slow tendency towards more untied aid. For example, the ratio of untied to partially tied to tied aid has changed from 100 : 28 : 110 in 1979 to 100 : 22 : 75 in 1993, representing an overall reduction of both tied and partially tied aid relative to untied aid over that period. In this respect, however, we must warn the reader of potential discrepancies between the official statistics and the tying of aid in practice. For example, officially tied aid from the Netherlands in the period 1970–80 as reported by DAC was 47 percent, which is well below the Jepma and De Haan (1984) estimate of 63 percent of formally *and* informally tied aid in the same period.

The data in table 8.1 are on bilateral aid flows, whereas part of official development assistance (ODA) is multilateral aid. In his OECD study Jepma (1991, p. 12) observes:

Tying percentages of multilateral aid are generally quite small, smaller in any case than those of bilateral aid . . . Thus a shift from bilateral to multilateral aid may be expected to induce some overall movement towards untying . . . During the 1980s, the share of multilateral aid of total ODA stabilized at approximately 25 per cent.

It is argued that tying is used by donors to support their own needy industries or to promote their exports. To estimate the true net increase in exports as a result of the tying of aid one needs to know the degree of fungibility, that is the amount of exports financed by aid which would have occurred anyway (Pack and Pack [1993]). This is essential in determining whether or not tying is in fact effective; see the discussion below in section 8.3. Given the rather high estimated average fungibility, ranging from about 50 percent (Healey and Clift [1980, p. 22]) and 60 percent (Krassowski [1965] and Hopkins [1970]) up to 90 percent (May and Dobson [1979, 1982a, 1982b]), and Jepma and Bartels's conclusion that ([1986], p. 52) "the difference in the commodity pattern between trade flows totally financed by tied aid and trade flows financed in some other way generally is small" leads us to conclude that tying appears not to be effective in general. Nonetheless, tied aid may be lucrative for individual producers; see Jepma (1991, pp. 58–9) for an overview of some lucid examples. We will return to the potential attractiveness of tied aid for individual producers in a more appropriate setting in the next chapter.

8.2   Tied aid with two countries

Michihiro Ohyama (1974) was the first to give proper attention to the economic analysis of tied aid. His approach was generalized, and interest in the issue was revitalized through a series of influential papers by Murray Kemp and Shoichi Kojima (1985a, 1985b, 1987). This section will be based on their work. We use part of their terminology by saying that aid is tied if it is spent inefficiently by the recipient in terms of individual preferences.[2] According to this definition, aid may be called "tied" not because the donor attaches conditions to the transfer but because the government of the recipient is unrepresentative or incompetent.

There are two countries, donor A and recipient B, and two private goods, x and y. Good x is used as the numéraire and p is the relative price of good y. The reader should keep in mind throughout this section that we know from the Samuelson theorem discussed in chapter 3 that in this setting transfer paradoxes (donor-enrichment and/or recipient-impoverishment) are not possible if aid is untied. As before E^J is country J's expenditure function and R^J is country J's revenue function. In contrast to the previous notation u^J is country J's utility derived from *privately* budgeted consumption, while v^J is country J's utility derived from *publicly* budgeted consumption. Initially, $v^J = 0$. Country J's welfare w^J is defined as the sum of privately and publicly budgeted utility:

$$w^J = u^J + v^J \tag{8.1}$$

The transfer is financed by the donor through lump-sum taxes. The aid is spent by the government of country B. It influences the welfare level w^B of country B, but does not enter its private budget constraint.[3] A proportion β of the aid is spent by the government of country B on the non-numéraire good y. The remainder of the transfer is spent on good x. It is assumed that if country A gives tied aid to country B it cannot require the government of country B to spend more on either good x or good y than the value of the transfer, that is $0 \leq \beta \leq 1$. There are no tariffs, quotas or other impediments to trade. The discussion is summarized in the following equations:

---

[2] Kemp and Kojima also say that aid is tied for the donor if it is financed inefficiently. We view this financial problem more as an issue for the public economics literature and thus do not use the term "tied aid" in that sense.

[3] The next section will comment on this modeling procedure.

$$E^A(p, u^A) = R^A(p) - T \tag{8.2}$$

$$E^B(p, u^B) = R^B(p) \tag{8.3}$$

$$m^A(p, u^A) + m^B(p, u^B) + \beta \frac{T}{p} = 0 \tag{8.4}$$

Equation (8.2) is the donor's budget constraint, equation (8.3) is the *private* budget constraint of the recipient and equation (8.4) is the market-clearing condition for good y, where $m^J \equiv E_p^J - R_p^J$ is the net private demand for good y from country J. Initially, $T = 0$. For clarity in the discussion below, and without loss of generality, we make the following assumption in this section:

Assumption I. Donor A exports good y, that is $m^A < 0$.

Totally differentiating equations (8.2)–(8.4), normalizing such that $E_u^J = 1$ and defining $M_p \equiv \sum_J m_p^J$ and $\Delta^{-1} \equiv -\sum_J \left(m_p^J - m^J m_u^J \right)$ we obtain

$$\begin{bmatrix} m^A & 1 & 0 \\ m^B & 0 & 1 \\ M_p & m_u^A & m_u^B \end{bmatrix} \begin{bmatrix} dp \\ du^A \\ du^B \end{bmatrix} = \begin{bmatrix} -1 \\ 0 \\ \frac{\beta}{p} \end{bmatrix} dT \tag{8.5}$$

Solving equation (8.5) gives

$$\det = \sum_J \left(m_p^J - m^J m_u^J \right) \equiv \frac{-1}{\Delta} < 0 \tag{8.6}$$

$$\frac{dp}{dT} = (\beta - pm_u^A) \frac{\Delta}{p} \tag{8.7}$$

$$\frac{du^A}{dT} = \left[M_p - \frac{m^B}{p} (pm_u^B - \beta) \right] \Delta \tag{8.8}$$

$$\frac{du^B}{dT} = -m^B(\beta - pm_u^A) \frac{\Delta}{p} = -m^B \frac{dp}{dT} \tag{8.9}$$

$$\frac{dw^B}{dT} = 1 + \frac{du^B}{dT} = 1 - m^B \frac{dp}{dT} = -\frac{du^A}{dT} = -\frac{dw^A}{dT} \tag{8.10}$$

The inequality in equation (8.6) indicates Walrasian stability. Equation (8.10), which is a reminder of the fact that total welfare consists of two parts, follows from the Pareto optimality of the initial equilibrium and the normalization $E_u^J = 1$. The main difference from the basic transfer model of untied aid analyzed in chapter 3 is the occurrence of the term β, that is the share of the transfer tied to the consumption of good y. This term β in a sense takes over the role of pm_u^B, which is the recipient's private marginal propensity to consume good y. From the assumption above that country A exports good y it follows from equation (8.7) that it is possible for the donor to improve its terms of trade relative to giving no aid at all by requiring that $\beta > pm_u^A$, unless the imported good x is an inferior good for country A.[4] The largest terms of trade gain for country A is reached when the entire transfer is spent on country A's export good, that is when $\beta = 1$. Similarly, it is easily seen by comparing equation (8.8) above with equation (3.7) that (since the recipient imports good y, that is $m^B > 0$) tying aid to good y can benefit the donor by choosing $\beta > pm_u^B$, unless $pm_u^B > 1$. In contrast, by comparing equation (8.9) with equation (3.8) we see that for the recipient untied aid is better than tied aid once the donor's tying restriction to its export good β exceeds a critical value. To summarize:

> **Proposition 25:** (Kemp and Kojima) The donor can improve its terms of trade relative to giving no aid by tying aid to its export good, unless the donor's import good is an inferior good. The donor can improve its terms of trade relative to giving untied aid by tying aid to its export good, unless the recipient's export good is an inferior good.

Now that we have established under what conditions the donor can improve its terms of trade by tying aid to the consumption of its export good, we have to investigate whether or not it is possible to have transfer paradoxes as a result of tied aid in the two-country context. From equation (8.8) and the definition of M_p it follows that the donor gains, that is $du^A/dT > 0$, if, and only if,

$$ m_p^A + m_p^B > \frac{m^B}{p}\left(pm_u^B - \beta\right) \tag{8.11} $$

If the recipient were an exporter of good y it would be easy to show that condition (8.11) implies a backward-bending offer curve for the recipient.[5] However, we have assumed above that the donor exports good y, such that the recipient must import it and $m^B > 0$. This makes

---

[4] Good x is an inferior good for country A if $\left(1 - pm_u^A\right) < 0$, or equivalently if $pm_u^A > 1$, so that it is impossible for β to exceed the value of pm_u^A because $\beta \le 1$.

[5] If $m^B < 0$ the own-price effect of the recipient's offer curve would be $\tilde{m}_p^B \equiv m_p^B - m^B m_u^B$. From $m^B < 0$ it then follows that condition (8.11) requires $\tilde{m}_p^B > m_p^A - \beta\left(m^B/p\right) > 0$, such that the recipient's offer curve is inelastic.

the analysis slightly more challenging. Since there are only two goods and the compensated net demand functions are homogeneous of degree zero, it follows that $-pm_p^B$ is the recipient's compensated cross-price effect for good x. Moreover, since the marginal propensities to consume sum to unity, it follows that $\left(1 - pm_u^B\right)$ is the recipient's marginal propensity to consume good x. From the dual version of the Slutsky equation (see the mathematical appendix), it follows that the uncompensated cross-price effect for the recipient's net demand of good x equals $\left[-pm_p^B - m^B\left(1 - pm_u^B\right)\right]$. Condition (8.11) can now be rewritten as

$$\left[-pm_p^B - m^B\left(1 - pm_u^B\right)\right] < pm_p^A - (1 - \beta)m^B < 0 \qquad (8.12)$$

where the last inequality follows from the assumption that $m^B > 0$. Thus, the term on the left-hand side of equation (8.12), that is the recipient's cross-price effect for the uncompensated net demand of good x, is negative. Therefore, its own uncompensated price effect is positive; see the mathematical appendix. Equivalently, the recipient's offer curve is inelastic. Although it is possible, in principle, that the donor's welfare increases as a result of a transfer of tied aid, it is implausible in the sense that it requires an inelastic offer curve for the recipient. Since the recipient's welfare increases if, and only if, the donor's welfare falls, we can conclude:

> **Proposition 26:** (Kemp and Kojima) The paradox of recipient-impoverishment and donor-enrichment as a result of an international transfer in a Walrasian-stable two-country world is possible if the transfer is tied, in contrast to where it is untied, but only if the recipient's offer curve is inelastic.

A necessary, but not sufficient, condition for the recipient to lose and the donor to gain from the tied transfer is $\beta > pm_u^A$. The intuition behind this potentially perverse outcome is not difficult to understand. If the donor forces the recipient to spend more on the donor's export good than the recipient would if it were to choose freely, the terms-of-trade effect (and thus the welfare change) is magnified in the donor's favor. The discussion above demonstrates that this change may be large enough to improve the donor's welfare level.

8.3   A discussion of tied aid

Some important observations can be made regarding the Kemp–Kojima formulation of tied aid, the first two of which were already explicitly noted by Kemp and Kojima.

(1) The model above can be viewed as a generalization of the "advantageous destruction" model of chapter 5. To see this, let country A discard a bundle of goods worth T, composed of $\beta(T/p)$ of good y and $(1 - \beta)T$ of good x. Then country A's budget constraint is as in equation (8.2), country B's budget constraint is unchanged as in equation (8.3) and the market-clearing condition for good y is as given in equation (8.4).

(2) Although the model above demonstrates that welfare paradoxes are possible in a Walrasian-stable two-country world in the case of tied international transfers, there are not two but three agents in the economy: the donor A, the private sector of recipient B and the government of country B. The results above can therefore be interpreted as a special case of the more general three-agent setting discussed in chapter 6. Kemp and Kojima (1985a, p. 726) suggest reducing the number of agents to two by extending the aid directly to individuals of country B, thus eliminating country B's government. The aid is, however, given conditional on *marginally* tied spending in the proportions β and $1 - \beta$. In view of point (4) below we are not convinced by this reasoning.

(3) The Kemp–Kojima model effectively analyzes the welfare and terms-of-trade consequences of the forced expenditure pattern of recipient country B's government. The spending of income of the recipient's private sector is not constrained. Although that is plausible, the assumption that the recipient's government forced spending pattern does not affect the private sector's spending decisions is less plausible. Presumably, the government distributes the goods x and y it purchases through its forced expenditure pattern to the private sector one way or another. As a result the private sector will adjust its own spending pattern. Suppose, for example, that I, being a citizen of recipient B, always want to consume five units of good x, no more and no less. Suppose, in addition, that I receive two units of good x from my government as a result of a tied aid distribution scheme. Will I not, as a result of this gift, purchase only three units, instead of five, from the private sector? In other words, the government's forced choice expenditure pattern will in general affect the private sector's expenditure pattern, unless our marginal spending patterns coincide.[6]

(4) Suppose, as suggested by Kemp and Kojima, that country A gives marginally tied aid to country B in a two-country world, that is country B is told by country A to spend the extra transfer income in the proportions β and $1 - \beta$. In line with the observations in point (3) above,

---

[6] That is, unless $\beta = pm_u^B$ in the model of section 8.2, in which case there is no difference between tied and untied aid.

we argue that (i) this condition is almost never a binding restriction, (ii) if the restriction is not binding there is no difference between marginally tied aid and untied aid, and (iii) if the condition is binding the economic outcome is usually different from the analysis in section 8.2 above. An example may clarify this argument.

> **Example 5** Suppose you earn $100 and I give you $10 under the condition that you spend $8 of the $10 on good x, and the remaining $2 on good y. We discuss three possibilities.
>
> (1) Suppose you always prefer to spend 40 percent of your income on good x and the remaining 60 percent on good y, that is your unconstrained preference is to spend $44 on good x and $66 on good y. You can now inform me that you used $8 of the $10 that I gave you on the purchase of good x, as I told you to, while you chose voluntarily to spend an additional $44 - $8 = $36. You make me believe that your marginal propensity to consume good x is 0.80 ($8 out of $10), while in reality it is only 0.40 [($44 - $40)/$10]. The only thing I can readily check to see if you indeed met my restriction is observe whether or not you spend at least $8 on the purchase of good x. This you do, and the end result is therefore the same whether or not aid is marginally tied. It is illustrated by Jepma (1991) that this happens in most cases, such that marginally tied aid is usually not an effectively binding restriction.
>
> (2) Suppose you always prefer to spend all of your income on the purchase of good y and nothing on the purchase of good x. Your unconstrained preference would be to spend $0 on good x and $110 on good y. This unconstrained preference does not meet the requirements I gave you, so that now marginal tying indeed does constrain you to spend $8 on the purchase of good x and the remaining $102 on the purchase of good y. Marginal tying effectively forced you to have a marginal propensity to consume good x of 0.80 rather than your preferred 0.
>
> (3) Suppose, finally, that you always prefer to spend 2 per cent of your income on good x and the remaining 98 percent on good y, that is your unconstrained preference is to spend $2.2 on good x and $107.8 on good y. This unconstrained preference does not meet the requirements I gave you, so that now marginal tying indeed does constrain you to spend $8 on the purchase of good x and the remaining $102 on the purchase of good y. In this case, however, marginal tying forced you to have a marginal propensity to consume good x of ($8 - $2)/$10 = 0.60. This is

higher than the 0.02 you would prefer, but lower than the 0.80 I thought I imposed on you through marginal tying.

It should be noted that the argumentation in the example above assumes that there can only be *ex post* verification of the tying restrictions and that the donor does not know the preferences (and/or the production functions in a production economy) of the recipient. If so, most marginally tied aid is not effectively tied, and if it is effectively tied, the tying is usually not in accordance with the restrictions the donor intended to impose, unless the recipient did not consume the good at all before the transfer. These issues are further discussed below and in the next chapter.

8.4   Marginally tied aid with three countries

One of the implications of the analysis in chapters 6 and 7 is that in a multi-country setting in which country A wishes to help country B there are circumstances under which this cannot be done either directly (country A gives a transfer to country B) or indirectly (country A gives a transfer to country C in order to help country B). This will be further discussed below.

Let us extend the analysis in section 8.2 to include a bystander, country C; see also Kemp and Kojima (1987). Thus, there are three countries, the donor A, the recipient B and the bystander C, and two private goods, x and y. Good x is used as the numéraire and p is the relative price of good y. As above E^J is country J's expenditure function, R^J is country J's revenue function, u^J is country J's utility derived from *privately* budgeted consumption, v^J is country J's utility derived from *publicly* budgeted consumption (initially $v^J = T = 0$) and country J's welfare w^J is defined as the sum of privately and publicly budgeted utility $w^J = u^J + v^J$. The transfer, financed through lump-sum taxes, is again spent by the government of country B. A proportion β, with $0 \leq \beta \leq 1$, of the aid is spent on good y and the remainder on good x. The model is summarized in the following equations:

$$E^A(p, u^A) = R^A(p) - T \tag{8.13}$$

$$E^B(p, u^B) = R^B(p) \tag{8.14}$$

$$E^C(p, u^C) = R^C(p) \tag{8.15}$$

$$m^A(p, u^A) + m^B(p, u^B) + m^C(p, u^C) + \beta\frac{T}{p} = 0 \tag{8.16}$$

Equation (8.13) is the donor's budget constraint, equation (8.14) is the *private* budget constraint of the recipient, equation (8.15) is the bystander's budget constraint and equation (8.16) is the market-clearing condition for good y, where $m^J \equiv E_p^J - R_p^J$ is country J's net private demand for good y. Totally differentiating equations (8.13)–(8.16), normalizing such that $E_u^J = 1$ and defining $M_p \equiv \sum_J m_p^J$ and $\Delta^{-1} \equiv -\sum_J \left(m_p^J - m^J m_u^J\right)$ we get:

$$
\begin{bmatrix}
m^A & 1 & 0 & 0 \\
m^B & 0 & 1 & 0 \\
m^C & 0 & 0 & 1 \\
M_p & m_u^A & m_u^B & m_u^C
\end{bmatrix}
\begin{bmatrix}
dp \\
du^A \\
du^B \\
du^C
\end{bmatrix}
=
\begin{bmatrix}
-1 \\
0 \\
0 \\
\frac{-\beta}{p}
\end{bmatrix}
dT
\tag{8.17}
$$

Solving equation (8.17) gives the same result as in equation (8.7) for the price change, while $du^A/dT = -1 - m^A(dp/dT)$, and $du^J/dT = -m^J(dp/dT)$ for $J = B, C$. More important, however, is the change in recipient B's total welfare as a result of tied aid:

$$
\frac{dw^B}{dT} = -\left(\frac{du^A}{dT} + \frac{du^C}{dT}\right)
$$
$$
= \left[M_p + m^C\left(m_u^C - m_u^A\right) + m^B\left(m_u^B - \frac{\beta}{p}\right)\right]\Delta
\tag{8.18}
$$

We can contrast this with the change in recipient B's welfare if country A gives untied aid to country B, either directly, denoted $du^B/dT_{AB}\,|_u$, or indirectly through giving untied aid to country C, denoted $du^B/dT_{AC}\,|_u$, where the u denotes untied aid and T_{IJ} denotes that the transfer flows from country I to country J. Using the results from chapter 6 the welfare consequences for country B of these alternative policies are given by

$$
\left.\frac{du^B}{dT_{AB}}\right|_u = \left[-M_p + m^C\left(m_u^C - m_u^A\right)\right]\Delta
\tag{8.19}
$$
$$
\left.\frac{du^B}{dT_{AC}}\right|_u = -m^B\left(m_u^C - m_u^A\right)\Delta
\tag{8.20}
$$

It is possible that country A cannot help country B either directly or indirectly, that is both $du^B/dT_{AB}\,|_u$ and $du^B/dT_{AC}\,|_u$ are negative. Under such circumstances it follows from equation (8.18), as the reader may verify, that it may nonetheless be possible for country A to help country B by giving tied aid. By comparing equations (8.18) and (8.19) it easily follows that this requires as a necessary but not sufficient condition that $m^B(pm_u^B - \beta) > 0$, that is the government of country B must spend more on country B's export good than country B's individuals would do privately. This makes perfect sense, as such a condition weakens country B's adverse terms-of-trade effect. To summarize:

> **Proposition 27:** (Kemp and Kojima) Suppose country A cannot help country B by giving untied aid in a three-country setting, either directly (an untied transfer from A to B) or indirectly (an untied transfer from A to C in order to help B), that is country B's welfare would decline as a result of both untied aid policies. Under such circumstances tied aid, rather than untied aid, may be a solution to the problem because tying aid to the recipient country B's export good may have a positive effect on country B's welfare level.

In short, section 8.2 demonstrated that tying aid can create transfer paradoxes in a two-country setting, while the present section demonstrates that tying aid can remove transfer paradoxes in a three-country setting. Also note that if donor A and recipient B export different commodities and country A can only help country B through *tied* aid in the above setting, then the impoverishment of the untied-aid recipient can only be circumvented by tying aid to the recipient's export good, that is unconventionally tying aid to the good *imported* by the donor.

8.5   The "forced choice" approach

Albert Schweinberger (1990) puts forth an interesting alternative to the modeling procedure for tied aid used by Kemp and Kojima. In Schweinberger's approach the "forced choices" due to the tying of aid may effectively restrain the spending pattern of the recipient's private sector, thus circumventing points (3) and (4) identified in section 8.3.

As in section 8.2 there are two countries, the donor A and the recipient B, and two goods, x and y. Good x is the numéraire and p is the relative price of good y. As before E^J is country J's expenditure function, R^J is country J's revenue function and u^J is country J's utility derived from privately budgeted consumption. In contrast to sections 8.2 and 8.4 there is no explicit public sector in recipient B. The transfer is financed by donor A through lump-sum taxes, thus

$$E^A(p, u^A) = R^A(p) - T \tag{8.21}$$

The aid is tied in the sense that a fraction β has to be spent on good y and the remainder on good x. One can envision this procedure as the government of either the recipient or the donor country purchasing the required quantities on the world market and distributing these in a lump-sum fashion to the recipient's private sector.[7] Alternatively, one can envision this procedure as a lump-sum transfer to country B's private sector, with the condition that at least βT of total expenditure has to be spent on good y and at least $(1 - \beta)T$ of total expenditure on good x. As before $0 \leq \beta \leq 1$. Throughout this section we make the following assumption.

> *Assumption II.* Preferences, endowments and parameter values are assumed to be such that the tying is effective on good y. As a result the recipient spends βT on good y to purchase $\beta T / p$ units.

Since tying is assumed to be effective on good y the recipient spends all the income from production plus the rest of the transfer, that is $(1 - \beta)T + R^B(p)$, on the purchase of good x, the numéraire.[8] Defining, as before, $m^A = E_p^A - R_p^A$ the market-clearing condition for good y is given by:

$$m^A(p, u^A) + \beta \frac{T}{p} - R_p^B(p) = 0 \tag{8.22}$$

The "forced choice" character of Schweinberger's approach follows directly from comparing (8.22) and (8.4).

8.5.1   The terms of trade and the donor

At this point it follows from equations (8.21) and (8.22), perhaps surprisingly, that we already have enough information to determine the terms-of-trade effect and the donor's welfare change as a result of a change in the transfer T, subject to the assumed effective tying on good y. Thus, p and u^A are determined independently of the preferences of country B (and thus u^B). Before we turn our attention to the modeling of effective tying of aid and the consequences for the recipient we first

---

[7] In this case, country B households cannot sell to foreigners the goods which were distributed to them by the government.

[8] Obviously, tying cannot be effective on both goods, but it could be effective on good x. Equally obviously, we *cannot*, as in sections 8.2 and 8.4, evaluate the consequences of a change in the transfer at the point $T = 0$ because the transfer is not effectively binding at that point.

investigate the impact of a change in T on p and u^A. Define $M_p \equiv m_p^A - R_{pp}^B - \beta T/p^2 < 0$ and $\Delta^{-1} \equiv -M_p + m^A m_u^A$; then totally differentiate equations (8.21) and (8.22) to get

$$\begin{bmatrix} m^A & 1 \\ M_p & m_u^A \end{bmatrix} \begin{bmatrix} dp \\ du^A \end{bmatrix} = \begin{bmatrix} -1 \\ -\dfrac{\beta}{p} \end{bmatrix} dT \tag{8.23}$$

Solving equation (8.23) gives

$$\det = \frac{1}{\Delta} > 0 \tag{8.24}$$

$$\frac{dp}{dT} = (\beta - pm_u^A) \frac{\Delta}{p} \tag{8.25}$$

$$\frac{du^A}{dT} = \left(M_p - \frac{\beta m^A}{p} \right) \Delta \tag{8.26}$$

The first thing to note, if we compare equation (8.25) with equation (8.7) in section 8.2, is that the Schweinberger approach to tied aid leads to the same effect on the terms of trade as the Kemp–Kojima approach to tied aid.[9] The second point of interest is that in the Kemp–Kojima approach donor-enrichment is possible, while donor-enrichment is *not* possible in the Schweinberger approach, as we will now demonstrate.[10] From equation (8.26) it follows that $du^A/dT < 0$ if, and only if, $M_p - \beta m^A/p < 0$ that is, using the definition of M_p, if and only if

$$\left(m_p^A - R_{pp}^B \right) - \frac{\beta}{p} \left(\frac{T}{p} + m^A \right) < 0 \tag{8.27}$$

A sufficient condition for the inequality in equation (8.27) is $T/p + m^A > 0$. Since $\beta \leq 1$ and using equation (8.22) it follows that

$$\frac{T}{p} + m^A > \beta \frac{T}{p} + m^A = R_p^B(p) > 0 \tag{8.28}$$

We have thus established

---

[9] But the derivatives will in general be evaluated at different equilibria. We address this issue more fully in the next chapter. Moreover, as discussed in section 8.3, a given amount of tied aid is always considered to be effectively tied in the Kemp–Kojima approach, while this is not automatically true in the Schweinberger approach.
[10] In his article Albert Schweinberger (1990) credits K. Abe three times for discovering and proving this point. Our proof is somewhat easier.

Proposition 28: (Schweinberger) The "forced choice" approach to tied aid gives rise to the same terms-of-trade effect of a change in tied aid as Kemp–Kojima's "marginal tying" approach. In contrast to the Kemp–Kojima approach, however, donor-enrichment is not possible in the "forced choice" approach in a Walrasian-stable, two-country world.

8.5.2   Effective tying and the recipient

We now discuss the effective tying of aid and the welfare consequences of a change in tied aid for the recipient. The effective tying of aid is essentially a binding rationing condition imposed on the recipient which forces it to consume at a different point on the budget constraint than in the absence of such rationing. Consequently, Schweinberger introduces "virtual" prices, that is those prices which would induce an unrationed consumer to behave in the same manner as when faced with a given rationing constraint.[11] Figure 8.1 illustrates the terminology and clarifies the issues in (y, x)-space. For ease of notation the superscript B will only be used in the equations.

The solid line $E - E/p$ is the recipient's budget constraint at the world price p for good y, where we recall that good x is the numéraire such that its price is one. The recipient's consumption point will be somewhere along this budget line. Income E at world price p must be equal to income from production plus the transfer, that is $E = R(p) + T$. In the absence of a rationing constraint the recipient would, given income E and price p, consume at the welfare-maximizing point D_0, that is reaching welfare level u_0 by consuming $x(p, E)$ units of good x and $y(p, E)$ units of good y. However, according to assumption II aid is effectively tied to the consumption of good y, such that the recipient must consume $\beta T/p$ units of good y, which is more than the $y(p, E)$ units of good y the recipient would consume in the absence of the rationing constraint. The remainder of the recipient's income, that is $E - p(\beta T/p) = E - \beta T = R(p) + (1 - \beta)T$, is spent on the consumption of good x. Consequently, the recipient consumes at point D_1 on the budget line $E - E/p$ in figure 8.1 reaching welfare level u_1, rather than at point D_0 reaching welfare level u_0. As illustrated in figure 8.1 we can now define the *virtual* price $\bar{p}$ and its concomitant virtual income $\bar{E}$ as that price and income level which would induce an unrationed recipient to consume at the point D_1 to reach welfare level u_1. Thus, by definition, we have

---

[11] Virtual prices were first suggested by Rothbarth (1940–1). The concept is extensively analyzed in Neary and Roberts (1980) for quantity constraints rather than expenditure constraints.

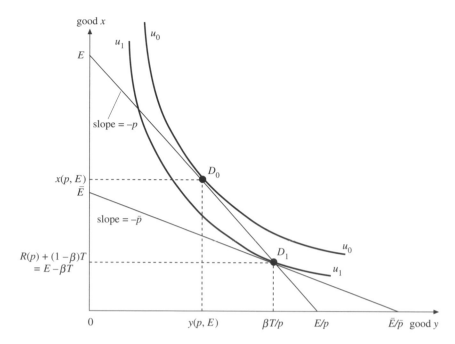

Figure 8.1.   *Forced choice*

$$\overline{E}_p^B(\overline{p}, u^B) = \beta \frac{T}{p} \tag{8.29}$$

Clearly, the world price p for good y is larger than the virtual price $\overline{p}$. Schweinberger uses this as the definition for effective tying to good y. As is evident from figure 8.1, $E = \overline{E} + (p - \overline{p})\beta T/p$, thus the recipient's budget constraint in terms of world prices can be written as

$$\overline{E}^B(\overline{p}, u^B) + (p - \overline{p})\beta \frac{T}{p} = R^B(p) + T \tag{8.30}$$

Totally differentiate equation (8.30), normalize $\overline{E}_u^B = 1$ and define $\eta \equiv (1 - \beta) + \beta \overline{p}/p$ to obtain

$$\left(\overline{E}_p^B(\overline{p}, u^B) - \beta \frac{T}{p}\right) d\overline{p} + du^B = -\left(\overline{p}\beta \frac{T}{p^2} - R_p^B(p)\right) dp + \eta dT \tag{8.31}$$

Now note that it follows from $p > \overline{p}$ that $\overline{p}/p < 1$, so that $\eta \equiv (1 - \beta) + \beta \overline{p}/p < (1 - \beta) + \beta = 1$. Use equation (8.29) to see that the $d\overline{p}$ term in equation (8.31) cancels. Rearrange equation (8.31) to

determine the change in the recipient's welfare level as a result of a
change in tied aid given in equation (8.32), where the change in the terms
of trade, dp/dT, is given in equation (8.25). For comparison we restate
the recipient's welfare change if aid is untied, denoted $du^B/dT\,|_u$, in
equation (8.33).

$$\frac{du^B}{dT} = \eta - \left(\frac{\bar{p}}{p}\bar{E}_p^B(\bar{p}, u^B) - R_p^B(p)\right)\frac{dp}{dT} \tag{8.32}$$

$$\frac{du^B}{dT}\bigg|_u = 1 - m^B\frac{dp}{dT}\bigg|_u \tag{8.33}$$

Comparing equations (8.32) and (8.33) it follows that, other things
being equal, in the absence of a change in the terms of trade tied aid is
worse for the recipient since $\eta < 1$. To the recipient's advantage, other
things being equal, an advantageous change in the terms of trade is
magnified or a disadvantageous terms-of-trade change is dampened
under tied aid compared to under untied aid since $\bar{p}/p < 1$. In general,
however, recipient-impoverishment is possible under effectively tied aid,
as Schweinberger concludes.

From the world welfare perspective one would think that there is an
improvement if the tying restriction becomes less binding. This is indeed
the case. First, from equation (8.21) it follows that $du^A = -m^A dp - dT$.
By adding du^B from equation (8.31) and using the definition of η and
equations (8.22) and (8.29), we obtain

$$du^A + du^B - \frac{\beta T(p - \bar{p})}{p}\left(\frac{dp}{p} - \frac{dT}{T}\right) \tag{8.34}$$

Thus, from equation (8.34) it follows that world welfare improves, that
is $du^A + du^B > 0$, if, and only if, the tying restriction becomes less
binding, that is $dp/p - dT/T > 0$.

Finally, the reader may totally differentiate equation (8.29) and plug in
previous results to determine the change in the virtual price $\bar{p}$ as a result
of a change in tied aid.

8.5.3 Tying to the numéraire and other complications

The above analysis assumes that tying is effective to the non-numéraire
good y; see assumption II. We now consider the alternative:

> *Assumption III.* Preferences, endowments and parameter values
> are assumed to be such that the tying is effective on good x. As a

result, the recipient spends $(1 - \beta)T$ on good x to purchase $(1 - \beta)T$ units since good x is the numéraire.

The recipient's total income in terms of good x equals $R^B(p) + T$. Since tying is effective on good x and he spends $(1 - \beta)T$ on this numéraire good, the remaining income, that is $R^B(p) + \beta T$, is spent on good y to purchase $(R^B(p) + \beta T)/p$ units. Thus, the donor's budget constraint is still given by equation (8.21) above, but the market-clearing condition for good y becomes

$$m^A(p, u^A) + \frac{R^B(p) + \beta T}{p} - R_p^B(p) = 0 \qquad (8.35)$$

Again we only need equations (8.21) and (8.35) to determine the terms of trade and the donor's welfare change. If we redefine $M_p \equiv m_p^A - R_{pp}^B - (R^B(p) + \beta T)/p^2 < 0$, normalize $E_u^A = 1$ and differentiate equations (8.21) and (8.35) we again obtain equation (8.23). Thus, the solution again leads to equations (8.24)–(8.26). This time $du^A/dT < 0$ if, and only if,

$$M_p - \beta \frac{m^A}{p} = \left(m_p^A - R_{pp}^B\right) - \frac{\beta}{p}\left(\frac{R^B(p) + \beta T}{\beta p} + m^A\right) < 0 \qquad (8.36)$$

A sufficient condition for inequality (8.36) to hold is $(R^B(p) + \beta T)/(\beta p) + m^A > 0$. If we use equation (8.35) and the fact that $\beta \leq 1$ we see that

$$\frac{R^B(p) + \beta T}{\beta p} + m^A > \frac{R^B(p) + \beta T}{p} + m^A = R_p^B(p) > 0 \qquad (8.37)$$

It thus follows from inequality (8.37) that donor-enrichment is also impossible if the tying is effective to the numéraire good x, in contrast to Schweinberger (1990, p. 460, note 6), so that both conclusions in the above proposition also hold under assumption III.

We can, of course, extend the analysis to include a bystander country. It should be obvious that if we do so the paradox of donor-enrichment cannot be excluded. More importantly, the Kemp–Kojima conclusion derived in section 8.4 that tied aid may circumvent the potential impossibility of one country helping another country in the three-country context through untied aid, either directly or indirectly, still holds. Using the same "forced choice" approach one can also analyze alternative tying conditions, such as to the recipient's production levels or the recipient's imports, effective to either the numéraire or non-numéraire good.

8.6   Conclusion

This chapter has demonstrated, using Kemp and Kojima's "marginal tying" approach, that the popularity of tied aid can in principle create transfer paradoxes in a Walrasian-stable, two-country world. This contrasts with the Samuelson theorem derived in chapter 3. On the other hand, the same approach also demonstrated that tied aid can circumvent transfer paradoxes in a three-country world by making it possible for one country to help another. Although the "marginal tying" procedure is analytically elegant it has some disadvantages, the most important of which is whether or not the marginal tying of aid is an effectively binding restriction; see section 8.3. In response to these disadvantages Albert Schweinberger introduced the "forced choice" approach in which virtual prices are defined to analyze the consequences of effectively binding tying restrictions. This approach allows us to derive some new results and demonstrates that the most important Kemp–Kojima conclusions still hold. Only the transfer paradox of donor-enrichment is not possible using the "forced choice" approach in a Walrasian-stable, two-country world (although recipient-impoverishment is possible).

9 Imperfect competition

9.1 Introduction

The analysis in previous chapters assumed perfect competition, constant returns to scale and price-taking behavior by the producers and consumers and therefore failed to take into account the developments over the past two decades in trade modeling which emphasize scale economies, imperfect competition and product differentiation. Traditional trade models cannot explain the empirical "stylized facts," while the models incorporating the above features, developed for example by Krugman (1979), Ethier and Horn (1984) or Markusen (1986), are able to explain these empirical observations.[1]

This chapter analyzes the transfer problem in a model which, in its basic form, has become widely accepted in the trade literature in the last two decades, incorporates the modern developments in international trade theory and by so doing embodies the stylized facts. For ease of exposition, attention is restricted to a two-country model involving just the donor and the recipient of the transfer. Incorporation of more countries, however, is straightforward; see Brakman and Van Marrewijk (1991b). As has become clear, differences in the demand structure of donor and recipient are the driving force behind any transfer effects (with the exception of the direct income effect). We focus our analysis on different spending behavior and different demand elasticities, respectively, for donor and recipient. These issues are most readily understood and analyzed directly, so that we will make only limited use of the dual approach in this chapter.

---

[1] Some "stylized facts" are the large trade flows characterized by intra-industry trade between developed countries and the smaller trade flows characterized by inter-industry trade between developing and developed countries, mostly an exchange of basic commodities for manufacturing varieties. The analysis in this chapter is based on Brakman and Van Marrewijk (1995).

The model distinguishes between two types of commodities, a basic commodity (called food) produced under constant returns to scale and a large number of manufactures produced under increasing returns to scale in monopolistic competition. There is an externality in the model since consumers like an increase in the number of varieties of manufactures produced, but producers of these varieties do not take this into consideration. In equilibrium, therefore, not enough manufactures are produced and our analysis is about second-best welfare economics. In the absence of distortions, lump-sum transfers only entail a movement along a given possibility locus, but with distortions there is a shift of the world utility possibility locus as well as a movement along it.

The tying of aid is modeled following the "forced choice" approach discussed in chapter 8. The donor gives a transfer to the recipient on the condition that it spends at least the amount of the transfer on the specified good or group of goods. If the recipient freely chooses to spend more on the good to which the transfer is tied, then the tying of aid is not an effectively binding restriction and the welfare effects are identical to those for untied aid.

We show that the imposition of a "fictitious" restriction (that is a restriction that is already fulfilled of tying aid to a specific manufactured good) can have real effects. In contrast to existing models this can explain the popularity of tied aid because as a result profits are made (which makes lobbying interesting) and the transfer itself is largely repatriated (hence one can appear to be more generous than one really is). Thus, the analysis supports the popular notion that tying of aid occurs because it increases the profits of particular firms or sectors.

9.2   The model

The basic model, extensively documented by Tirole (1988, ch. 7), is by now well known in international economic theory and has been developed, for example, by Dixit and Norman (1980) and Krugman (1979) to explain intra-industry trade. There is a "developed" country A and a "less developed" country B. Country A (the donor) makes a transfer to country B (the recipient). The transfer can be in the form of tied aid or untied aid. There are no tariffs, quotas or other barriers to trade. On the demand side two types of commodities are distinguished: a standard basic commodity (or commodity bundle) which will be called food F and serves as numéraire, and a range of differentiated manufactured goods. The manufactured goods will be denoted X_i for $i = 1, ..., n$. From the consumer's point of view the manufactured goods are close but imperfect substitutes. Preferences are of the Spence–Dixit–Stiglitz type.

$$u^k = \left[\sum_{i=1}^{n} (X_i^k)^{\beta_k}\right]^{\frac{\alpha_k}{\beta_k}} (F^k)^{1-\alpha_k}, \ k = A, B \tag{9.1}$$

with $0 < \alpha_k < 1$ and $0 < \beta_k < 1$. Naturally, X_i^k is the amount of manufactured good i which is consumed by country k and F^k is the amount of food consumed by country k. Moreover, n is the number of manufactured goods varieties which are available in the market. Hence β_k is a monotone transformation of the elasticity of substitution for manufactured goods ($\beta_k = 1 - 1/\varepsilon_k$, where ε_k is the elasticity of substitution for manufactured goods in country k) and α_k represents the share of income spent on the consumption of manufactured goods. If the number of varieties is large, as we will assume, the Marshallian price elasticity of demand can be approximated by the elasticity of substitution for manufactured goods; see Horn (1984) for this approximation. We first develop the model under assumption I below and investigate differences in spending patterns between rich and poor countries. The consequences of different demand elasticities will also be briefly discussed in what follows.

> *Assumption I.* The elasticity of demand is the same in both countries, that is $\beta_A = \beta_B = \beta$, while the developed country spends a larger share of income on manufactured goods, that is $\alpha_A > \alpha_B$.

The basic good F is produced in both countries using constant returns to scale technology. All factor markets are perfectly competitive. The production of manufactured goods X_i requires special techniques and skilled labor and can only take place in the developed country A. Total income of country k is denoted by I_k. As country B cannot produce manufactured goods it will only produce food F in the amount I_B, which also represents its income because food is the numéraire. The production of manufactured goods is characterized by (internal) increasing returns to scale, where the non-convexity only occurs on the corner. Hence production of each variety within the manufacturing sector will be undertaken by just one firm. It is most convenient to model the production process in two stages.[2]

---

[2] The results derived below, however, also hold for an appropriately defined one-stage modeling procedure that uses only one factor of production, labor say. The advantages of this two-stage approach, also used by Ethier and Horn (1984), are that different inputs, like labor, land and capital, can lead to the strictly concave production possibility curve above and that there is a clear choice of inputs devoted to the constant returns to scale

First, standard factors of production (capital and labor, say) are used to produce food F and an intermediate good M under constant returns. This first step then leads to a standard production possibility curve $G(M)$, with negative first and second derivatives. Hence $G(M)$ gives the amount of food country A can produce if it produces M of the intermediate good. Obviously, there is an upper bound, $\overline{M}$ say, to the amount of intermediates country A can produce, which is dictated by the available amount of factors of production and technology. The tangent to the production possibility curve equals *minus* the price r of intermediates, that is $r = -G'(M)$.

Second, the intermediate good M is used to produce manufactured goods X_i, each variety of which uses the same production technique. Internal increasing returns to scale are represented by the real fixed costs a (in terms of intermediates) and the (constant) marginal costs b (also in terms of intermediates). In equilibrium all firms will produce the same quantity of output, that is $X_i = X$ for all i. Accordingly, we can write this as (recall that n equals the number of firms or varieties of manufactured goods available in the economy)

$$M = n(a + bX) \tag{9.2}$$

Let p be the price of manufactured goods (which in equilibrium will be the same for all varieties); then we have from the conditions of profit maximization for each manufacturing variety (marginal cost equals marginal revenue)

$$p\beta = rb \tag{9.3}$$

From the fact that total profits in each industry are zero (otherwise new firms would enter the market) we have[3]

$$pX = \frac{rM}{n} \tag{9.4}$$

Using equations (9.2)–(9.4) we can derive the output of each firm in an industry (which thus is indeed the same for all varieties)

$$X = \frac{a\beta}{b(1 - \beta)} \tag{9.5}$$

part of the economy (food) on the one hand and the increasing returns to scale part of the economy (manufactures) on the other hand.

[3] Note that we abstract from the integer problem, as is usual in this type of model.

Applying equations (9.2) and (9.5) gives the number of varieties n as a function of the production of intermediates M:

$$n = \frac{(1 - \beta)}{a} M \tag{9.6}$$

The demand functions for manufacturing products X_i^k and food F^k for country k, which can be derived from utility maximization using the fact that the price of all varieties is the same, are

$$X_i^k = \frac{\alpha_k I_k}{pn} \tag{9.7}$$

$$F^k = (1 - \alpha_k)I_k \tag{9.8}$$

Market-clearing conditions and country A's income are[4]

$$X = \frac{(\alpha_A I_A + \alpha_B I_B)}{pn} \tag{9.9}$$

$$G(M) + I_B = (1 - \alpha_A)I_A + (1 - \alpha_B)I_B \tag{9.10}$$

$$I_A = G(M) + rM \tag{9.11}$$

The model is determined (by Walras's law) by the equilibrium condition for the food sector and the production possibility curve. It is easy to incorporate transfers into the model, simply by subtracting T from A's income and adding it to B's income. Define the functions $L(M)$ and $R_u(M|T)$ for convenience as follows:

$$L(M) \equiv (1 - \alpha_A)rM = -(1 - \alpha_A)G'(M)M \tag{9.12}$$

$$R_u(M|T) \equiv \alpha_A G(M) + [\alpha_B I_B - (\alpha_A - \alpha_B)T] \tag{9.13}$$

The function $L(M)$ denotes the demand for food from the manufacturing sector in country A and is thus equal to the donor's net demand for food. Similarly, $R_u(M|T)$ reflects the net supply of food from the food sector. Since country B only produces food, these functions correspond to the international trade flows. Using these two definitions, the model, now incorporating transfers, can be reduced to the following single equation (use $r = -G'(M)$ and equation [9.11]):

$$L(M) = R_u(M|T) \tag{9.14}$$

---

[4] Note that in equilibrium there are no profits in the manufactured goods sector in country A, hence $pnX = rM$ and $I_A = G(M) + rM$.

Since we are interested in the welfare consequences of transfers we also state the indirect utility function v_k for country k, which is given by (I_k^d is country k's disposable income)

$$v_k = K_k p^{-\alpha_k} n^{\phi_k} I_k^d \tag{9.15}$$

$$\text{where } K_k \equiv \alpha_k^{\alpha_k} (1 - \alpha_k)^{(1-\alpha_k)} \quad \text{and} \quad \phi_k \equiv \alpha_k \frac{(1 - \beta_k)}{\beta_k}$$

9.3 Untied aid

First, we discuss untied aid. *A priori* one might expect this form of aid to be most beneficial for the recipient. Given the initial size of the transfer, the initial equilibrium quantity of intermediates M produced is determined by the unique point of intersection of the (upward-sloping) $L(M)$ curve and the (downward-sloping) $R_u(M)$ curve (where the u indicates untied aid) as defined in equation (9.14) above.[5] An increase in untied aid does not affect the $L(M)$ curve, but shifts the $R_u(M)$ curve down by the amount $(\alpha_A - \alpha_B)$ times the change in the transfer. This reduces the equilibrium production of intermediates M, which in turn reduces the number of varieties n produced, and so on. These qualitative conclusions hold for discrete changes in the size of the transfer. The change in the production level of intermediates relative to the change in the transfer depends also on the (change in) the slopes of the $L(M)$ curve and the $R_u(M)$ curve. To gauge the size of this and related relative changes we use (local) calculus techniques. Differentiating equation (9.14) leads to

$$\frac{\widehat{M}}{\widehat{T}} = -\frac{(\alpha_A - \alpha_B)}{[1 + (1 - \alpha_A)\sigma]} < 0 \tag{9.16}$$

$$\text{where } \sigma \equiv \frac{M G'(M)}{G''(M)} > 0, \quad \widehat{T} = \frac{dT}{M} \quad \text{and} \quad \widehat{M} = \frac{dM}{M}$$

Hence σ is the elasticity of substitution in the supply of intermediates and $\widehat{T}$ denotes the change of the transfer in relation to total world spending on manufactured goods. All other "^" signs in this chapter refer to relative changes, for example $\widehat{M} = dM/M$. Since $r = -G'(M)$ we have $\widehat{r} = \sigma \widehat{M}$, and since it follows from equations (9.3) and (9.6) that $\widehat{p} = \widehat{r}$ and $\widehat{n} = \widehat{M}$, we obtain:

---

[5] Examples of these curves are given in figures 9.1 and 9.2. Note that the R curve is concave and that $L(0) = 0$.

Proposition 29: Under assumption I an untied transfer induces (i) a price decrease for all manufactured goods, (ii) a decrease in the number of varieties in the manufactured goods industry, and (iii) an increase in the production and consumption of food.

This proposition can be given the usual interpretation. If country A transfers income to country B and country B spends a smaller proportion of this income on manufactures than country A does, then the price of manufactures falls. In this setting, that causes a concomitant fall in the number of varieties n produced in the world economy.

The relative change in indirect utility can be calculated from equation (9.15). Let ω_k be the share of the domestically produced value of manufactured products in disposable income, that is $\omega_A = rM/I_A$ and $\omega_B = 0$. Since country A is a net exporter of manufactured goods while country B is a net importer we have $\omega_A - \alpha_A > 0$ and $\omega_B - \alpha_B < 0$. Let η_k be country k's disposable income over the world value of manufactured products, that is $\eta_A = I_A^d/rM$ $(= 1/\omega_A$ in this two-country world) and $\eta_B = I_B^d/rM$ $(\neq 1/\omega_B)$. Then we obtain $I_A^d = \omega_A \hat{r} - T/\eta_A$ and $I_B^d = T/\eta_B$ and welfare effects

$$\widehat{v_A} = (\omega_A - \alpha_A)\widehat{p} + \phi_A \widehat{n} - \frac{\widehat{T}}{\eta_A} < 0 \tag{9.17}$$

$$\widehat{v_B} = (\omega_B - \alpha_B)\widehat{p} + \phi_B \widehat{n} + \frac{\widehat{T}}{\eta_B} \tag{9.18}$$

Note that, in contrast to the traditional transfer models discussed in previous chapters, the welfare effects consist of *three* rather than *two* components. There is not only the terms-of-trade effect and the income effect, but also a "love-of-variety" effect. The latter is the positive externality associated with the production of manufactured goods (not taken into consideration by the producers) resulting from an increase in the number of varieties n produced in the world economy. Hence in (the non-Pareto-optimal) equilibrium there is an under-production of the number of manufactured goods. This under-production will be exacerbated by an *increase* in the transfer as it further *reduces* the number of varieties produced. Note that this externality, the love-of-variety effect, is smaller the easier it is to substitute one manufactured good for another (that is, β_k increases and therefore ϕ_k falls).[6]

[6] The distortion due to imperfect competition does not quite disappear if β_k approaches one and therefore ϕ_k approaches zero because then the number of varieties becomes small and we cannot "abstract from the integer problem" (see note 3) anymore as the market

The donor's welfare is reduced for three reasons: (i) there is a negative terms-of-trade effect $((\omega_A - \alpha_A)\widehat{p} < 0)$ because the price of manufactured goods falls and the donor is a net exporter of these goods, (ii) there is a negative variety effect because the fall in the price of manufactured goods induces a reduction in the number of varieties produced ($\phi_A \widehat{n} < 0$), and (iii) there is a negative income effect due to the transfer itself $(-\widehat{T}/\eta_A < 0)$.[7]

The recipient is faced with two positive effects and one negative effect. As the recipient is a net exporter of food the terms-of-trade effect is positive, as is, of course, its direct income effect. In fact, the latter effect will usually be quite large as the recipient's income tends to be small compared to the world expenditures on manufactured goods. The love-of-variety effect is negative, however, as the number of varieties declines. Therefore the net welfare effect for the recipient is inconclusive because the love-of-variety effect may potentially dominate both the terms-of-trade effect and the direct income effect. A sufficient condition for $\widehat{v_B}$ to be positive is $(\varepsilon - 1)\sigma > 1$, with $\varepsilon \equiv 1/(1 - \beta)$ representing the elasticity of demand for a particular product in the manufacturing sector.[8] Therefore the recipient's welfare improves if the product of demand and supply elasticities is sufficiently high. Empirical work in a similar framework by Gasiorek et al. (1991) reports rather large values for the elasticity of demand, ranging from 5.8 to 35. If we take ε close to 6, the lowest estimate of Gasiorek et al., then an elasticity of supply of intermediates exceeding 0.2 would be sufficient to guarantee that the recipient gains from the transfer. This condition will appear frequently throughout the rest of the chapter, so we will give it a name.

> *Elasticity condition.* We say the elasticity condition holds if, and only if, $(\varepsilon - 1)\sigma > 1$, that is if, and only if, the demand for manufactured goods and the supply of intermediates are sufficiently elastic. This is equivalent to requiring that the terms-of-trade effect dominates the love-of-variety effect.

Using this terminology we derive the following proposition.

---

will move into a form of oligopoly or monopoly. Addressing this issue would require the modeling of varieties as a continuum of goods.

[7] It should be clear that if we extend the model to three or more countries, those countries not directly involved in the transfer will only face the terms-of-trade effect and the love-of-variety effect; see Brakman and Van Marrewijk (1991b).

[8] This condition is derived by combining the first two terms on the right-hand side of equation (9.18).

Proposition 30: Under assumption I the welfare effects of untied aid are always negative for the donor. The elasticity condition is sufficient to ensure that the recipient gains from untied aid.

9.4 Tied aid

This section discusses, in turn, two forms of generic tied aid: aid tied to food ("humanitarian" aid) and aid tied to manufactured goods in general.

9.4.1 Aid tied to food

First, we look at "humanitarian" aid, that is aid tied to the consumption of food. The recipient maximizes equation (9.1) subject to the two restrictions

$$\left(\sum_{i=1}^{n} p_i X_i^B \right) + F^B \leq I_B + T \tag{9.19}$$

$$F^B \geq T \tag{9.20}$$

The first restriction is the budget constraint and the second is the tying-of-aid constraint, representing the donor's condition that the recipient should spend at least the amount of the transfer on food consumption. Obviously, if the transfer is relatively small the recipient will voluntarily choose to spend more on food than the size of the transfer and the second restriction, equation (9.20), will not be binding. As a result the same demand relations as before are operative, that is equations (9.7) and (9.8) still hold. Consequently, within a certain range of transfers the tying-of-aid restriction is said to be "not effective" and within this range the effects of tied aid on welfare, prices, the number of varieties, etc. are the same as those for untied aid analyzed in the previous section. The analysis of tied aid becomes interesting if the tying-of-aid restriction is effective and the second restriction is binding. In that case the following demand relations hold:

$$X_i^B = \frac{I_B}{pn} \quad \text{for} \quad i = 1, ..., n \tag{9.21}$$

$$F^B = T \tag{9.22}$$

These demand relations lead to the indirect utility function:

$$v_B = p^{-\alpha_B} n^{\phi_B} I_B^{\alpha_B} T^{(1-\alpha_B)} \tag{9.23}$$

The food market equilibrium becomes[9]

$$G(M) + I_B = (1 - \alpha_A)(I_A - T) + T \tag{9.24}$$

For convenience, define the function $R_{tf}(M|T)$, where tf denotes aid tied to food, as:

$$R_{tf}(M|T) = \alpha_A G(M) + [I_B - \alpha_A T]$$

Using this definition, equation (9.24), $r = -G'(M)$, the definition of $L(M)$ in equation (9.12) and equation (9.11), the equilibrium production level of intermediates M if aid is effectively tied to food can be determined as:

$$L(M) = R_{tf}(M|T) \tag{9.25}$$

Equilibrium conditions (9.14) (for untied aid) and (9.25) (for aid tied to food) differ only in the term appearing in square brackets in the R-function. The discussion above is illustrated in figure 9.1. Suppose the initial equilibrium is at point E_0 with the initial transfer T_0 (which could be zero). An increase of the transfer from T_0 to T_1 shifts the R-curve down to $R_u(M|T_1)$ if aid is untied and results in equilibrium E_1, as analyzed in the previous section. Now note that an increase in the transfer from T_0 to T_1 where aid is tied to food but the tying restriction, equation (9.20), is just effective also results in a downward shift of the R-curve to $R_{tf}(M|T_1) = R_u(M|T_1)$ and therefore also results in equilibrium E_1. We therefore suppose that at T_1 the tying-to-food restriction, equation (9.20), becomes just binding, that is $(1 - \alpha_B)(I_B + T_1) = T_1$. A further increase of the transfer from T_1 to T_2 results in a further downward shift of the R-curve to $R_u(M|T_2)$ and equilibrium E_2^u if aid is untied, but to a larger downward shift to $R_{tf}(M|T_2) < R_u(M|T_2)$ and equilibrium E_2^{tf} if aid is tied to food. Therefore we can conclude that, independently of the size of the transfer, aid tied to food leads to larger decreases in the price of manufactures, the number of varieties produced, etc. than untied aid, provided the tying restriction (9.20) is effective. To put it differently, tying aid to food results in a "magnification effect." Figure 9.1 also clarifies another important aspect of tied aid. If we want to gauge the

[9] Note that country B's preferences do not play a role in determining the terms of trade, but country B's technology does; see Schweinberger (1990).

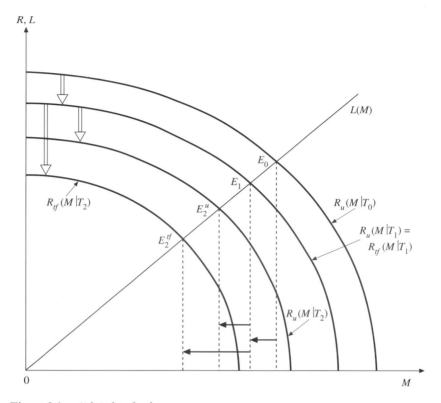

Figure 9.1   *Aid tied to food*

impact of aid tied to food relative to that of untied aid by comparing
the size of various relative changes using calculus techniques, as we did
in the previous section, we can do that usefully only at one point. We
noted above that if the transfer is small (the tying-of-aid restriction is
not effective) there is no difference between the effects of the two types
of aid. If the transfer is large (the tying-of-aid restriction is effective),
however, there is a difference. Suppose that we compare the effect of a
small change in the transfer when aid is tied relative to that when aid is
untied, starting from an initially large transfer like T_2 in figure 9.1. This
would be like comparing apples and oranges since we would be
comparing changes at two different initial equilibria, E_2^{tf} and E_2^{u}
respectively, which affects, in particular, the elasticity of substitution σ
in the supply of intermediates. Therefore, the initial transfer must be
large enough such that there is a difference between tied aid and untied
aid, whereas the transfer must be small enough in order to evaluate

both at the same initial equilibrium point. The only initial transfer that satisfies both these criteria is transfer T_1 in figure 9.1 in which the tying-of-aid restriction (9.20) is just binding. Evaluation at that point (E_1 in figure 9.1) also implies that equation (9.18) still holds (see the appendix to this chapter). A further advantage of this approach is that the modeling of tied aid can then also be given the Kemp–Kojima interpretation of marginal tying (see chapter 8), since the outcome of the two approaches then coincides. Let the symbol $|_{tf}$ indicate aid effectively tied to food. Differentiation of equation (9.25) and comparison to the results of the previous section lead to

$$\hat{r}\,|_{tf} = \hat{p}\,|_{tf} = \sigma\hat{n}\,|_{tf} = \sigma\hat{M}\,|_{tf} = \frac{\alpha_A}{(\alpha_A - \alpha_B)}\hat{r} < \hat{r} < 0 \qquad (9.26)$$

From this equation and the above discussion it is clear that the price and variety changes are larger (in absolute value) if aid is tied to food instead of untied. More precisely, these changes are $\alpha_A/(\alpha_A - \alpha_B) > 1$ times as large. This is easy to understand as the recipient is forced, through the tying of aid, to spend the entire increase of the transfer exclusively on food consumption, rather than just the fraction $(1 - \alpha_B)$. The welfare changes are given by

$$\widehat{v_A}\,|_{tf} = (\omega_A - \alpha_A)\hat{p}\,|_{tf} + \phi_A\hat{n}\,|_{tf} - \frac{\hat{T}}{\eta_A} < \widehat{v_A} < 0 \qquad (9.27)$$

$$\widehat{v_B}\,|_{tf} = (\omega_B - \alpha_B)\hat{p}\,|_{tf} + \phi_B\hat{n}\,|_{tf} + \frac{\hat{T}}{\eta_B} \qquad (9.28)$$

Hence welfare for the donor decreases to a greater extent because of a larger terms-of-trade effect and a larger love-of-variety effect. The recipient of the transfer has a larger welfare gain from the tying of aid to food, which forces it to use its monopoly power, relative to that from untied aid, if, and only if, the elasticity condition holds, that is if, and only if, the terms-of-trade (monopoly) effect dominates the love-of-variety effect. One could therefore say that humanitarian aid is truly humanitarian if, and only if, the elasticity condition holds.

Proposition 31: Under assumption I, aid tied to food compared to untied aid causes (i) a larger welfare decrease for the donor, (ii) larger decreases in the price and number of manufactured goods, and (iii) a larger welfare gain for the recipient if, and only if, the elasticity condition holds.

9.4.2   Aid tied to manufactures in general

Sometimes, aid is not tied to a specific good (as discussed in the next section), but the tying is 'coordinated' between donors to manufactures in general (see Jepma [1991] for examples of multi-country tying and chapter 7 for an analysis). It should come as no surprise that this case represents the mirror image of aid tied to food. The tying-of-aid constraint becomes

$$\sum_{i=1}^{n} p_i X_i^B \geq T \tag{9.29}$$

If this constraint is not effective, that is if the transfer is small, then generic tying of aid to manufactures has the same implications as untied aid because restriction (9.29) is not binding. If the transfer is large enough, that is if restriction (9.29) is binding, the demand relations are (in equilibrium)

$$X_i^B = \frac{T}{pn} \quad \text{for} \quad i = 1, ..., n \tag{9.30}$$

$$F^B = I_B \tag{9.31}$$

And the market-clearing condition for food becomes

$$G(M) + I_B = (1 - \alpha_A)(I_A - T) + I_B \tag{9.32}$$

Again, for convenience, define the function $R_{tm}(M|T)$, where tm denotes aid tied to manufactures in general, as

$$R_{tm}(M|T) = \alpha_A G(M) + [(1 - \alpha_A)T]$$

Using this definition, equation (9.32), $r = -G'(M)$, the definition of $L(M)$ in equation (9.12) and equation (9.11), the equilibrium production level of intermediates M where aid is effectively tied to manufactures in general can be determined as

$$L(M) = R_{tm}(M|T) \tag{9.33}$$

Equilibrium conditions (9.14) (for untied aid) and (9.33) (for aid tied to manufactures in general) also differ only in the term appearing in brackets in the R-function. The situation is illustrated in figure 9.2. Starting from the initial equilibrium at point E_0 with the initial transfer T_0 (which could be zero) an increase of the transfer from T_0 to T_1 shifts the R-curve down

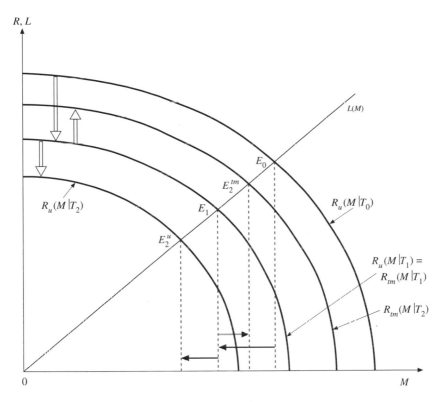

Figure 9.2.   *Aid tied to manufactures in general*

to $R_u(M|T_1)$ if aid is untied and results in equilibrium E_1, as analyzed in section 9.3. Similarly, an increase in the transfer from T_0 to T_1 where aid is tied to manufactures in general and the tying restriction (9.29) is just effective also results in a downward shift of the R-curve to $R_{tm}(M|T_1) - R_u(M|T_1)$ and therefore also results in equilibrium E_1. We therefore suppose that at T_1 the tying-to-manufactures restriction (9.29) becomes just binding, that is $\alpha_B(I_B + T_1) = T_1$. A further increase of the transfer from T_1 to T_2 results in a further downward shift of the R-curve to $R_u(M|T_2)$ and equilibrium E_2^u where aid is untied. In contrast, a further increase of the transfer from T_1 to T_2 leads to an upward shift to $R_{tm}(M|T_2) > R_{tm}(M|T_1) = R_u(M|T_1) > R_u(M|T_2)$ and equilibrium E_2^{tm} where aid is tied to manufactures. Therefore, we can conclude that, independently of the size of the transfer, aid tied to manufactures in general leads to opposite effects for the price of manufactures, the number of varieties produced, etc. than does untied aid, provided the tying restriction (9.29) is effective. To put it differently, tying aid to manufactures in general leads to a "reversal effect." For the reasons discussed in the previous subsection, we evaluate derivatives at the same initial equilibrium, in which the tying-of-aid restriction (9.29) is just binding. Let the symbol $|_{tm}$ indicate aid effectively tied to manufactures in general. Differentiation of equation (9.33) and comparison with the results of the previous section leads to

$$\hat{r}\,|_{tm} = \hat{p}\,|_{tm} = \sigma\hat{n}\,|_{tm} = \sigma\hat{M}\,|_{tm} = -\frac{(1-\alpha_A)}{(\alpha_A - \alpha_B)}\hat{r} > 0 > \hat{r} \qquad (9.34)$$

From this it is immediately clear that the price and variety changes are *positive* rather than *negative* if aid is tied to manufactures in general instead of untied. This follows from the fact that the recipient is forced, through the tying of aid, to spend the increase of the transfer exclusively on the consumption of manufactures, rather than just the fraction α_A, which is what the donor would have spent on manufactures from that part of its income. This, then, leads to an increase in the demand for manufactures and hence an increase in their price and the quantity supplied through an increase in the number of varieties. The welfare changes are given by

$$\widehat{v_A}\,|_{tm} = (\omega_A - \alpha_A)\hat{p}\,|_{tm} + \phi_A\hat{n}\,|_{tm} - \frac{\hat{T}}{\eta_A} > \widehat{v_A} \qquad (9.35)$$

$$\widehat{v_B}\,|_{tm} = (\omega_B - \alpha_B)\hat{p}\,|_{tm} + \phi_B\hat{n}\,|_{tm} + \frac{\hat{T}}{\eta_B} \qquad (9.36)$$

The donor is now faced with a positive terms-of-trade effect and a positive love-of-variety effect, but a negative direct income effect. Its welfare decrease will be smaller than if aid is untied. Indeed, the donor may even gain through the tying of aid to manufactures if the love-of-variety effect dominates the direct income effect. The recipient, on the other hand, is confronted with two positive effects and one negative effect. As before, its direct income effect is positive because it receives the transfer. The terms-of-trade effect is now negative as the price of manufactured goods rises, an effect which may be counterbalanced by the positive love-of-variety effect if the elasticity condition does not hold. The benefit of tying aid to manufactures is the increase in the number of varieties n produced, a positive externality for all countries involved. Aid tied to manufactures will therefore lead to an outward shift of the utility possibility locus, rather than an inward shift (as would be the case with untied aid or aid tied to food).

Proposition 32: Under assumption I, aid tied to manufactures in general compared to untied aid induces (i) a price increase for all manufactured goods, (ii) an increase in the number of varieties in the manufactured goods industry, (iii) a smaller welfare loss (or possibly a welfare gain) for the donor, and (iv) a smaller welfare gain for the recipient if, and only if, the elasticity condition holds.

It has become clear from the above propositions that some transfer paradoxes cannot be ruled out. In particular, if aid is untied or tied to food the recipient's welfare may fall (and hence everyone is worse off), while if aid is tied to manufactures the donor's welfare may rise (and hence everyone may gain). Simulations suggest that these paradoxes only occur for very small values of β (close to 0.01), and hence very low values of ε $(= 1/(1 - \beta))$, and are largely independent of the other parameters in the model; see Brakman and Van Marrewijk (1991b) for details. Low values of β correspond to an elasticity of demand close to 1, much lower than the lowest empirical estimate (5.8) found by Gasiorek et al. (1991).

9.5 A fictitious restriction?

The previous section discussed generic tied aid, that is aid tied to food in general or to manufactures in general. In reality, however, if aid is tied it is usually tied to a specific good produced in the donor country. For example, Japan gives aid to Indonesia provided the money is used to buy tractors in Japan.[10] Without loss of generality we assume the specific good to be good X_1. Suppose, then, in the same vein as in the previous section, that the world is in an initial equilibrium in which country A gives untied aid to country B and that this transfer is just large enough for country B to pay for the purchase of manufactured good X_1, which is imported from country A, that is $T = p[\alpha_B(I_B + T)/pn]$. One might be tempted to argue that the mere proclamation by country A that henceforth aid is tied to the purchase of manufactured good X_1 would *not* alter the equilibrium in the world economy since the restriction imposed is already fulfilled by the current equilibrium (and therefore appears to be a fictitious restriction). This reasoning would be wrong, however, as we will now explain.

---

[10] The transfer is, of course, still given in terms of the numéraire, with equation (9.37) as tying restriction.

The recipient solves the maximization problem subject to the budget constraint and the tying-of-aid constraint

$$p_1 X_1^B \geq T \qquad (9.37)$$

If the tying-of-aid constraint is binding, expenditures on good X_1 are equal to the transfer and the remainder of the income is used to buy the other $(n-1)$ manufactured goods and food, which leads to the following demand relations for the recipient

$$X_1^B \geq \frac{T}{p_1} \qquad (9.38)$$

$$X_i^B \geq \frac{\alpha_B I_B}{p(n-1)} \quad \text{for} \quad i = 2, ..., n \qquad (9.39)$$

$$F^B = (1 - \alpha_B) I_B \qquad (9.40)$$

The producer of good X_1 can take advantage of the restriction being imposed upon the consumers in the less developed country. If he could charge different prices in the two countries he could set the price in country B arbitrarily high and still receive revenue T because demand for manufactured good X_1 in country B is now unit-elastic (while a higher price means lower quantity demanded and hence lower cost). We assume, however, that consumer arbitrage between the two countries forces the producer of good X_1 to charge the same price in both countries. Let ε_k^i be the elasticity of demand for manufactured good $i = 1, ..., n$ in country $k = A, B$; let ε_i be the overall elasticity of demand for manufactured good i, and let θ_i be the share of sales of manufactured good i in country A, that is $\theta_i = X_i^A / (X_i^A + X_i^B)$. Then the following relation holds:

$$\varepsilon_i = \theta_i \varepsilon_A^i + (1 - \theta_i) \varepsilon_B^i \quad \text{for} \quad i = 1, ..., n \qquad (9.41)$$

Therefore, the overall elasticity of demand ε_i is a weighted average of the elasticities of demand in the two countries. For all producers $i = 2, ..., n$ we have $\varepsilon_k^i = 1/(1 - \beta)$ for both countries $k = A, B$, and hence $\varepsilon_i = 1/(1 - \beta) = \varepsilon$, say. For the producer of good X_1, however, $\varepsilon_A^1 = 1/(1 - \beta) > 1 = \varepsilon_B^1$ and hence $\varepsilon_1 < \varepsilon$. Since all producers equate marginal revenue and marginal cost according to the rule

$$p_i \left(1 - \frac{1}{\varepsilon_i}\right) = rb \qquad (9.42)$$

this implies that the producer of good X_1 charges a higher price than his competitors, which allows him to make a profit. As a result the sales of each competitor $i = 2, ..., n$ at the old price will increase slightly, which leads to profits, which in turn causes an increase in the price and the number of varieties produced.

> **Proposition 33:** The imposition of an "imaginary" constraint, tying aid to a specific manufactured good, causes (i) a price increase for all manufactured goods, (ii) an increase in the number of varieties, (iii) a higher price for the manufactured good to which aid is tied than for the other manufactured goods, and (iv) profits for the producer of the good to which aid is tied.

The "fictitious" restriction has real effects because it affects the elasticity of demand for the "privileged" producer. Obviously, the possibility of the "privileged" producer having positive profits if aid is tied to the production of its good explains both the envy of other producers, who will object to this practice, and the existence of lobby groups for certain producers trying to acquire the "privileged" status. Effectively, the tying of aid to a specific good manufactured by the donor largely repatriates the transfer in terms of profits for this manufactured good industry. Therefore, countries involved to a large extent in this type of tied-aid practice appear much more generous than they really are.

9.6 Differences in demand elasticity

Naturally, under assumption I, a manufacturing firm, in the absence of tariffs, quotas or transport costs, will *automatically* charge the same price in both countries because the elasticity of demand is the same in both countries. Even if demand elasticities differ between countries a producer will be forced to charge the same price in both countries through consumer arbitrage if consumers in country A (B) can purchase goods in country B (A), as we assumed in the previous section. We will now briefly investigate the consequences of differences in demand elasticity between donor and recipient. For clarity in exposition we will use assumption II, but it is of course trivial to change the relation between β_A and β_B.[11]

---

[11] Empirical evidence does not support assumption II (nor the alternative, that is, demand is more elastic in less developed countries). Just restricting ourselves, for example, to the large developed countries (Germany, France, Italy, the United Kingdom, the United States and Japan) compared to the less developed countries (Rest of the World) in table 19 of Stalioner (1987) shows that in sixteen instances demand is more elastic in the developed countries, while in fourteen instances demand is more elastic in the less developed countries. One would therefore have to investigate the consequences of aid on a case-by-case basis.

Assumption II: The elasticity of demand is higher in the developed country than in the less developed country, that is $\beta_A > \beta_B$, while the share of income spent on manufactured goods is identical in both countries, that is $\alpha_A = \alpha_B = \alpha$.

Suppose, furthermore, that the producer of a manufactured good can take advantage of the different elasticities of demand in each market and can set different prices in different markets. This implies, from the marginal revenue equals marginal cost condition, that the price charged for manufactured goods will be higher in country B than in country A.

$$p_A \beta_A = rb \tag{9.43}$$

$$p_B \beta_B = rb \tag{9.44}$$

The zero-profit condition changes to

$$p_A X^A + p_B X^B = \frac{rM}{n} \tag{9.45}$$

where X^k is consumption in country k, which is given by

$$X^A = \frac{\alpha(I_A - T)}{p_A n} \tag{9.46}$$

$$X^B = \frac{\alpha(I_B + T)}{p_B n} \tag{9.47}$$

Equilibrium in the food market gives

$$I_B + G(M) = (1-\alpha)[(I_A - T) + (I_B + T)] = (1-\alpha)(I_A + I_B) \tag{9.48}$$

and is therefore *independent* of the size of the transfer. Equilibrium in the food market, using $I_A = G(M) + rM$, reduces to

$$\alpha(I_B + G(M)) + (1 - \alpha)G'(M)M = 0 \tag{9.49}$$

which determines the quantity of intermediates M produced. This, then, gives in turn F, r, p_A, p_B and I_A. Solving for the number of varieties n we get

$$n = (1 - \beta_B)\frac{M}{a} - (\beta_A - \beta_B)\frac{\alpha}{ra}(I_A - T) \tag{9.50}$$

From equation (9.50) it readily follows that an increase in the transfer T leads to an increase in the number of varieties n produced if, and only if, the donor's demand is more elastic than the recipient's demand ($\beta_A > \beta_B$).

Proposition 34: Under assumption II and price discrimination an increase in the transfer from country A to country B (i) does not change the equilibrium prices of food and intermediates, nor the equilibrium production quantities of food and intermediates, (ii) increases the number of varieties produced, and (iii) leads to a welfare gain for the recipient.

The results of this proposition are intuitively straightforward to explain. Suppose that country A increases the transfer to country B. Since donor and recipient spend the same proportion of this income on food consumption the equilibrium condition in the food market is not changed; hence the production level of food and intermediates is not affected by the transfer. This means that the price of intermediates, the income level I_A and the prices for manufactures charged in the different countries do not change. Only the consumption levels in countries A and B and the number of varieties produced change.

Recall the spending levels of countries A and B on a representative manufactured good, that is look at equations (9.46) and (9.47). Given the produced number of varieties (n), an increase in the transfer T will shift demand away from country A to country B where the price is higher (because demand is less elastic in country B). This will therefore increase revenues without increasing costs, which attracts new firms into the market, thereby reducing the quantity demanded from an individual producer at a given price level so that profits are again zero. Under these conditions, then, a transfer leads to an increase in the number of varieties produced and to an outward shift of the utility possibility locus. The donor is confronted with a negative income effect and a positive love-of-variety effect, while the recipient is confronted with a positive income effect and a positive love-of-variety effect (and therefore gains from an increase in the transfer). What happens if the manufacturer cannot charge different prices in the two markets? Basically the same results hold, because an increase in the transfer does not affect the food market equilibrium condition, while demand has shifted to the country with a lower demand elasticity which therefore raises prices and the number of intermediates produced.

9.7 Conclusion

Chapter 8 demonstrated the possibility of transfer paradoxes if aid is tied in a Walrasian-stable, two-good, two-country framework. This chapter derived the same result in a popular, non-Pareto-optimal trade model which also incorporates increasing returns to scale and imperfect competition. We obtained three additional results.

First, there are three, rather than two, welfare effects; that is, in addition to the well-known terms-of-trade effect and direct income effect, there is a love-of-variety effect which may potentially dominate the other two effects. This third welfare effect becomes less important if the elasticity of substitution for manufactured goods increases.

Second, if the elasticity of demand is the same in the two countries but the donor spends more on manufactures than the recipient (i) the price of manufactures and the number of varieties decreases and the donor always loses if aid is untied, while the recipient gains if an elasticity condition is fulfilled, (ii) untied aid leads to an inward shift of the utility possibility locus, (iii) the results in i and ii are magnified if aid is tied to food and reversed if aid is tied to manufactures in general, (iv) welfare paradoxes are possible if the elasticity of demand is close to 1, and (v) the imposition of tied aid with respect to a specific manufactured good increases the price of the good and enables the producer of that good to make a profit, thereby largely repatriating the transfer.

Third, if the donor's demand is more elastic than the recipient's (with identical spending patterns) then an increase in aid does not change the terms-of-trade but increases both the number of varieties produced and the welfare level of the recipient (and leads to an outward shift of the utility possibility locus).

9.A   Appendix: effective tying

This appendix shows that equation (9.18) still holds if aid is tied to food and the tying constraint is just effective, that is if $(1 - \alpha_B)(I_B + T) = T$. The demand relations for country B are

$$X_i^B = \frac{I_B}{pn} \quad \text{for} \quad i = 1, ..., n \tag{9.51}$$

$$F^B = T \tag{9.52}$$

which leads to the indirect utility function

$$v_B = p^{-\alpha_B} n^{\phi_B} I_B^{\alpha_B} T^{1-\alpha_B} \tag{9.53}$$

Differentiating equation (9.53) results in (I_B is given)

$$\widehat{v_B} = -\alpha_B \widehat{p} + \phi_B \widehat{n} + (1 - \alpha_B) \frac{dT}{T}$$

$$= -\alpha_B \widehat{p} + \phi_B \widehat{n} + (1 - \alpha_B) \left(\frac{rM}{\cdot T} \right) \left(\frac{dT}{rM} \right)$$

$$= \alpha_B \widehat{p} + \phi_B \widehat{n} + (1 - \alpha_B) \left(\frac{rM}{I_B + T} \right) \left(\frac{I_B + T}{T} \right) \widehat{T}$$

$$= -\alpha_R \widehat{p} + \phi_R \widehat{n} + (1 - \alpha_B) \left(\frac{1}{\eta_B} \right) \left(\frac{I_B + T}{T} \right) \widehat{T}$$

$$= -\alpha_B \widehat{p} + \phi_B \widehat{n} + \left(\frac{1}{\eta_B} \right) \widehat{T}$$

where the last equality holds because $(1 - \alpha_B)[(I_B + T)/T] = 1$ if tying is just effective. Showing that equation (9.18) still holds if aid is tied to manufactures in general if the tying is just effective is entirely analogous.

10 Dynamics, money and the balance of payments

10.1 Introduction

The dynamic issues involved with international transfers have been largely ignored in the previous chapters. This chapter will only partially fill this gap as it is beyond the scope of this book to give an extensive treatment of dynamic optimization in the multitude of economic growth frameworks with a variety of behavioral assumptions. We start the discussion as close as possible to the dual framework used most often in the book, first by investigating complete futures markets and then by looking at financial transfers and the balance of payments in a context of Hicksian temporary equilibria. We then continue the analysis within a neoclassical, continuous-time dynamic optimization framework to look at the effects of transfers over time and the optimal timing of transfers, with or without cooperation.

10.2 Quasi dynamics with complete futures markets

Payments imbalances over time need not reflect real disequilibria, but can simply reflect differences between countries in the demand for future versus present consumption. The many-goods model of chapter 4 can have a dynamic interpretation if we distinguish between goods available at different periods as different commodities; see Arrow and Debreu (1954) and Debreu (1959). If prices for future sales and deliveries had a comparable basis, say at the initial date, there would be one budget constraint, implying that the present value of sales would have to be at least as great as the present value of purchases. At different time periods there can then be either trade deficits or surpluses, but the present value of all trade deficits would have to be non-positive. Thus, the generalization of Samuelson's theorem derived in chapter 4 concerning welfare effects for donor and recipient in a perfectly competitive two-country world also holds if this is given a dynamic interpretation in present-value terms with complete futures markets.

To make the argumentation more precise, suppose there are two countries, donor A and recipient B. There is an arbitrary number N of traded goods in each period, with index $i = 1, ..., N$, and an arbitrary number M of periods, with index $t = 1, ..., M$. Let p^{it} be the present-value price of good i delivered in period t as of period 1, let $\mathbf{p}^t = (p^{1t}, ..., p^{Nt})'$ be the vector of present value prices for goods delivered in period t as of period 1 and let $\mathbf{p} = (\mathbf{p}^1, ..., \mathbf{p}^M)'$ be the total vector of present-value prices. The function E^J is the minimum expenditure necessary to achieve utility u^J at relative price $\mathbf{p}$ in country J, while R^J is the maximum revenue obtainable at price $\mathbf{p}$ in country $J = A, B$. The expenditure and revenue functions capture the intertemporal consumption and production plans. If we let $\mathbf{m}^J$ denote the planned net demands (that is imports) for country J, such that $\mathbf{m}^J \equiv E^J_{\mathbf{p}} - R^J_{\mathbf{p}}$, and $\mathbf{m}^{Jt} \equiv (m^{J1t}, ..., m^{JNt})'$ the import vector with delivery date t for $t = 1, ..., M$, then the budget constraint implies $\mathbf{p}'\mathbf{m}^J = \sum_t \mathbf{p}'_t \mathbf{m}^J_t = 0$. The individual terms $\mathbf{p}'_t \mathbf{m}^J_t$ represent the present values of country J's trade deficits at different dates.

$$E^A(\mathbf{p}, u^A) = R^A(\mathbf{p}) - T \tag{10.1}$$

$$E^B(\mathbf{p}, u^B) = R^B(\mathbf{p}) + T \tag{10.2}$$

$$\mathbf{m}^A(\mathbf{p}, u^A) + \mathbf{m}^B(\mathbf{p}, u^B) = \mathbf{0} \tag{10.3}$$

The set of structural equations is (10.1)–(10.3), which is identical to section 4.5 if we choose one of the goods as numéraire. The analysis can therefore proceed along the same lines.

> **Proposition 35:** Samuelson's theorem, which states that the donor loses and the recipient gains from an international transfer in a perfectly competitive, two-good, two-country and Walrasian stable world, generalizes to an arbitrary number of traded goods and an arbitrary number of periods if futures markets are perfect.

10.3   Financial transfers and the balance of payments

Although it is true, as explained in the previous section, that the many-goods model of chapter 4 can have a dynamic interpretation which explains the trade balance, this is not a very satisfactory framework for discussing the balance of payments. Although time is mentioned explicitly it is essentially a static framework in which payments imbalances are part of complete plans made at the beginning of time (people who are not yet born have to make plans and specify contracts). Payments are not ordinary payments. They are claims for specific goods in specific time periods, not general financial assets. It is preferable, therefore, to have a theory of the balance of payments with assets as a general store of purchasing power and regular national and international payments.

In this section we will follow Dixit and Norman (1980, ch. 7) by investigating the balance of payments in the context of Hicksian temporary equilibria. Agents have access to markets for spot commodities today and a financial asset called money. The financial asset is held for buying commodities on the spot market tomorrow, and thus the demand for money is influenced by expectations about future commodity prices. These expectations may be inconsistent across consumers and may turn out to be wrong as the future unravels. If there is perfect foresight, a sequence of Hicksian temporary equilibria coincides with the equilibrium which would obtain with perfect forward markets.

We introduce money holdings in a two-period model. Residents in a country acquire claims on each other held in their own country's money. The authorities supply this money in exchange for foreign money. There is an inflow of money supply at a rate equal to a country's trade surplus, which leads to an adjustment process like Hume's specie-flow mechanism. There is a spot commodity with price p^J relative to money as the numéraire in country J. There is no storage or money-holding by producers, so they have the usual revenue function $R^J(p^J)$ with supply $R_p^J(p^J)$ of the spot commodity. Consumers demand spot commodities and money, labeled 0, which is held for buying commodities in the future. We assume that the expected future price $_ep^J$ reflects current spot prices in a linearly homogeneous way to avoid money illusion; see equation (10.7) where ψ^J is homogeneous of degree one. Thus the expenditure function is $E^J(_ep^J, p^J, u^J)$, with E_p^J the demand for spot commodities and $E_0^J \equiv E_{_ep^J}^J$ the demand for real cash balances. If we let l^J denote the initial money-holdings and T^J the value of the transfer, both denominated in country J's currency, then this gives budget constraints (10.4) and (10.5) for donor and recipient, respectively. The market-clearing condition for spot commodities is given in (10.6). Finally, to link the money supplies in the two countries we introduce the fixed exchange rate ϵ in equation (10.8). An increase in ϵ is a devaluation of the recipient's currency. Equations (10.4)–(10.8) can then be thought of as describing a short-run equilibrium with a fixed exchange rate.

$$E^A(_ep^A, p^A, u^A) = R^A(p^A) + (l^A - T^A) \tag{10.4}$$

$$E^B({_\epsilon}p^B, p^B, u^B) = R^B(p^B) + (l^B + T^B) \tag{10.5}$$

$$m^A({_\epsilon}p^A, p^A, u^A) + m^B({_\epsilon}p^B, p^B, u^B) = 0 \tag{10.6}$$

$${_\epsilon}p^J = \psi^J(p^J) \quad \text{for } J = A, B \tag{10.7}$$

$$p^B = \epsilon p^A \tag{10.8}$$

Multiplying (first) the donor's budget constraint, equation (10.4), by the exchange rate ϵ, using (secondly) linear homogeneity of the expenditure and revenue functions in prices, (thirdly) linear homogeneity of ψ^A and (fourthly) $\epsilon p^A = p^B$ and $\epsilon T^A = T^B$ give, in turn:

$$\epsilon E^A(\psi^A(p^A), p^A, u^A) = \epsilon R^A(p^A) + \epsilon(l^A - T^A)$$

$$E^A(\epsilon \psi^A(p^A), \epsilon p^A, u^A) = R^A(\epsilon p^A) + (\epsilon l^A - \epsilon T^A)$$

$$E^A(\psi^A(\epsilon p^A), \epsilon p^A, u^A) = R^A(\epsilon p^A) + (\epsilon l^A - \epsilon T^A)$$

$$E^A(\psi^A(p^B), p^B, u^A) = R^A(p^B) + (\epsilon l^A - T^B)$$

If we now, for convenience, define $p \equiv p^B$ and $T = T^B$ we can simplify equations (10.4)–(10.8) to

$$E^A(\psi^A(p), p, u^A) = R^A(p) + (\epsilon l^A - T) \tag{10.9}$$

$$E^B(\psi^B(p), p, u^B) = R^B(p) + (l^B + T) \tag{10.10}$$

$$m^A(\psi^A(p), p, u^A) + m^B(\psi^B(p), p, u^B) = 0 \tag{10.11}$$

Let l denote the world supply of money at the beginning of the period, that is $\bar{l} = \epsilon l^A + l^B$. Then differentiating (10.9)–(10.11) gives equation (10.12).[1] Solving (10.12) gives (10.13)–(10.16), where the inequality in (10.13) represents stability.

$$\begin{bmatrix} \frac{\epsilon l^A - T}{p} & 1 & 0 \\ \frac{l^B + T}{p} & 0 & 1 \\ 0 & m_u^A & m_u^B \end{bmatrix} \begin{bmatrix} dp \\ du^A \\ du^B \end{bmatrix} = \begin{bmatrix} -1 \\ 1 \\ 0 \end{bmatrix} d'T \tag{10.12}$$

$$\det = -[(\epsilon l^A - T)m_u^A + (l^B + T)m_u^B]\frac{1}{p} \equiv \frac{-1}{\Delta} < 0 \tag{10.13}$$

$$\frac{dp}{dT} = (m_u^B - m_u^A)\Delta > 0 \quad \text{iff} \quad m_u^B > m_u^A \tag{10.14}$$

---

[1] Differentiating equation (10.10) with respect to p, for example, gives $E_0^B \psi_p^B + E_p^B - R_p^B$. Using $p\psi_p^B E_p^B + pE_p^B = E$ and $pR_p^B = R$ (from homogeneity of E^B and R^B) and (10.10) gives $E_0^B \psi_p^B + E_p^B - R_p^B = (l^B + T)/p$.

$$\frac{du^A}{dT} = -\frac{\bar{l}}{p} m_u^B \Delta \tag{10.15}$$

$$\frac{du^B}{dT} = \frac{\bar{l}}{p} m_u^A \Delta \tag{10.16}$$

Equation (10.14) gives the usual conclusion that the price of spot commodities increases if, and only if, the recipient's marginal propensity to consume spot commodities exceeds the donor's marginal propensity to consume spot commodities. Moreover, from equations (10.15) and (10.16) it follows that the donor's welfare falls (respectively, the recipient's welfare increases) if, and only if, the recipient's (respectively, the donor's) marginal propensity to consume spot commodities is positive. Not surprisingly, the size of the welfare change is related to the real value of the world money stock.

> **Proposition 36:** A financial transfer in a stable Hicksian temporary equilibrium increases the price level of spot commodities if, and only if, the recipient's marginal propensity to consume spot commodities is larger than the donor's. This does not give rise to transfer paradoxes if the demand for spot commodities is normal for both countries.

What is the influence of a transfer on the trade balance in this model, or, more appropriately, on the current account? Country J's trade surplus, TB^J say, is the value of the net excess supply of commodities, or $TB^J = p^J(R_p^J - E_p^J)$. Using linear homogeneity of the revenue and expenditure functions, that is $R_p^J p^J = R^J$ and $E_0^J {}_e p^J + E_p^J p^J = E^J$, equation (10.7), the relation between current expenditure and current revenue in equations (10.4) and (10.5) and the fact that the transfer is given from country A to country B gives country J's spot current account, CA^J say, in equation (10.17).[2]

$$CA^J = E_0^J({}_e p^J, p^J, u^J)\psi^J(p^J) - l^J \tag{10.17}$$

Thus, a country will have a spot current account surplus if its demand for nominal cash-holdings exceeds its current nominal cash-holdings. Since ψ^J is homogeneous of degree one, E_0^J is homogeneous of degree zero in prices and the sum of the marginal propensities to consume is equal to one, that is $E_{0u}^J \psi^J = 1 - p^J m_u^J$, it follows from (10.17) that:

---

[2] That is, $CA^A = TB^A - T^A$ and $CA^B = TB^B + T^B$.

$$\frac{dCA^J}{dT^J} = \left(1 - p^J m_u^J\right) \frac{du^J}{dT^J} \tag{10.18}$$

Thus, if the demand for spot commodities is normal and we do not have any transfer paradoxes (see the above proposition), then the donor's spot current account deteriorates and the recipient's spot current account improves. Intuitively, if the demand for spot and future commodities are both normal goods for the donor, then the donor wishes to spread out the consequences of its transfer over the two periods involved. Similar reasoning holds, necessary changes being made, for the recipient of the transfer.

> **Proposition 37:** A financial transfer in a stable Hicksian temporary equilibrium leads to a deterioration of the donor's spot current account and an improvement in the recipient's spot current account if the demand for spot commodities is normal for both countries.

10.4 Aid over time

The previous two sections were still essentially static in nature, although time was mentioned explicitly. Moreover, the analysis used discrete time, in contrast to the vast majority of the economic growth literature in which time is continuous. The remainder of this chapter amends these two shortcomings, first by introducing and explaining the workings of the neoclassical growth model and then by applying this model to the hitherto unanswered question of the optimal timing of aid.

10.4.1 The neoclassical growth model

Consider a closed economy, with a constant population L in which production Y is derived using capital and labor from a constant returns to scale production function $F(K(\tau), L)$, where $K(\tau)$ is the level of the capital stock at time τ.[3] As indicated by this notation the capital stock may change over time, and thus is implicitly a function of time. We will suppress this dependence in the remainder of the chapter, except where it may be confusing. Moreover, in the remainder of this chapter we will assume that there is a benevolent and omniscient central planner to solve dynamic optimization problems. For information on this aspect and on dynamic optimization we refer the reader to the mathematical appendix.

---

[3] We use τ to denote time because T and t are reserved to denote transfers.

If we let lower-case letters denote per capita values it follows that production per capita y is a function of capital per capita k since $y \equiv Y/L = F(K, L)/L = F(K/L, 1) = F(k, 1) \equiv f(k)$. The function f is assumed to satisfy the Inada conditions, that is, the second derivative is negative and the first derivative is positive and approaches zero (respectively, infinity) if per capita capital approaches infinity (respectively, zero). Per capita production y can be used either for consumption c or investment in the capital stock i; see equation (10.20). The capital stock k rises over time owing to investment and falls owing to exponential depreciation at the rate δ; see equation (10.21) where an overdot denotes the rate of change over time. A consumer derives welfare W from consumption c, from the initial time, zero to infinity, at the instantaneous utility level $u(c)$, a function with the same properties as f, and subject to a constant rate of time preference ρ; see equation (10.19). The objective is to maximize welfare (10.19), subject to the budget constraint (10.20), the law of motion for capital (10.21) and the initial level of the capital stock (10.22).

$$\max_{c,i} \quad W = \int_0^\infty e^{-\rho\tau} u(c(\tau)) \, d\tau \tag{10.19}$$

$$y = f(k) = c + i \tag{10.20}$$

$$\dot{k} = i - \delta k \tag{10.21}$$

$$k(0) = k_0, \quad \text{given.} \tag{10.22}$$

To solve this problem we can use a procedure quite similar to defining a Lagrangian if we substitute (10.20) in (10.21) and define the current-value Hamiltonian in (10.23), where ψ is the co-state variable, that is the shadow price of capital (see the mathematical appendix). The optimality conditions are given in (10.24)–(10.27), subject to (10.22). Equation (10.24) simply indicates that the shadow price of investing in the capital stock is equal to the marginal utility of consumption forgone. Equation (10.26) gives the rate of change of this shadow price over time, which depends on the marginal productivity of capital.

$$H(c, k, \psi) = u(c) + \psi(f(k) - \delta k - c) \tag{10.23}$$

$$(H_c = 0) \qquad u_c(c) = \psi \tag{10.24}$$

$$\left(\dot{k} = H_\psi \right) \qquad \dot{k} = f(k) - \delta k - c \tag{10.25}$$

$$\left(\dot{\psi} = \rho\psi - H_k \right) \qquad \dot{\psi} = [(\rho + \delta) - f_k(k)]\psi \tag{10.26}$$

$$\lim_{\tau \to \infty} e^{-\rho\tau} \psi(\tau) k(\tau) = 0 \tag{10.27}$$

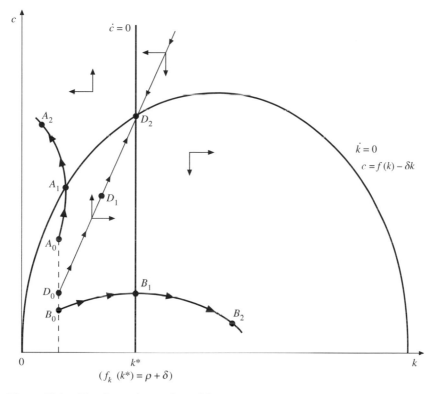

Figure 10.1   *Neoclassical growth model*

Define $\sigma(c) \equiv -c\,u_{cc}/u_c > 0$, the elasticity of marginal utility, as a local measure of the curvature of the utility function. The optimization problem can be illustrated graphically if we differentiate (10.24), that is $u_c(c(\tau)) = \psi(\tau)$, with respect to time τ and use (10.26) to get (10.28).

$$u_{cc}(c(\tau))\,\dot{c}(\tau) = \dot{\psi}(\tau), \quad \text{thus}$$

$$\dot{c} = -\frac{c}{\sigma(c)}\frac{\dot{\psi}}{\psi} = \frac{c}{\sigma(c)}[f_k(k) - (\rho + \delta)] \tag{10.28}$$

Equations (10.25) and (10.28) are two differential equations in the control variable c and the state variable k. We can use these, together with the initial condition (10.22) and the transversality condition (10.27), to characterize the solution of the optimization problem. This is done in figure 10.1. The vertical line at k^* which solves $f_k(k^*) = (\rho + \delta)$ denotes combinations of k and c for which $\dot{c} = 0$. According to (10.28) c is increasing to the left and decreasing to the right of this line, as indicated by the upward (respectively downward) arrows in figure 10.1. Similarly, the curve $c = f(k) - \delta k$ gives combinations of k and c for which $\dot{k} = 0$. According to (10.25) k is increasing below and decreasing above this curve, as indicated by the rightward (respectively leftward) arrows in figure 10.1.

The initial level of the capital stock k_0 is given and cannot be changed instantaneously. The level of consumption $c(0)$ is a control variable and can be changed; however, once chosen, the evolution of c over time is dictated by (10.25) and (10.28). Figure 10.1 illustrates the consequences of three potential choices for $c(0)$: a high level of initial consumption (trajectory $A_0 A_1 A_2$), a low level of initial consumption (trajectory $B_0 B_1 B_2$) and an intermediate level of initial consumption (trajectory $D_0 D_1 D_2$). If a high consumption level is chosen, capital accumulates slowly until point A_1 is reached and then starts to decline. Ultimately, the capital stock would become negative, which is not a viable economic solution. Similarly, if a low consumption level is chosen then the consumption level rises slowly until point B_1 is reached and then starts to decline. Ultimately, the consumption level would become negative, which is not a viable economic solution either. If the level of consumption is chosen precisely right, that is neither too high nor too low, then we would move along the so-called saddle-path $D_0 D_1 D_2$. Both the level of consumption and the capital stock increase over time until the long-run equilibrium D_2 is reached in which both $\dot{c} = 0$ and $\dot{k} = 0$. With a constant level of c is associated a constant level of ψ such that the transversality condition (10.27) is satisfied, as required.

10.4.2 Continuous transfers in the neoclassical growth model

Suppose then, in the spirit of Chacholiades (1978, ch. 14), that this country continuously transfers T units of production abroad, or t units per capita. This changes equation (10.20) to (10.29), which in turn changes equation (10.25) to (10.30), but it does not affect equation (10.28).

$$y = f(k) = c + i + t \tag{10.29}$$
$$\dot{k} = f(k) - \delta k - c - t \tag{10.30}$$

The economics of the transfer is illustrated in figure 10.2. At time $\tau = 0$ the economy possesses $k(0)$ units of capital. If it did not transfer any production abroad, the economy would consume $c(0)$ at time $\tau = 0$, slowly increasing together with the capital stock along the saddle-path

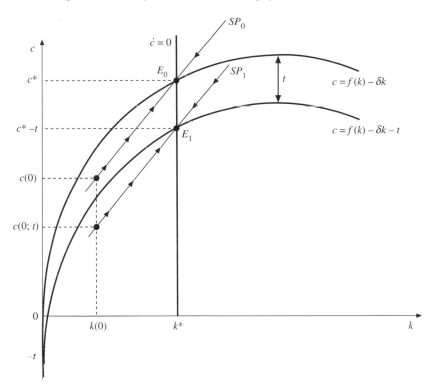

Figure 10.2   *Neoclassical growth model and transfers*

SP_0 to the long-run equilibrium at E_0. In the long run the economy
would consume c^* units per capita. If the economy, however, continuously transfers t units of production this shifts the $\dot{k} = 0$ curve down by
the amount of the per capita transfer, but does not affect the $\dot{c} = 0$ curve.
At time $\tau = 0$ the economy would consume $c(0; t)$ per capita to put the
economy on the new saddle-path SP_1 to reach long-run equilibrium E_1.
Very little can be concluded in general about the position of $c(0; t)$
relative to $c(0)$, but the new long-run equilibrium per capita consumption
level is exactly t units below the old long-run equilibrium c^* because the
efficiency criterion, $f_k(k^*) = \rho + \delta$, the so-called modified golden rule
which determines the long-run per capita capital stock, has not been
affected by the transfer. In this dynamic optimization framework we can
therefore slightly sharpen Chacholiades's (1978, ch. 14) analysis to
conclude that there is no long-run secondary burden from a continuous
transfer.

Proposition 38: (Chacholiades) A continuous transfer per capita in a neoclassical dynamic optimization framework reduces the long-run consumption per capita of the paying country exactly by the amount of the transfer per capita. The reverse holds for the recipient.

10.5   The timing of aid

An issue which hitherto has been left unexplored is the optimal timing of aid. Suppose, then, that there are two economies, A and B, as described in the dynamic optimization framework of the previous section, identical in all respects except for the initial level of the capital stock, which is privately immobile between countries.[4] Since the two countries produce the same goods and have the same time preference, there is no reason for the two countries to trade. Assume, furthermore, that country A has a larger initial level of the capital stock which is below the modified golden rule level, that is $k_{B0} < k_{A0} < k^*$. The analysis in the previous subsection makes it clear that, as a result of this assumption, country A's consumption level is higher than country B's in isolation until the long-run equilibrium is reached. Thus, country A has a higher welfare level and can be called the wealthy country. Finally, suppose that the government of country A wants to help the residents of country B by transferring part $\Omega \equiv k_B(0) - k_{B0}$ of country A's capital stock at time $\tau = 0$ and/or transferring $\omega(\tau)$ of production from A to B at time τ. The government of country A maximizes (10.31) below; that is, it cares about the inhabitants of country B but less so than about its own inhabitants, as measured by the parameter $0 < \lambda < 1$. The smaller the parameter λ, the less the government of A cares about the inhabitants of B. Obviously, the restrictions on the evolution of the capital stocks and their initial level, as given in (10.32)–(10.34), also have to be taken into consideration. Equation (10.32) shows that the donor's capital stock in period τ increases by the extent to which total production $f(k_A)$ exceeds the sum of depreciation δk_A, consumption c_A and flow transfer of goods $\omega(\tau)$ to country B at time τ. The same holds, necessary changes being made, for equation (10.33). Equation (10.34) shows that the initial stocks of capital can be redistributed between the two countries by means of an initial stock capital transfer.

---

[4] This section is based on Kemp *et al.* (1990), to which the reader is referred for a two-good extension. For complications arising in general from not so well-behaved production and utility functions, see Van Marrewijk and Verbeek (1993) and the references therein.

$$\max \int_0^\infty e^{-\rho\tau}[u(c_A(\tau)) + \lambda u(c_B(\tau))]\,d\tau \,, \quad \text{s.t.} \tag{10.31}$$

$$\dot{k}_A = f(k_A) - \delta k_A - c_A - \omega \tag{10.32}$$

$$\dot{k}_B = f(k_B) - \delta k_B - c_B + \omega \tag{10.33}$$

$$k_{A0}, k_{B0} \text{ given}; \quad k_A(0) + k_B(0) \le k_{A0} + k_{B0} \tag{10.34}$$

10.5.1 Cooperation

Kemp *et al.* (1990) refer to a situation in which the direction of the transfer is not restricted, that is the transfer can be from A to B or from B to A at any time, as one of cooperation. The current-value Hamiltonian is given in (10.35), which leads to necessary conditions (10.36)–(10.40).

$$H = u(c_A) + \lambda u(c_B) + \psi_A(f(k_A) - \delta k_A - c_A - \omega)$$
$$+ \psi_B(f(k_B) - \delta k_B - c_B + \omega) \tag{10.35}$$

$$(H_{c_A} = 0) \qquad u_c(c_A) = \psi_A \tag{10.36}$$

$$(H_{c_B} = 0) \qquad \lambda u_c(c_B) = \psi_B \tag{10.37}$$

$$(H_\omega = 0) \qquad \psi_A = \psi_B \tag{10.38}$$

$$(\dot{\psi}_A = \rho\psi_A - H_{k_A}) \qquad \dot{\psi}_A = [(\rho + \delta) - f_k(k_A)]\psi_A \tag{10.39}$$

$$(\dot{\psi}_B = \rho\psi_B - H_{k_B}) \qquad \dot{\psi}_B = [(\rho + \delta) - f_k(k_B)]\psi_B \tag{10.40}$$

The optimal solution to this problem is intuitively straightforward.[5] Combining (10.38)–(10.40) gives the efficiency criterion that the marginal product of capital should be the same in both countries, and thus the level of the capital stock should be the same in both countries, that is $k_A(\tau) = k_B(\tau)$ for all τ. This, then, determines the initial *positive* transfer of the capital stock from country A to country B, that is $\Omega - (k_{A0} - k_{B0})/2 > 0$. On the other hand, combining (10.36)–(10.38) and keeping in mind that $\lambda < 1$ demonstrates that the marginal utility of consumption must be higher for recipient B than for donor A, and thus the consumption level must be higher for donor A than for recipient B, that is $c_A(\tau) > c_B(\tau)$ for all τ. This, combined with the above information on the equality of the capital stocks and equations (10.32) and (10.33), implies that the continuous flow of aid $\omega(\tau)$ is *negative* for all τ, that is production flows from B to A. At first sight this may be a

---

[5] If we say "for all τ" in the following, we mean "for almost all τ" in the sense of measure theory, that is for all τ, except possibly on sets of measure zero.

surprising distribution of the transfer over time: a large initial transfer from A to B, followed by a stream of transfers from B to A. However, this is precisely the time profile which follows if country B borrows a large sum initially which is paid back (with or without interest payments) over time, a very frequently used form of aid indeed.

> **Proposition 39:** (Kemp *et al.*; cooperation) The optimal timing of aid from wealthy country A to poor country B if the two countries cooperate is a large initial transfer from A to B (to equalize the marginal product of capital), followed by a stream of payments from B to A.

We need to tie up one loose end in this subsection before proceeding to the analysis of non-cooperation. The full cooperation between countries A and B is modeled by giving full control to the government of country A. It is clear that if the parameter λ is extremely low, say it approaches zero, then the government of A would give (almost) no consumption to the inhabitants of country B, and thus the welfare of country B could be arbitrarily low. However, the government of country B has an outside option by not participating in the transfer scheme at all, which would give its inhabitants a certain welfare level, $\bar{W}_B$ say. This welfare level $\bar{W}_B$ is equivalent to the welfare level it would reach in the cooperative transfer scheme for some minimum level, $\underline{\lambda}$ say, of the parameter λ. For any value of λ above $\underline{\lambda}$ country B is willing to cooperate. We could argue similarly that there is a maximum value, $\bar{\lambda}$ say, of the parameter λ for which country A is willing to cooperate. Since there is an efficiency gain from cooperation there would be a non-degenerate interval $[\underline{\lambda}, \bar{\lambda}]$ in which both countries would be willing to cooperate, and thus both strictly gain in the interior of this interval. On the other hand, country A may be genuinely interested in helping the inhabitants of country B, in which case λ could exceed $\bar{\lambda}$. Obviously, as long as λ remains below one, country A is the wealthier of the two countries.

10.5.2   Non-cooperation

Kemp *et al.* (1990) refer to a situation in which the direction of the transfer is restricted to one direction only, that is from A to B and *not* vice versa, as one of non-cooperation. This restriction, which obviously ensures that the welfare level of the inhabitants of country B can only rise at the expense of those of country A, is given in equation (10.41). Taking the inequality constraint (10.41) into consideration implies that equation (10.38) changes to equation (10.42).

$$\Omega \geq 0 ; \quad w(\tau) \geq 0 \tag{10.41}$$

$$(H_w \leq 0; \ w H_w = 0) \qquad \psi_B \leq \psi_A ; \quad w(\psi_B - \psi_A) = 0 \tag{10.42}$$

We can now demonstrate, not unexpectedly in light of the results of the preceding subsection, that the non-cooperative restriction implies that $w(\tau) = 0$ for all τ. Suppose, on the contrary, that $w > 0$ for a non degenerate interval $[\tau_1, \tau_2]$. This implies from (10.42) that $\psi_A = \psi_B$ and from (10.39) and (10.40) that $k_A = k_B$. Using this together with (10.32) and (10.33) then indicates that $c_A + w = c_B - w$. Using the restriction on the direction of the transfer this gives

$$c_A(\tau) = c_B(\tau) - 2w(\tau) < c_B(\tau) , \quad \text{for } \tau \in [\tau_1, \tau_2] \tag{10.43}$$

On the other hand, we already saw in the previous subsection that if $\psi_A = \psi_B$, equations (10.36) and (10.37) together with $\lambda < 1$ indicate that the marginal utility of B must be higher than the marginal utility of A. This implies that A's consumption level must be higher than B's consumption level, which gives

$$c_A(\tau) > c_B(\tau) , \quad \text{for } \tau \in [\tau_1, \tau_2] \tag{10.44}$$

Obviously, equations (10.43) and (10.44) cannot both hold at the same time and this contradiction implies that there cannot be an interval for which w is positive.

> **Proposition 40:** (Kemp *et al.*; non-cooperation) The optimal timing of aid from wealthy country A to poor country B if the two countries do not cooperate (transfers are exclusively from A to B and not vice versa) is to offer all aid at the outset (that is, give the transfer at once).

Intuitively, since the marginal product of capital is higher for the recipient than for the donor, it is optimal to give all aid at once. The size of the initial transfer is of course determined by the size of the parameter λ. In this case λ has to exceed a threshold level, $\tilde{\lambda}$ say, to ensure that the initial transfer is positive. For $\lambda \in \left(\tilde{\lambda}, 1 \right)$ we can conclude that $\Omega \in (0, (k_{A0} - k_{B0})/2)$, where the upper bound arises because an initial transfer exceeding that level without future return payments would make the recipient wealthier than the donor.

10.6 Conclusion

The dynamic analysis in this chapter arrived at a number of important and intuitively appealing conclusions. First, we demonstrated that the dual framework used in the body of the book can be given a dynamic interpretation if futures markets are complete. Second, if futures markets are not complete and agents hold money to purchase future consumption goods, we showed not only (i) that Samuelson's theorem holds if spot commodities are normal goods, but also (ii) that the donor's spot current account deteriorates and the recipient's improves as a result of the transfer. This is in accordance with the generally held belief that a transfer reduces the donor's current account. Third, in a dynamic optimization framework we showed (i) that a continuous per capita transfer reduces the long-run per capita consumption by exactly the amount of the per capita transfer, (ii) that it is optimal to give a large initial transfer from the rich to the poor country followed by a stream of reverse payments from the poor to the rich country if the two countries cooperate, and (iii) that it is optimal to give the transfer at once if the two countries do not cooperate. The last two results on the optimal timing of transfers follow from the efficiency criterion to equalize as much as possible the marginal product of capital for donor and recipient. Based on that logic it is not surprising that the optimal timing of aid is an uninteresting problem in an endogenous growth type model with constant returns to accumulable factors (a broad concept of the capital stock). Since any initial transfer of the capital stock does not affect the marginal product of capital in either country there is in general a continuum of combinations of initial transfers and subsequent flows to solve the optimal timing problem, even if the two countries do not cooperate.[6]

[6] The reader can easily verify this statement using the methodology of section 10.5 by putting $f(k) = Ak$ and $u(c) = \log(c)$.

Mathematical appendix

We briefly review some elementary mathematical terminology and results on duality theory. All statements in this chapter are for sufficiently differentiable, real-valued functions, defined on real space.

A.1 Some reminders

Convex. A set X is convex if, and only if, all linear combinations of two arbitrary points belonging to the set X also belong to the set X. That is, if $x \in X$ and $\bar{x} \in X$, then $[\lambda x + (1 - \lambda)\bar{x}] \in X$ for all scalars $\lambda \in [0, 1]$.

Convex function. A function f defined on a convex set X is (strictly) convex if, and only if, the linear combination of the f-value of two (different) arbitrary points belonging to the set X (strictly) exceeds the f-value of the linear combination itself. That is, if $x \in X$ and $\bar{x} \in X$ then $\lambda f(x) + (1 - \lambda)f(\bar{x}) \geq f(\lambda x + (1 - \lambda)\bar{x})$ for all scalars $\lambda \in [0, 1]$, with strict inequality for strictly convex functions. The function f is convex if, and only if, the Hessian matrix of second-order derivatives is positive semi-definite.

Concave function. A function f defined on a convex set X is (strictly) concave if, and only if, $-f$ is (strictly) convex. Equivalently, a function f defined on a convex set X is (strictly) concave if, and only if, the linear combination of the f-value of two (different) arbitrary points belonging to the set X (strictly) falls short of the f-value of the linear combination itself. That is, if $x \in X$ and $\bar{x} \in X$ then $\lambda f(x) + (1 - \lambda)f(\bar{x}) \leq f(\lambda x + (1 - \lambda)\bar{x})$ for all scalars $\lambda \in [0, 1]$, with strict inequality for strictly concave functions. The function f is concave if, and only if, the Hessian matrix of second-order derivatives is negative semi-definite.

Upper contour set. The upper contour set $X^{\rho f}$ of a function f defined on a set X for a real value ρ is the set of all points in X such that the f-value is at least equal to ρ. That is $X^{\rho f} = \{x \in X \mid f(x) \geq \rho\}$.

Quasi-concave function. A function f defined on a convex set X is (strictly) quasi-concave if, and only if, all its upper contour sets are (strictly) convex.

Homogeneity. A function f is homogeneous of degree γ if, and only if, the f-value of a positive proportional increase t of a point x is equal to the product of t^γ and the f-value of the point x. This complicated wording means that $f(tx) = (t)^\gamma f(x)$ for all positive t. Thus, if f is homogeneous of degree zero, then $f(tx) = f(x)$. This holds, for example, for an expenditure-minimizing consumption combination to yield a certain utility level, where a doubling of the consumption prices does not affect the expenditure-minimizing consumption combination (but, of course, doubles the expenditure). Similarly, if f is homogeneous of degree one, then $f(tx) = tf(x)$. This holds, for example, if f is a constant returns to scale production function and x are inputs, where a doubling of inputs also doubles the output.

Euler's theorem 1. If f is a differentiable homogeneous function of degree γ, then $\sum_j x^j f_{x^j}(x) = \gamma f(x)$. This follows simply from differentiating $f(tx) = (t)^\gamma f(x)$ with respect to t and evaluating at $t = 1$. In particular, if f is a differentiable homogeneous function of degree one, then $\sum_j x^j f_{x^j}(x) = f(x)$. The result is very useful. Suppose, for example, that f is an increasing returns to scale production function, such that $\gamma > 1$. Then, paying each input x^j its marginal product f_{x^j} is impossible because this would require a total payment of $\sum_j x^j f_{x^j}$ which (using Euler's theorem 1) is more than the total that is produced: $\sum_j x^j f_{x^j}(x) = \gamma f(x) > f(x)$.

Euler's theorem 2. If f is a differentiable homogeneous function of degree γ, then its derivatives are homogeneous of degree $\gamma - 1$. This follows simply from differentiating $f(tx) = (t)^\gamma f(x)$ with respect to x^i and dividing by t, from which $f_{x^i}(tx) = (t)^{\gamma-1} f_{x^i}(x)$. An important implication is that the slopes of the level surfaces of a homogeneous function, e.g. $-f_{x^1}(x)/f_{x^2}(x)$, are constant along rays through the origin, since

$$\frac{f_{x^1}(tx)}{f_{x^2}(tx)} = \frac{(t)^{\gamma-1} f_{x^1}(x)}{(t)^{\gamma-1} f_{x^2}(x)} = \frac{f_{x^1}(x)}{f_{x^2}(x)}$$

Homothetic. A function f is homothetic if it is a monotonic transformation of a homogeneous function. That is, f is homothetic if, and only if, there exists a monotonic function g and a homogeneous function h such that $f(x) = g(h(x))$. It is easy to see that the slopes of the level surfaces of a homothetic function are also constant along rays through the origin. A frequently used application is the assumption of homothetic preferences such that the income expansion path at given prices is a straight line through the origin. A further important implication is that a price increase for one good always means that the relative consumption of that good decreases. That is, if c^2/c^1 is the consumption of good 2 relative to good 1 before a price rise of good 2 and $\overline{c^2/c^1}$ after the price rise, then $c^2/c^1 > \overline{c^2/c^1}$.

A.2   Revenue function

Let $v = (v^1, ..., v^m)'$ be a vector of primary inputs and let $x = (x^1, ..., x^n)'$ be an output vector of goods. The state of technology determines which combinations $(\mathbf{x}, \mathbf{v})$ are feasible. We assume that the technology is convex; that is, if the two combinations $(\mathbf{x}, \mathbf{v})$ and $(\overline{\mathbf{x}}, \overline{\mathbf{v}})$ are both feasible, then so is its linear combination $(\lambda \mathbf{x} + (1 - \lambda)\overline{\mathbf{x}}, \lambda \mathbf{v} + (1 - \lambda)\overline{\mathbf{v}})$ for all scalars $\lambda \in [0, 1]$. This rules out, in particular, increasing returns to scale. Production decisions maximize total profit for given prices $\mathbf{p}$ and available inputs $\mathbf{v}$. Clearly, the optimal output depends on $\mathbf{p}$ and $\mathbf{v}$, say $\mathbf{x} = \mathbf{x}(\mathbf{p}, \mathbf{v})$. The corresponding maximum value of output, called the *revenue function* R and assumed to be twice continuously differentiable, is also a function of $\mathbf{p}$ and $\mathbf{v}$:

$$R(\mathbf{p}, \mathbf{v}) = \max_{\mathbf{x}}\{\mathbf{p}'\mathbf{x} \mid (\mathbf{x}, \mathbf{v}) \quad \text{is feasible}\} = \mathbf{p}'\mathbf{x}(\mathbf{p}, \mathbf{v})$$

The revenue function has the following properties (derivatives are indicated by subscripts):
(1) R is convex as a function of $\mathbf{p}$; thus, $\mathbf{R}_{\mathbf{pp}}(\mathbf{p}, \mathbf{v})$ is positive semi-definite.
(2) The derivative of R with respect to p^i gives the optimal supply x^i of good i; thus, $\mathbf{R}_{\mathbf{p}}(\mathbf{p}, \mathbf{v}) = \mathbf{x}(\mathbf{p}, \mathbf{v})$.
(3) R is homogeneous of degree one in $\mathbf{p}$; thus, using Euler's theorem, $\mathbf{p}'\mathbf{R}_{\mathbf{p}}(\mathbf{p}, \mathbf{v}) = \mathbf{R}_{\mathbf{p}}(\mathbf{p}, \mathbf{v})$.
(4) R_{p^i} is homogeneous of degree zero in $\mathbf{p}$ for each i; thus, $\mathbf{p}'\mathbf{R}_{\mathbf{pp}}(\mathbf{p}, \mathbf{v}) = \mathbf{0}$.
(5) R is concave as a function of $\mathbf{v}$; thus, $\mathbf{R}_{\mathbf{vv}}(\mathbf{p}, \mathbf{v})$ is negative semi-definite.
(6) The derivative of R with respect to v^i gives the shadow price (or demand price) w^i for this factor (equal to the factor price in a competitive equilibrium); thus, $\mathbf{R}_{\mathbf{v}}(\mathbf{p}, \mathbf{v}) = \mathbf{w}(\mathbf{p}, \mathbf{v})$.
(7) The effect of a change in price p^j on factor price w^i is equal to the effect of a change in input v^i on output supply x^j; this follows simply from $w^i_{p^j}(\mathbf{p}, \mathbf{v}) = R_{v^i p^j}(\mathbf{p}, \mathbf{v}) = R_{p^j v^i}(\mathbf{p}, \mathbf{v}) = x^j_{v^i}(\mathbf{p}, \mathbf{v})$.
(8) w^i is homogeneous of degree one in $\mathbf{p}$; thus, $\mathbf{w}(\mathbf{p}, \mathbf{v}) = \mathbf{R}_{\mathbf{vp}}(\mathbf{p}, \mathbf{v})\mathbf{p}$.

(9) If there are constant returns to scale x^i is homogeneous of degree one in $\mathbf{v}$; thus, $\mathbf{x}(\mathbf{p}, \mathbf{v}) = \mathbf{R}_{\mathbf{vp}}(\mathbf{p}, \mathbf{v})\mathbf{p}$.

To prove property 1, suppose $\bar{\mathbf{p}}$ is the convex linear combination of $\bar{\mathbf{p}}$ and $\tilde{\mathbf{p}}$, $\bar{\mathbf{p}} = \lambda\bar{\mathbf{p}} + (1 - \lambda)\tilde{\mathbf{p}}$ for some $\lambda \in [0, 1]$, and let $\bar{\tilde{\mathbf{x}}}$, $\bar{\mathbf{x}}$ and $\tilde{\mathbf{x}}$ be the corresponding revenue-maximizing bundles. By definition $R(\bar{\mathbf{p}}, \mathbf{v}) = \bar{\mathbf{p}}'\bar{\mathbf{x}} \geq \bar{\mathbf{p}}'\bar{\tilde{\mathbf{x}}}$ and $R(\tilde{\mathbf{p}}, \mathbf{v}) = \tilde{\mathbf{p}}'\tilde{\mathbf{x}} \geq \tilde{\mathbf{p}}'\bar{\tilde{\mathbf{x}}}$. Thus, using these two simple facts, it follows that $R(\bar{\mathbf{p}}, \mathbf{v}) = \bar{\mathbf{p}}'\bar{\tilde{\mathbf{x}}} = [\lambda\bar{\mathbf{p}} + (1 - \lambda)\tilde{\mathbf{p}}]'\bar{\tilde{\mathbf{x}}} = \lambda\bar{\mathbf{p}}'\bar{\tilde{\mathbf{x}}} + (1 - \lambda)\tilde{\mathbf{p}}'\bar{\tilde{\mathbf{x}}} \leq \lambda R(\bar{\mathbf{p}}, \mathbf{v}) + (1 - \lambda)R(\tilde{\mathbf{p}}, \mathbf{v})$.

The intuition behind the convexity of the revenue function in prices is fairly obvious. Suppose we graph revenue as a function of a single price only, with all the other prices held constant. If the price of the good rises revenue will never go down, but it will go up at an increasing rate. Why? Suppose that, after the price rise, we just behave passively and continue to produce what we made before. Then revenue would go up linearly. The maximum revenue must exceed this "passive" strategy since we can adjust the composition of the commodity bundle advantageously. Therefore, revenue is convex in prices.

To prove property 2, let $\bar{\mathbf{x}}$ be the revenue-maximizing bundle at prices $\bar{\mathbf{p}}$. Define the function

$$g(\mathbf{p}) = R(\mathbf{p}, \mathbf{v}) - \mathbf{p}'\bar{\mathbf{x}}$$

Since $R(\mathbf{p}, \mathbf{v})$ is maximum revenue this function is always non-negative. At $\mathbf{p} = \bar{\mathbf{p}}$ we have $g(\mathbf{p}) = 0$. At this minimum value of $g(\mathbf{p})$ its derivative must be zero:

$$g_{p^i}(\mathbf{p}) = R_{p^i}(\mathbf{p}, \mathbf{v}) - \bar{x}^i = 0$$

Thus, the revenue-maximizing output bundle is given simply by the vector of derivatives of the revenue function. The economic intuition is again obvious. If we are producing at a revenue-maximizing point and the price of one of the goods increases, there will be a direct effect in that the revenue of the good with the higher price will rise (proportional to the production level of that good). There would also be an indirect effect in that we would want to change the output mix. Since we are operating at a revenue-maximizing point, no such changes are profitable for very small (infinitesimal) changes in price.

Property 3 is obvious since the parameter $\mathbf{p}$ does not affect the constraint. Increasing every price by the same factor θ, therefore, does not affect the composition of the revenue-maximizing bundle such that revenue must go up by the same factor θ. Property 4 is an immediate consequence of property 3.

The proof of property 5 is similar to that of property 1. Fix the price level $\mathbf{p}$ and suppose that $\bar{\mathbf{x}}$ and $\tilde{\mathbf{x}}$ maximize revenue for $\bar{\mathbf{v}}$ and $\tilde{\mathbf{v}}$ at that price level. Since the technology is convex the convex linear combination of $\bar{\mathbf{x}}$ and $\tilde{\mathbf{x}}$, say $\hat{\mathbf{x}} = \lambda\bar{\mathbf{x}} + (1-\lambda)\tilde{\mathbf{x}}$, can be produced using the convex linear combination of $\bar{\mathbf{v}}$ and $\tilde{\mathbf{v}}$, say $\hat{\mathbf{v}} = \lambda\bar{\mathbf{x}} + (1-\lambda)\tilde{\mathbf{x}}$. Since the revenue-maximizing bundle at $\hat{\mathbf{v}}$ must be no less than the revenue of any possible producible combination (in particular, the revenue of producing $\hat{\mathbf{x}}$) this gives $R(\mathbf{p}, \hat{\mathbf{v}}) = R(\mathbf{p}, \lambda\bar{\mathbf{v}} + (1-\lambda)\tilde{\mathbf{v}}) \geq \mathbf{p}'\hat{\mathbf{x}} = \mathbf{p}'[\lambda\bar{\mathbf{x}} + (1-\lambda)\tilde{\mathbf{x}}] = \lambda\mathbf{p}'\bar{\mathbf{x}} + (1-\lambda)\mathbf{p}'\tilde{\mathbf{x}} = \lambda R(\mathbf{p}, \bar{\mathbf{v}}) + (1-\lambda)R(\mathbf{p}, \tilde{\mathbf{v}})$.

The concavity of the revenue function in the constraints is the mirror image of the convexity of the revenue function in prices. The proof of properties 6–9 is straightforward.

Example A.1 Consider maximizing revenue for a country that produces two goods, x^1 and x^2, with prices p^1 and p^2, one factor of production (labor) supplied perfectly inelastically up to l, subject to the production functions: $x^1 = (l^1)^\alpha$, $x^2 = (l^2)^\alpha$, where $l^1 + l^2 = l$ and $0 < \alpha < 1$. Define $\delta = 1/(1-\alpha) > 1$, then standard maximization of $p^1x^1 + p^2x^2$ keeping these restrictions in mind leads to

$$l^i(p^1, p^2, l) = [(p^1)^\delta + (p^2)^\delta]^{-1}(p^i)^\delta l \text{ for } i = 1, 2$$

The revenue function is therefore defined as

$$R(p^1, p^2, l) = p^1x^1(p^1, p^2, l) + p^2x^2(p^1, p^2, l) = [(p^1)^\delta + (p^2)^\delta]^{1/\delta}l^\alpha$$

which is obviously homogeneous of degree one in $\mathbf{p}$ (property 3). Differentiation of the revenue function gives

$$R_{p^i}(p^1, p^2, l) - [(p^1)^\delta + (p^2)^\delta]^{-\alpha}(p^i)^{\alpha\delta}l^\alpha - [l^i(p^1, p^2, l)]^\alpha$$
$$= x^i(p^1, p^2, l) \quad (property\ 2)$$

In a competitive economy the wage rate is equal to the marginal value product of labor in either sector:

$$w = p^i\alpha(l^i)^{\alpha-1} = \alpha p^i\{[(p^1)^\delta + (p^2)^\delta]^{-1}(p^i)^\delta l\}^{\alpha-1}$$
$$= \alpha[(p^1)^\delta + (p^2)^\delta]^{1/\delta}l^{\alpha-1} = R_l(p^1, p^2, l) \quad (property\ 6)$$

Clearly, w is homogeneous of degree one in $\mathbf{p}$ (property 8) such that $w = p^1R_{lp^1}(p^1, p^2, l) + p^2R_{lp^2}(p^1, p^2, l)$. The reader may verify properties 1, 4, 5 and 7 above. Property 9 does not hold since the technology in this example does not exhibit constant returns to scale.

A.3   Indirect utility function

Let $\mathbf{d} = (d^1, ..., d^n)'$ be a vector of consumption goods and let $f(\mathbf{d})$ be the utility level attained from consuming this bundle of goods, where f is assumed to be strictly quasi-concave. The consumer wishes to maximize his utility for a given level of income y at given goods prices $\mathbf{p}$. Clearly, the resulting optimal choice of consumption depends on prices $\mathbf{p}$ and income y; it is called the (Marshallian) demand function $\mathbf{d}(\mathbf{p}, y)$. Substituting the optimal choice of consumption in the utility function gives the maximum utility attainable at prices $\mathbf{p}$ and income y; it is called the *indirect utility function W*:

$$W(\mathbf{p}, y) = \max_{\mathbf{d}} \{ f(\mathbf{d}) \mid \mathbf{p}'\mathbf{d} = y \} = f(\mathbf{d}(\mathbf{p}, y))$$

The indirect utility function has the following properties:
(1) W is non-increasing in $\mathbf{p}$.
(2) W is non-decreasing in y.
(3) W is quasi-convex in $\mathbf{p}$.
(4) W is homogeneous of degree zero in $(\mathbf{p}, y)$.
    We will illustrate the remaining part of the appendix using the simplest Cobb–Douglas utility function. The proof of most statements in the sequel are analogous to those given in section A.2.

> **Example A.2** Consider maximizing utility $f(\mathbf{d}) = (d^1)^{\alpha_1}(d^2)^{\alpha_2}$, with $\alpha_1 + \alpha_2 = 1$, subject to the budget constraint $p^1 d^1 + p^2 d^2 = y$. Simple maximization leads to the Marshallian demand functions $d^i(\mathbf{p}, y) = (\alpha_i)(p^i)^{-1}y$, such that the indirect utility function is given by $W(\mathbf{p}, y) = (\alpha_1)^{\alpha_1}(\alpha_2)^{\alpha_2}(p^1)^{-\alpha_1}(p^2)^{-\alpha_2}y$. The four properties above are now readily verified.

A.4   Expenditure function

The consumer's dual problem of maximizing utility for given income and prices is minimizing expenditure E to attain utility level u at given prices $\mathbf{p}$. The solutions to this problem are the compensated (Hicksian) demand functions and depend, of course, on prices $\mathbf{p}$ and utility u to be attained, say $\mathbf{c}(\mathbf{p}, u)$. The corresponding minimal expenditure $\mathbf{p}'\mathbf{c}(\mathbf{p}, u)$ is defined as the *expenditure function E*:

$$E(\mathbf{p}, u) = \min_{\mathbf{c}}\{\mathbf{p}'\mathbf{c} \mid f(\mathbf{c}) \geq u\} = \mathbf{p}'\mathbf{c}(\mathbf{p}, u)$$

The expenditure function has the following properties:
(1) E is a rising function of u.
(2) E is non-decreasing in $\mathbf{p}$.
(3) E is homogeneous of degree one in $\mathbf{p}$.
(4) E is concave in $\mathbf{p}$; thus $\mathbf{E_{pp}}$ is negative semi-definite.
(5) The derivative of E with respect to p^i is equal to compensated demand c^i; thus $\mathbf{E_p}(\mathbf{p}, u) = \mathbf{c}(\mathbf{p}, u)$.

Example A.3 Consider minimizing expenditure $p^1 c^1 + p^2 c^2$ for achieving Cobb Douglas utility level u, that is, subject to $f(\mathbf{c}) = (c^1)^{\alpha 1}(c^2)^{\alpha 2} \geq u$, with $\alpha_1 + \alpha_2 = 1$. Straightforward expenditure minimization leads to the Hicksian demand functions $c^j(\mathbf{p}, u) = (\alpha_j)^{\alpha i}(\alpha_i)^{-\alpha i}(p^i)^{\alpha i}(p^j)^{-\alpha i}u$, $i \neq j$, such that the expenditure function is given by $E(\mathbf{p}, u) = (\alpha_1)^{-\alpha 1}(\alpha_2)^{-\alpha 2}(p^1)^{\alpha 1}(p^2)^{\alpha 2}u$ (use the fact that $\alpha_1 + \alpha_2 = 1$; note the similarity in structure of the indirect utility function and the expenditure function). The reader may now verify the five properties of the expenditure function above, especially property 5.

A.5   Relations between the indirect utility function and the expenditure function

An elementary consistency condition on the relation between the indirect utility function and the expenditure function is that income y just suffices to achieve utility level u, that is:

$$y = E(\mathbf{p}, u)$$

For fixed prices $\mathbf{p}$ this gives a relation between income y and utility u, from which it follows that $(\partial u / \partial y) = 1/E_u(\mathbf{p}, u)$ such that $1/E_u(\mathbf{p}, u)$ gives the marginal utility of income.

The following four identities are obvious:
(1) $E(\mathbf{p}, W(\mathbf{p}, y)) = y$; the minimal expenditure to reach utility $W(\mathbf{p}, y)$ is y.
(2) $W(\mathbf{p}, E(\mathbf{p}, u)) = u$; the maximal utility from income $E(\mathbf{p}, u)$ is u.
(3) $c^i(\mathbf{p}, u) = d^i(\mathbf{p}, E(\mathbf{p}, u))$; the Hicksian demand at utility u is the same as the Marshallian demand at income $E(\mathbf{p}, u)$.
(4) $d^i(\mathbf{p}, y) = c^i(\mathbf{p}, W(\mathbf{p}, y))$; the Marshallian demand at income y is the same as the Hicksian demand at utility $W(\mathbf{p}, y)$.

Example A.4 Using the expenditure and revenue functions derived in examples A.2 and A.3 it is trivial to establish identities 1 and 2. Since $d^i(\mathbf{p}, y) = (\alpha_i)(p^i)^{-1}y$ (see example A.2) it follows from example A.3 that

$$d^i(\mathbf{p}, E(\mathbf{p}, u)) = (\alpha_i)(p^i)^{-1}\{(\alpha_1)^{-\alpha1}(\alpha_2)^{-\alpha2}(p^1)^{\alpha1}(p^2)^{\alpha2}u\}$$
$$= (\alpha_j)^{\alpha i}(\alpha_i)^{-\alpha i}(p^i)^{\alpha i}(p^j)^{-\alpha i}u = c^j(\mathbf{p}, u) \qquad \text{(identity 3)}.$$

Similarly, by reversed reasoning using examples A.2 and A.3 it follows that

$$c^j(\mathbf{p}, W(\mathbf{p}, y)) = (\alpha_j)^{\alpha i}(\alpha_i)^{-\alpha i}(p^i)^{\alpha i}(p^j)^{-\alpha i}\{(\alpha_1)^{\alpha1}(\alpha_2)^{\alpha2}(p^1)^{-\alpha1}(p^2)^{-\alpha2}y\}$$
$$= (\alpha_i)(p^i)^{-1}y = d^i(\mathbf{p}, y) \qquad \text{(identity 4)}$$

Differentiating the first identity above with respect to y and the second identity with respect to u gives

$$E_u(\mathbf{p}, W(\mathbf{p}, y))W_y(\mathbf{p}, y) = 1$$
$$W_y(\mathbf{p}, E(\mathbf{p}, u))E_u(\mathbf{p}, u) = 1$$

Differentiating the first identity above with respect to price p^i, and then using the derivative property of the expenditure function gives

$$E_{p^i}(\mathbf{p}, W(\mathbf{p}, y)) + E_u(\mathbf{p}, W(\mathbf{p}, y))W_{p^i}(\mathbf{p}, y) = 0$$
$$c^i(\mathbf{p}, W(\mathbf{p}, y)) + E_u(\mathbf{p}, W(\mathbf{p}, y))W_{p^i}(\mathbf{p}, y) = 0$$

Using $E_u W_y = 1$ and the fourth identity above, and rearranging leads to

- Roy's identity: $$d^i(\mathbf{p}, y) = -\frac{W_{p^i}(\mathbf{p}, y)}{W_y(\mathbf{p}, y)}$$

Differentiating the third identity above with respect to price p^j, and then using the derivative property of the expenditure function gives

$$c^i_{p^j}(\mathbf{p}, u) = d^i_{p^j}(\mathbf{p}, E(\mathbf{p}, u)) + d^i_y(\mathbf{p}, E(\mathbf{p}, u))E_{p^j}(\mathbf{p}, u)$$
$$c^i_{p^j}(\mathbf{p}, u) = d^i_{p^j}(\mathbf{p}, E(\mathbf{p}, u)) + d^i_y(\mathbf{p}, E(\mathbf{p}, u))c^j(\mathbf{p}, u)$$

Substituting $E(\mathbf{p}, u) = y$, $W(\mathbf{p}, y) = u$ and the third identity above, and then rearranging, gives the Slutsky equation in its conventional formulation:

- conventional Slutsky equation:

$$d^i_{p^j}(\mathbf{p}, y) = c^i_{p^j}(\mathbf{p}, W(\mathbf{p}, y)) - d^j(\mathbf{p}, y)d^i_y(\mathbf{p}, y)$$

where the Slutsky equation decomposes the response of the Marshallian demand curve to price changes into the classic substitution effect (the first term) and the income effect (the second term).

Alternatively, differentiating the fourth identity above with respect to price p^j, and then using Roy's identity, gives

$$d^i_{p^j}(\mathbf{p}, y) = c^i_{p^j}(\mathbf{p}, W(\mathbf{p}, y)) + c^i_u(\mathbf{p}, W(\mathbf{p}, y)) W_{p^j}(\mathbf{p}, y)$$

$$d^i_{p^j}(\mathbf{p}, y) = c^i_{p^j}(\mathbf{p}, W(\mathbf{p}, y)) - c^i_u(\mathbf{p}, W(\mathbf{p}, y))d^j(\mathbf{p}, y) W_y(\mathbf{p}, y)$$

Substituting $W(\mathbf{p}, y) = u$, $E(\mathbf{p}, u) = y$, $E_u W_y = 1$ and the fourth identity above gives the Slutsky equation in its dual formulation:

- dual Slutsky equation: $d^i_{p^j}(\mathbf{p}, E(\mathbf{p}, u)) = c^i_{p^j}(\mathbf{p}, u) - \dfrac{c^j(\mathbf{p}, u)}{E_u(\mathbf{p}, u)} c^i_u(\mathbf{p}, u)$

The main text in the book uses this formulation of the Slutsky equation, with a slight simplification because we usually normalize such that $E_u(\mathbf{p}, u) - 1$.

Finally, the marginal propensity to consume good i, μ_i say, is defined as the change in the expenditure on good i as a result of a change in the income level, that is $\mu_i = p^i d^i_y(\mathbf{p}, y)$. From the identity $\mathbf{p}'\mathbf{d}(\mathbf{p}, y) = y$ it follows that $\mathbf{p}'\mathbf{d}_y(\mathbf{p}, y) = 1$, that is, the sum over all goods of the marginal propensities to consume is unity: $\sum_i p^i d^i_y(\mathbf{p}, y) = \sum_i \mu_i = 1$. From the third identity above it follows that

- Marginal propensity to consume good i:

$$\mu_i = p^i d^i_y(\mathbf{p}, E(\mathbf{p}, u)) = \frac{p^i c^i_u(\mathbf{p}, u)}{E_u(\mathbf{p}, u)}$$

and thus

$$\sum_i \frac{p^i c^i_u(\mathbf{p}, u)}{E_u(\mathbf{p}, u)} = 1$$

The main text of the book usually normalizes such that $E_u(\mathbf{p}, u) - 1$, in which case $p^i c^i_u(\mathbf{p}, u)$ is identical to good i's marginal propensity to consume and $\sum_i p^i c^i_u(\mathbf{p}, u) = 1$. Moreover, the main text of the book usually applies this relationship and the Slutsky equation to the *net* demand for goods. Verification of the statements regarding the marginal propensity to consume, Roy's identity and the two formulations of the Slutsky equation for the examples A.2 and A.3 is left to the reader.

A.6   Constant elasticity of substitution

A well-known special production or utility function which is frequently used in analytic and numerical examples is the constant elasticity of substitution (CES) function. The CES function is convenient to work with and contains several other functions as special cases. We will demonstrate this using a CES utility function and derive its dual expenditure function. Let the consumer's utility function U be of the following CES type:

$$U(c^1, c^2) = \left[(a_1 c^1)^\rho + (a_2 c^2)^\rho \right]^{\frac{1}{\rho}} \text{ where } \rho \in (-\infty, 1] \setminus \{0\} \quad \text{(A.1)}$$

A.6.1   The CES name

We first demonstrate the origin of the name CES. Since the utility function in equation (A.1) is homogeneous of degree one it suffices to analyze expenditure minimization to reach unit utility. To achieve any other arbitrary utility level we just increase or decrease our expenditure proportionally. Thus we must ultimately solve the following unit expenditure minimization problem e:

$$e(p^1, p^2) = \min_{c^1, c^2} p^1 c^1 + p^2 c^2 \text{ s.t. } \left[(a_1 c^1)^\rho + (a_2 c^2)^\rho \right]^{1/\rho} = 1 \quad \text{(A.2)}$$

If λ is the Lagrange multiplier the first-order conditions are

$$p^1 = a_1 \lambda \left[(a_1 c^1)^\rho + (a_2 c^2)^\rho \right]^{\frac{1}{\rho} - 1} (a_1 c^1)^{\rho - 1} \quad \text{(A.3)}$$

$$p^2 = a_2 \lambda \left[(a_1 c^1)^\rho + (a_2 c^2)^\rho \right]^{\frac{1}{\rho} - 1} (a_2 c^2)^{\rho - 1} \quad \text{(A.4)}$$

Taking the ratio of equations (A.3) and (A.4)

$$\frac{p^1}{p^2} = \left(\frac{a_1}{a_2} \right)^\rho \left(\frac{c^1}{c^2} \right)^{\rho - 1} ; \quad \text{hence} \quad \frac{c^1}{c^2} = \left(\frac{a_1}{a_2} \right)^{\frac{\rho}{1-\rho}} \left(\frac{p^1}{p^2} \right)^{\frac{1}{\rho - 1}} \quad \text{(A.5)}$$

There are two goods, c^1 and c^2, with concomitant prices, p^1 and p^2. For every price ratio p^1/p^2 there is a different expenditure-minimizing combination of consumption goods c^1/c^2. An important characteristic of an iso-utility curve is the ease with which it can substitute one good for another as a result of a relative price change. This characteristic is called the elasticity of substitution, σ_c say, and is defined as the (negative) of the change in relative consumption of goods as a result of a change in the relative price:

$$\sigma_c \equiv -\frac{\partial\left(\frac{c^1}{c^2}\right)\frac{p^1}{p^2}}{\partial\left(\frac{p^1}{p^2}\right)\frac{c^1}{c^2}} \tag{A.6}$$

From the second part of equation (A.5) it follows, using the definition above, that for the CES class of utility functions defined in equation (A.1) the elasticity of substitution is equal to

$$\sigma_c = \frac{1}{1-\rho} \tag{A.7}$$

which is, not surprisingly given the name CES, a constant. Thus, for the CES class of utility functions the ease with which a consumer can substitute one good for another is everywhere the same along the iso-utility curve. Since $\rho \in (-\infty, 1] \setminus \{0\}$ it follows that σ_c is positive, more precisely $\sigma_c \in (0, \infty) \setminus \{1\}$.

A.6.2   Some special cases

As mentioned in the introduction to this section the CES function contains some interesting other functions as special cases. For illustrative purposes we assume $a_1 = a_2 = 0.5$ in this subsection. The three special cases discussed below are illustrated in figure A.1.[1]
  (1) *The linear utility function* ($\rho = 1$). Simple substitution yields

$$U(c^1, c^2) = a_1 c^1 + a_2 c^2$$

The elasticity of substitution for the linear utility function is infinite.
  (2) *The Cobb Douglas utility function* ($\lim_{\rho \to 0}$). It can be shown that equation (A.1) reduces to

$$U(c^1, c^2) = \left(c^1\right)^{a_1} \left(c^2\right)^{a_2}$$

---

[1] A simple proof on the claims for the second and third special cases below can be found in Varian (1992, ch. 1).

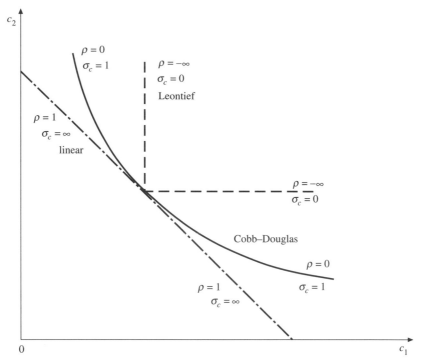

Figure A.1. *Special cases of the utility function*

The elasticity of substitution for the Cobb–Douglas utility function is one.

(3) *The Leontief (fixed proportion) utility function* ($\lim_{\rho \to -\infty}$). It can be shown that equation (A.1) reduces to

$$U(c^1, c^2) = \min\{c^1, c^2\}$$

The elasticity of substitution for the Leontief utility function is zero.

A.6.3   The expenditure function

We now derive the unit utility expenditure function dual to the utility function of equation (A.1). Multiply the first part of equation (A.5) by c^1/c^2 to get equation (A.8). Add 1 to both sides of equation (A.8) to get equation (A.9). Since $p^1 c^1 + p^2 c^2 = e(p^1, p^2)$ and $(a_1 c^1)^\rho + (a_2 c^2)^\rho = 1$, equation (A.9) reduces to equation (A.10). Solve equation (A.10) for

c^2 to get equation (A.11). Multiply by p^2 to get equation (A.12). Analogously to (A.12), equation (A.13) follows for $p^1 c^1$. Add equations (A.12) and (A.13) to get equation (A.14).

$$\frac{p^1 c^1}{p^2 c^2} = \frac{(a_1 c^1)^\rho}{(a_2 c^2)^\rho} \tag{A.8}$$

$$\frac{p^1 c^1 + p^2 c^2}{p^2 c^2} = \frac{(a_1 c^1)^\rho + (a_2 c^2)^\rho}{(a_2 c^2)^\rho} \tag{A.9}$$

$$\frac{e(p^1, p^2)}{p^2 c^2} = \frac{1}{(a_2 c^2)^\rho} \tag{A.10}$$

$$c^2 = \left[e(p^1, p^2) \right]^{\frac{1}{1-\rho}} (a_2)^{\frac{\rho}{1-\rho}} (p^2)^{\frac{1}{\rho-1}} \tag{A.11}$$

$$p^2 c^2 = \left[e(p^1, p^2) \right]^{\frac{1}{1-\rho}} \left(\frac{p^2}{a_2} \right)^{\frac{\rho}{\rho-1}} \tag{A.12}$$

$$p^1 c^1 = \left[e(p^1, p^2) \right]^{\frac{1}{1-\rho}} \left(\frac{p^1}{a_1} \right)^{\frac{\rho}{\rho-1}} \tag{A.13}$$

$$p^1 c^1 + p^2 c^2 = \left[e(p^1, p^2) \right]^{\frac{1}{1-\rho}} \left[\left(\frac{p^1}{a_1} \right)^{\frac{\rho}{\rho-1}} + \left(\frac{p^2}{a_2} \right)^{\frac{\rho}{\rho-1}} \right] \tag{A.14}$$

Finally, note again that $p^1 c^1 + p^2 c^2 = e(p^1, p^2)$ and solve equation (A.14) for the unit utility expenditure function $e(p^1, p^2)$ we are looking for.

$$e(p^1, p^2) = \left[\left(\frac{p^1}{a_1} \right)^{\frac{\rho}{\rho-1}} + \left(\frac{p^2}{a_2} \right)^{\frac{\rho}{\rho-1}} \right]^{\frac{\rho-1}{\rho}} \tag{A.15}$$

We immediately note that the structure of the CES utility function in equation (A.1) is exactly the same as the structure of the expenditure function in equation (A.15), with the role of parameter ρ from equation (A.1) replaced by the parameter $\frac{\rho}{\rho-1}$ in equation (A.15). Since we saw that the utility function has a constant elasticity of substitution in consumption, σ_c (equal to $\frac{1}{1-\rho}$; see equation [A.7]), it is obvious that the expenditure function has a constant elasticity of substitution in prices, σ_e say. Recalling that $\frac{\rho}{\rho-1}$ in equation (A.15) plays the role of ρ in equation (A.1) and using the formula for σ_c in equation (A.7) it is easy to see that

$$\sigma_e = \frac{1}{1 - \left(\frac{\rho}{\rho-1} \right)} = 1 - \rho = \frac{1}{\sigma_c} \tag{A.16}$$

Equation (A.16) very clearly demonstrates the duality of consumption and prices. If the consumption elasticity of substitution is high, then the price elasticity of substitution is low, and vice versa. Finally, since equation (A.15) gives the unit utility expenditure function, the expenditure function itself, that is the minimum outlays at prices p^1 and p^2 to achieve utility u, is given by

$$E(p^1, p^2) = \left[\left(\frac{p^1}{a_1} \right)^{\frac{\rho}{\rho - 1}} + \left(\frac{p^2}{a_2} \right)^{\frac{\rho}{\rho - 1}} \right]^{\frac{\rho - 1}{\rho}} u \tag{A.17}$$

A.6.4   Some derivatives

To avoid cumbersome notation we assume in this subsection that $a_1 = a_2 = 1$ and we define $\eta \equiv \rho/(\rho - 1)$. Thus, like ρ, we have $\eta \in (-\infty, 1] \setminus \{0\}$, while η approaches one (minus infinity) if ρ approaches minus infinity (one). This reduces the expenditure function in equation (A.17) to

$$E(p^1, p^2) = \left[(p^1)^\eta + (p^2)^\eta \right]^{\frac{1}{\eta}} u \tag{A.18}$$

Now note that

$$E_{p^1}(p^1, p^2) = \left[(p^1)^\eta + (p^2)^\eta \right]^{\frac{1}{\eta} - 1} (p^1)^{\eta - 1} u \tag{A.19}$$

The reader may wish to check that this is indeed the Hicksian demand for good 1. Define $\Omega \equiv \left[(p^1)^\eta + (p^2)^\eta \right]^{\frac{1}{\eta}}$ for notational convenience. It follows that

$$E_{p^1 p^1}(p^1, p^2) = (1 - \eta)\Omega^{-2}(p^1)^{2\eta - 2} u - (1 - \eta)\Omega^{-1}(p^1)^{\eta - 2} u$$

Collect terms

$$E_{p^1 p^1}(p^1, p^2) = -(1 - \eta)\Omega^{-2}(p^1)^{\eta - 2} u \left[-(p^1)^\eta + (p^1)^\eta + (p^2)^\eta \right]$$

Hence

$$E_{p^1 p^1}(p^1, p^2) = -(1 - \eta)\left[(p^1)^\eta + (p^2)^\eta \right]^{\frac{1}{\eta} - 2} (p^1)^{\eta - 2}(p^2)^\eta u < 0 \tag{A.20}$$

For the second-order cross-price derivative we get

$$E_{p^1 p^2}(p^1, p^2) = (1 - \eta)\left[(p^1)^\eta + (p^2)^\eta\right]^{\frac{1}{\eta}-2}(p^1)^{\eta-1}(p^2)^{\eta-1}u > 0 \qquad (A.21)$$

Finally, the reader may wish to verify that indeed $E_{p^1 p^1} E_{p^2 p^2} - \left(E_{p^1 p^2}\right)^2 = 0$.

A.7 Dynamic optimization

Economic agents are frequently interested in solving dynamic optimization problems. Producers, for example, may be looking for optimal investment opportunities, consumers may wish to solve an optimal savings problem, while the government may try to maximize its chances of re-election by solving a dynamic "fine-tuning" problem. Various methods to solve dynamic problems, such as dynamic programming and the calculus of variations, have been developed over the years. For most purposes, however, the maximum principle of optimal control, developed by a team of Russian mathematicians (Lev Pontryagin *et al.*, 1962), is most useful as it can directly deal with general constraints on the control variables. This overview is brief. For further details, and many examples and applications, we refer the interested reader to, for example, Intriligator (1971), Blanchard and Fisher (1989) or Barro and Sala-I-Martin (1995).

A.7.1 Problem statement

Equations (A.22)–(A.25) describe a general dynamic optimization problem. The economic agent wants to maximize an objective function, given in (A.22), over a certain time period by choosing a *control variable* c for each instant of time t. The initial time is denoted 0, while the length of the time horizon T may be infinite. The overdot in equation (A.23) denotes the derivative with respect to time t. The constraint in (A.23), called the *transition equation* or *equation of motion*, is therefore dynamic and describes the evolution of the economy over time as represented by the change in the *state variable* k. Actually, there is a continuum of constraints, one for every point in time between 0 and T. The initial level of the state variable at time 0 is given in equation (A.24), while (A.25) indicates that the state variable cannot be negative at the end of the planning horizon.

$$\max_{c(t)} W(0) = \int_0^T U(c(t), k(t), t)dt + F(k(T), T), \quad \text{s.t.} \quad \text{(A.22)}$$

$$\dot{k}(t) = G(c(t), k(t), t) \tag{A.23}$$

$$k(0) = k_0 > 0, \quad \text{given} \tag{A.24}$$

$$k(T) \geq 0 \tag{A.25}$$

In general, the control variable c can be changed instantaneously (at least within a certain range) while the state variable k adjusts slowly over time, that is without discontinuities. Think of a car where you can immediately push the gas pedal to the floor (representing the control variable), but it takes some time before the speed of the car has increased from 50 to 80 kilometers per hour (representing the state variable). Similarly, if you push the brake pedal as hard as you can it will still take a while before the car stops. Note that the objective function depends on, or is influenced by, the control variable, the state variable and calendar time. In the car example, these may influence fuel efficiency, the need for speed and the time you want to arrive at your destination, respectively.

A.7.2   First-order conditions

This subsection gives a "heuristic" derivation of the first-order conditions for a dynamic optimization problem. The maximum principle can be considered the extension of the Lagrange multiplier method to such dynamic optimization problems. Proceeding in a way analogous to static problems we add a new variable $\psi(t)$, called the co-state variable, associated with the differential equation constraint in equation (A.23)[2] The co-state variable, which can be interpreted as the shadow price of the state variable, thus varies over time, such that the inner product of the co-state variable and the constraint are put under the integral sign and the Lagrangian is given in (A.26).

$$L = \int_0^T \left\{ U(c(t), k(t), t) + \psi(t) \left[G(c(t), k(t), t) - \dot{k}(t) \right] \right\} dt + F(k(T), T) \tag{A.26}$$

We now proceed in two steps. As in the static optimization problem, a saddle point of the Lagrangian, maximizing with respect to the control variable c and minimizing with respect to the co-state variable ψ, would yield the solution.

---

[2] Alternative names for co-state variables are "multipliers," "adjoint variables," "dual variables," and "auxiliary variables."

First, a change of the co-state variable trajectory to $\psi(t) + \Delta\psi(t)$, where $\Delta\psi(t)$ is any continuous function of time, would change the Lagrangian by

$$\Delta L = \int_0^T \Delta\psi \left[G(c(t), k(t), t) - \dot{k}(t) \right] dt \qquad (A.27)$$

Setting the change in the Lagrangian equal to zero, the first-order necessary condition for minimizing L by choice of ψ requires that the equation of motion is satisfied:

$$\dot{k}(t) = G(c(t), k(t), t) \qquad (A.28)$$

Second, define the first two expressions in (A.26) to be the *Hamiltonian function* $\hat{H}$ as given in (A.29). Now note that the term $-\psi(t)\dot{k}(t)$ in equation (A.26) can be integrated by parts to yield (A.30).

$$\hat{H}(c, k, \psi, t) \equiv U(c, k, t) + \psi G(c, k, t) \qquad (A.29)$$

$$L = \int_0^T \left\{ \hat{H}(c, k, \psi, t) + \dot{\psi}k \right\} dt + F(k(T), T) - [\psi(T)k(T) \quad \psi(0)k(0)] \, (A.30)$$

Consider now a change in the control trajectory from $c(t)$ to $c(t) + \Delta c(t)$ with a corresponding change in the state trajectory from $k(t)$ to $k(t) + \Delta k(t)$. The change in the Lagrangian is

$$\Delta L = \int_0^T \left\{ [H_c]\Delta c + \left[H_k + \dot{\psi} \right]\Delta k \right\} dt + [F_k - \psi(T)]\Delta k(T) \quad (A.31)$$

For a maximum, the change in the Lagrangian must vanish for any $\Delta c(t)$, implying that

$$\dot{H}_c - 0 \quad \text{for} \quad 0 \leq t \leq T \qquad (A.32)$$

$$\dot{\psi} = -\hat{H}_k \quad \text{for} \quad 0 \leq t \leq T \qquad (A.33)$$

$$\psi(T) = F_k \qquad (A.34)$$

Thus equations (A.32)–(A.34) are necessary for an optimum to the dynamic optimization problem. Moreover, an inequality constraint in a static optimization problem gives rise to a complementary-slackness condition. The same holds for this dynamic optimization problem since the state variable cannot be negative at the end of the planning horizon:

$$\psi(T)k(T) = 0 \qquad\qquad (A.35)$$

This so-called *transversality condition* indicates that if some of the state variable is left at the end of the period ($k(T) > 0$), then its shadow price must be zero ($\psi(T) = 0$). Alternatively, if the state variable has a positive value at the end of the planning horizon ($\psi(T) > 0$), then none of it must be left in the end ($k(T) = 0$). Finally, if the planning horizon is infinite rather than finite, then the transversality condition becomes

$$\lim_{t\to\infty} \psi(t)k(t) = 0 \qquad\qquad (A.36)$$

A.7.3 A cookbook procedure

To summarize the procedure of the previous subsection: if you want to find the solution to the dynamic problem (A.22)–(A.25) you start by defining the Hamiltonian $\hat{H}$, using the co-state variable ψ:

$$\hat{H} = U(c,k,t) + \psi(t)G(c,k,t) \qquad\qquad (A.37)$$

Then you take the derivative of the Hamiltonian with respect to the control variable and set it equal to zero (equation [A.38]), and the derivative with respect to the state variable and set it equal to *minus* the change of the co-state variable over time (equation [A.39]). Finally, depending on whether or not the planning horizon is finite, the transversality condition is given by the first or second part of equation (A.40), respectively.

$$\hat{H}_c = U_c + \psi G_c = 0 \qquad\qquad (A.38)$$
$$\hat{H}_k = U_k + \psi G_k = -\dot{\psi} \qquad\qquad (A.39)$$
$$\psi(T)k(T) = 0 \quad \text{or} \quad \lim_{t\to\infty} \psi(t)k(t) = 0 \qquad\qquad (A.40)$$

Combining equations (A.38) and (A.39) with the evolution of the state variable over time (equation [A.23]) gives two differential equations in the variables k and ψ. We need two boundary conditions for the system to be determinate. These are given by the initial condition on $k(0)$ (see equation [A.24]) and the terminal (transversality) condition (see equation [A.40]). Alternatively, we can in principle use (A.38) to rewrite the problem into differential equations for the state variable k and the control variable c, again using the initial and terminal condition to get a determinate solution.

A.7.4   Current-value Hamiltonian

Economic dynamic problems frequently, but not always, do not depend directly on time once a discount factor is taken into account, that is, the objective function is of the form given in equation (A.41).

$$\max_{c(t)} W(0) = \int_0^T e^{-\rho t} U(c(t), k(t)) dt + F(k(T), T) \qquad \text{(A.41)}$$

If the constraints are again given in (A.23)–(A.25) the Hamiltonian would be

$$\hat{H} = e^{-\rho t} U(c, k) + \psi(t) G(c, k, t) \qquad \text{(A.42)}$$

where the shadow price $\psi(t)$ measures the value of the state variable in time-0 utils. It can be useful to measure the state variable at time t in time-t utils. This can be done by defining $q(t) \equiv \psi(t) e^{\rho t}$, such that (A.42) becomes

$$\hat{H} = e^{-\rho t} [U(c, k) + q(t) G(c, k, t)] \qquad \text{(A.43)}$$

If we now define the *current-value Hamiltonian H* as

$$H = U(c, k) + q(t) G(c, k, t) \qquad \text{(A.44)}$$

the reader may wish to verify that the cookbook procedure of the previous subsection when applied to the current-value Hamiltonian gives the conditions (A.45)–(A.47) below.

$$H_c = U_c + q G_c = 0 \qquad \text{(A.45)}$$
$$H_k = U_k + q G_k = \rho q - \dot{q} \qquad \text{(A.46)}$$
$$e^{-\rho T} q(T) k(T) = 0 \quad \text{or} \quad \lim_{t \to \infty} e^{-\rho t} q(t) k(t) = 0 \qquad \text{(A.47)}$$

Applications of the current-value Hamiltonian are given in chapter 10, starting with the neoclassical growth model in section 10.4.

References

Abe, K. 1992, Tariff reform in a small open economy with public production, *International Economic Review* 33: 209–22.

Abrams, B. A. and Lewis, K. A. 1993, Human rights and the distribution of U. S. foreign aid, *Public Choice* 77: 815–21.

Ansari, J. and Singer, H. 1982, *Rich and Poor Countries*, 3rd. edn., London, George Allen & Unwin.

Arrow, K. J. and Debreu, G. 1954, Existence of an equilibrium for a competitive economy, *Econometrica* 22: 265–90.

Association of German Economic Research Institutes 1991–5, The economic situation in Germany, *Intereconomics* 26–30: 305–8, 301–4, 309–12, 309–12 and 313–16, respectively.

Aumann, R. J. and Peleg, B. 1974, A note on Gale's example, *Journal of Mathematical Economics* 1: 209–11.

Barro, R. J. and Sala-I-Martin, X. 1995, *Economic Growth*, New York, McGraw-Hill.

Bastable, C. F. 1889, On some applications of the theory of international trade, *Quarterly Journal of Economics* 4: 1–17.

Beladi, H. 1990, Unemployment and immiserizing transfer, *Journal of Economics* 52: 253–65.

Berthélemy, J.-C. 1988, The transfer paradox in a non-Walrasian context, *Weltwirtschaftliches Archiv* 124: 420–34.

Bhaduri, A. and Skarstein, R. 1996, Short-period macroeconomic aspects of foreign aid, *Cambridge Journal of Economics* 20: 195–206.

Bhagwati, J. N. 1958, Immiserizing growth: a geometrical note, *Review of Economic Studies* 25: 201–5.

   1967, The tying of aid, in J. N. Bhagwati and R. S. Eckans (eds.), *Foreign Aid*, Harmondsworth, Penguin: 235–93.

   1968, Distortions and immiserizing growth: a generalization, *Review of Economic Studies* 35: 481–5.

   1969, Optimal policies and immiserizing growth, *American Economic Review* 59: 967–70.

   1982, Directly unproductive profit-seeking (DUP) activities, *Journal of Political Economy* 90: 988–1002.

Bhagwati, J. N., Brecher, R. A. and Hatta, T. 1983, The generalized theory of transfers and welfare: bilateral transfers in a multilateral world, *American Economic Review* 73: 606–18.

1984, The paradoxes of immiserizing growth and donor-enriching "recipient-immiserizing" transfers: a tale of two literatures, *Weltwirtschaftliches Archiv* 120: 228–43.

1985, The generalized theory of transfers and welfare: exogenous (policy-imposed) and endogenous (transfer-induced) distortions, *Quarterly Journal of Economics* 20: 697–714.

Blanchard, O. J. and Fischer, S. 1989, *Lectures on Macroeconomics*, Cambridge, Mass., MIT Press.

Blaug, M. 1978, *Economic Theory in Retrospect*, Cambridge, Cambridge University Press.

Bosworth, A. B. 1993, *Conquest and Empire: The Reign of Alexander the Great*, Cambridge, Cambridge University Press.

Brakman, S. and Garrretsen, H. 1994, Can East Germany catch up? in U. Blien, H. Herrmann and M. Koller (eds.), *Regional Entwicklung und Regionale Arbeitspolitik*, Nuremberg, Institut für Arbeitsmarkt- und Berufsforschung der Bundesanstalt für Arbeit.

Brakman, S. and Marrewijk, C. van 1991a, A note on endogenous transfers, *Journal of Economics* 54: 171–8.

1991b, On the economics of tied aid, Research Memorandum no. 444, University of Groningen.

1993, Transfer problems in a multi-country world: endogenous, optimal and coordinated aid, *Asian Journal of Economics and Social Studies* 12: 41–57.

1995, Transfers, returns to scale, tied aid and monopolistic competition, *Journal of Development Economics* 47: 333–54.

Brecher, R. A. and Bhagwati, J. N. 1982, Immiserizing transfers from abroad, *Journal of International Economics* 13: 353–64.

Carr, W. 1987, *A History of Germany 1815–1985*, 3rd. edn., London, Edward Arnold.

Chacholiades, M. 1978, *International Trade Theory and Policy*, New York, McGraw-Hill.

Chichilnisky, G. 1980, Basic goods, the effects of commodity transfers and the international economic order, *Journal of Development Economics* 7: 505–19.

1983, The transfer problem with three agents once again, *Journal of Development Economics* 13: 237–48.

Chichilnisky, G. and Heal, G. 1986, *The Evolving International Economy*, Cambridge, Cambridge University Press.

Chipman, J. S. 1974, The transfer problem once again, in Horwich and Samuelson (eds.): 19–78.

Choi, J.-Y. and Yu, S. H. E. 1987, Immiserizing transfers under variable returns to scale, *Canadian Journal of Economics* 20: 634–45.

De Nederlandse Bank, 1954, *Jaarverslag 1954*, Amsterdam.

Debreu, G. 1959, *Theory of Value*, The Cowles Foundation, Monograph 17, New Haven, Yale University Press.

Dixit, A. K. 1983, The multi-country transfer problem, *Economics Letters* 13: 49–53.

Dixit, A. K. and Norman, V. 1980, *Theory of International Trade*, Cambridge, Cambridge University Press.

Eichengreen, B. 1992, Transfer problem, in P. Newman, M. Milgate and J. Eatwell (eds.), *The New Palgrave Dictionary of Money and Finance*, London, Macmillan.

Eichengreen, B. (ed.) 1985, *The Gold Standard in Theory and History*, London, Methuen.

Elliot, G. A. 1938, Transfer of means-of-payment and the terms of international trade, *Canadian Journal of Economics and Political Science* 4: 481–92.

Ethier, W. J. and Horn, H. 1984, A new look at economic integration, in Kierzkowski (ed.): 207–29.

Feiwel, G. R. (ed.) 1985, *Issues in Contemporary Microeconomics and Welfare*, London, Macmillan.

Fluckiger, Y. 1987, The theory of transfers in a multilateral world: the customs union case, *International Trade Journal* 11: 173–92.

Fries, T. 1983, The possibility of an immiserizing transfer under uncertainty, *Journal of International Economics* 15: 297–311.

Gale, D. 1974, Exchange equilibrium and coalitions: an example, *Journal of Mathematical Economics* 1: 63–6.

Garretsen, H. 1992, *Keynes, Coordination and Beyond*, Aldershot, Edward Elgar.

Gasiorek, M., Smith, A. and Venables, A. J. 1991, Completing the internal market in the EC: factor demands and comparative advantage, in Winters and Venables (eds.): 9–30.

Geanakoplos, J. and Heal, G. 1983, A geometric explanation of the transfer paradox in a stable economy, *Journal of Development Economics* 13: 223–36.

Grilli, E. R. and Riess, M. 1992, EC aid to associated countries: distribution and determinants, *Weltwirtschaftliches Archiv* 128: 202–20.

Guesnerie, R. and Laffont, J.-J. 1978, Advantageous reallocations of initial resources, *Econometrica* 46: 835–41.

Gunning, J. W. 1983a, Basic goods, the effects of commodity transfers and the international economic order, *Journal of Development Economics* 13: 197–203.

  1983b, The transfer problem: a rejoinder, *Journal of Development Economics* 13: 249–50.

Hammond, N. G. L. 1989, *Alexander the Great: King, Commander and Statesman*, Bristol, Bristol Press.

Harris, J. R. and Todaro, M. P. 1970, Migration, unemployment and development: a two-sector analysis, *American Economic Review* 60: 126–42.

Hatzipanayotou, P. and Michael, M. 1995, Foreign aid and public goods, *Journal of Development Economics* 47: 455–67.

Healey, J. and Clift, C. 1980, The developmental rationale for aid re-examined, *ODI Review* 21: 14–34.

Hollander, J. H. 1918, International trade under depreciated paper: a criticism, *Quarterly Journal of Economics* 32: 674–90.

Hopkins, A. 1970, Aid and the balance of payments, *Economic Journal* 80: 1–22.

Horn, H. 1984, Product diversity, trade and welfare, in Kierzkowski (ed.): 51–68.

Horwich, G. and Samuelson, P. A. (eds.) 1974, *Trade, Stability and Macro-economics*, New York, Academic Press.

Hume, D. 1985 [1752], *Of the Balance of Trade*, reprinted (abridged) in Eichen-green (ed.): 39–48.

Ide, T. and Takayama, A. 1990a, Marshallian stability and long-run equilibrium in the theory of international trade with factor market distortions and variable returns to scale, *Economic Letters* 33: 101–8.

1990b, Variable returns to scale and the global correspondence principle in the theory of international trade, *Economics Letters* 33: 301–8.

Imlah, A. H. 1958, *Economic Elements in the Pax Britannica*, Cambridge, Mass., Harvard University Press.

International Monetary Fund 1996, *Balance of Payments Statistics Yearbook* 47. Washington, D. C.

1997, *World Economic Outlook* (May), Washington, D. C.

Intriligator, M. D. 1971, *Mathematical Optimization and Economic Theory*, Englewood Cliffs, Prentice-Hall.

Jepma, C. J. 1991, *The Tying of Aid*, Paris, OECD.

Jepma, C. J. and Bartels, C. P. A. 1986, *Economic Impacts of Untying of Foreign Aid of EC countries*, report for the Netherlands' General Directorate of International Cooperation, The Hague.

Jepma, C. J. and Haan, H. de 1984, De binding van de Nederlandse ontwikke-lingshulp, in C. J. Jepma, H. de Haan and M. C. Quist (eds.), *Ontwikkelingshulp en het Nederlandse bedrijfs-leven*, Leiden, Stenfert Kroese: 7–36.

Johnson, H. G. 1955, The transfer problem: a note on criteria for changes in the terms of trade, *Economica* 22: 113–21.

1956, The transfer problem and exchange stability, *Journal of Political Economy* 64: 212–25.

Jones, R. W. 1970, The transfer problem revisited, *Economica* 37: 178–84.

1975, Presumption and the transfer problem, *Journal of International Economics* 5: 263–74.

1985, Income effects and paradoxes in the theory of international trade, *Economic Journal* 95: 330–44.

Kemp, M. C. 1964, *The Pure Theory of International Trade*, Englewood Cliffs, Prentice-Hall.

1984, A note on the theory of international transfers, *Economics Letters* 14: 259–62.

1992, The static welfare economics of foreign aid: a consolidation, in Savoie and Brecher (eds.): 289–314.

1995, *The Gains from Trade and the Gains from Aid*, London, Routledge.

Kemp, M. C. and Abe, K. 1994, The transfer problem in a context of public goods, *Economics Letters* 45: 223–6.

Kemp, M. C. and Kojima, S. 1985a, Tied aid and the paradoxes of donor-enrichment and recipient-impoverishment, *International Economic Review* 26: 721–9.

1985b, The welfare economics of foreign aid, in Feiwel (ed.): 470–83.

1987, More on the welfare economics of foreign aid, *Journal of the Japanese and International Economies* 1: 97–109.

Kemp, M. C. and Shimomura, K. 1991, "Trade" or "aid"? in Takayama *et al.* (eds.): 19–35.

Kemp, M. C., van Long, N. and Shimomura, K. 1990, On the optimal timing of foreign aid, *Kobe Economic and Business Review* 35: 31–49.

Kemp, M. C. and Wong, K. 1993, Paradoxes associated with the administration of foreign aid, *Journal of Development Economics* 42: 197–204.

Keynes, J. M. 1929a, The German transfer problem, *Economic Journal* 39: 1–7.

1929b, The reparations problem: a discussion. II: A rejoinder, *Economic Journal* 39: 179–82.

1929c, Mr. Keynes' views on the transfer problem. III: A reply, *Economic Journal* 39: 404–8.

1936, *The General Theory of Employment, Interest and Money*, London, Macmillan.

Khan, M. A. 1982, Tariffs, foreign capital and immiserizing growth with urban unemployment and specific factors of production, *Journal of Development Economics* 10: 245–56.

Kierzkowski, H. (ed.) 1984, *Monopolistic Competition and International Trade*, Oxford, Clarendon Press.

Krassowski, A. 1965, *Aid and the UK Balance of Payments*, London.

Krugman, P. 1979, Increasing returns, monopolistic competition and international trade, *Journal of International Economics* 9: 469–79.

Lahiri, S. and Raimondos, P. 1995, Welfare effects of aid under quantitative trade restrictions, *Journal of International Economics* 39: 297–315.

Léonard, D. and Manning, R. 1983, Advantageous reallocations: a constructive example, *Journal of International Economics* 15: 291–5.

Leontief, W. 1936, A note on the pure theory of transfers, in *Explorations in Economics: Notes and Essays Contributed in Honor of F. W. Taussig*, New York, McGraw-Hill: 84–91.

Li, J. and Mayer, W. 1990, The transfer problem with supply effects: presumptions for terms of trade changes, *Canadian Journal of Economics* 23: 896–907.

McDougall, I. 1965, Non-traded goods and the transfer problem, *Review of Economic Studies* 32: 67–84.

Machlup, F. 1966, *International Monetary Economics*, London, George Allen & Unwin.

Majumdar, M. and Mitra, T. 1985, A result on the transfer problem in international trade theory, *Journal of International Economics* 19: 161–70.

Markusen, J. R. 1986, Explaining the volume of trade, *American Economic Review* 76: 1002–11.

Marrewijk, C. van and Verbeek, J. 1993, On opulence-driven poverty traps, *Journal of Population Economics* 6: 67–81.

May, R. S. and Dobson, N. C. 1979, The impact of the United Kingdom's bilateral aid programme on British industry, *ODI Review* 2: 1–22.

1982a, Some trade aspects of aid: the British experience, *National Westminster Bank Quarterly Review*: 46–58.

1982b, The U. K. development aid programme and the British domestic industry, *Intereconomics* 17: 20–5.

Metzler, L. A. 1942, The transfer problem reconsidered, *Journal of Political Economy* 50: 397–414.

Michael, M. S. and Marrewijk, C. van 1998, Foreign aid tied to capital transfers and economic development, *Review of Development Economics* 2: 61–75.

Mill, J. S. 1848, *Principles of Political Economy*, London, Longmans, Green and Co.

Mundell, R. A. 1960, The pure theory of international trade, *American Economic Review* 50: 67–110.

Neary, J. P. 1981, On the Harris–Todaro model with intersectoral capital mobility, *Economica* 48: 219–34.

Neary, J. P. and Roberts, K. W. S. 1980, The theory of household behavior under rationing, *European Economic Review* 13: 15–42.

Ohlin, B. 1928a, The reparations problem. I: The economic development in Germany since the stabilization and the Dawes plan, *Index* [Svenska Handelsbanken, Stockholm] April: 2–13.

1928b, The reparations problem. II: General views on international movements of capital, *Index* [Svenska Handelsbanken, Stockholm] June: 2–33.

1929a, The reparations problem: a discussion; transfer difficulties, real and imagined, *Economic Journal* 39: 172–83.

1929b, Mr. Keynes' views on the transfer problem. II: A rejoinder from Professor Ohlin, *Economic Journal* 39: 400–4.

Ohyama, M. 1974, Tariffs and the transfer problem, *KEIO Economic Studies* 11: 29–45.

Opeskin, B. R. 1996, The moral foundations of foreign aid, *World Development* 24: 21–44.

Pack, H. and Pack, J. R. 1993, Foreign aid and the question of fungibility, *Review of Economics and Statistics* 75: 258–65.

Pigou, A. C. 1932, The effect of reparations on the real ratio of international interchange, *Economic Journal* 42: 532–43.

1950, Unrequited imports, *Economic Journal* 60: 241–54.

Polemarchakis, H. 1983, On the transfer paradox, *International Economic Review* 24: 749–60.

Pontryagin, L. S., Boltyanskii, V. G., Gamkredlidze, R. V. and Mishchenko, E. F. 1962, *The Mathematical Theory of Optimization*, New York, Interscience Publishers.

Ravallion, M. 1983, Commodity transfers and the international economic order: a comment, *Journal of Development Economics* 13: 205–12.

Ricardo, D. 1810, *The High Price of Bullion: A Proof of the Depreciation of Bank Notes*, in Viner (1955): 295–6.

Rothbarth, E. 1940–1, The measurement of changes in real income under conditions of rationing, *Review of Economic Studies* 8: 100–7.

Rueff, M. J. 1929, Mr. Keynes' views on the transfer problem, *Economic Journal* 39: 388–99.

Safra, Z. 1983, The transfer paradox: stability, uniqueness and smooth preferences, mimeo, Harvard University.

1984, On the frequency of the transfer paradox, *Economics Letters* 15: 209–12.

Saghafi, M. M. and Nugent, J. B. 1983, Foreign aid in the form of commodity transfers that increase the income gap between rich and poor countries: the Chichilnisky theorem revisited, *Journal of Development Economics* 13: 213–16.

Samuelson, P. A. 1941, The stability of equilibria: comparative statics and dynamics, *Econometrica* 9: 97–120.

1947, *Foundations of Economic Analysis*, Cambridge, Mass., Harvard University Press.

1952, The transfer problem and transport costs: the terms of trade when impediments are absent, *Economic Journal* 62: 278–304.

1954, The transfer problem and transport costs. II: Analysis of effects of trade impediments, *Economic Journal* 64: 264–89.

Savoie, D. and Brecher, I. (eds.) 1992, *Equity and Efficiency in Economic Development: Essays in Honor of Benjamin Higgins*, Montreal, McGill-Queen's University Press.

Schumpeter, J. A. 1954, *History of Economic Analysis*, London, George Allen & Unwin.

Schweinberger, A. G. 1990, On the welfare effects of tied aid, *International Economic Review* 31: 457–62.

Silberberg, E. 1990, *The Structure of Economics: A Mathematical Analysis*, 2nd. edn., New York, McGraw-Hill.

Silberling, N. J. 1924, Financial and monetary policy of Great Britain during the Napoleonic wars. II: Ricardo and the bullion report, *Quarterly Journal of Economics* 39: 397–439.

Skidelsky, R. 1992, *John Maynard Keynes: The Economist as Saviour 1920–1937*, London, Macmillan.

Smith, A. 1981 [1776], *An Inquiry into the Nature and Causes of the Wealth of Nations*, Liberty Classics, Indianapolis (reprint of Oxford University Press edition [1976]).

Srinivasan, T. N. and Bhagwati, J. N. 1983a, On transfer paradoxes and immiserizing growth, part I: comment, *Journal of Development Economics* 13: 217–22.

1983b, Postscript, *Journal of Development Economics* 13: 251–2.

1984, On transfer paradoxes and immiserizing growth, part II, *Journal of Development Economics* 15: 111–15.

Stalioner, A. 1987, Estimation and simulation of international trade linkages in the QUEST model, *European Economy* 31.

Stern, R. M. 1973, *The Balance of Payments: Theory and Economic Policy*, London, Macmillan.

Takayama, A. 1994, *Analytical Methods in Economics*, New York, Harvester Wheatsheaf.

Takayama, A., Ohyama, M. and Ohta, H. (eds.) 1991, *Trade Policy and International Adjustments*, London, Academic Press.

Taussig, F. W. 1917, International trade under depreciated paper: a contribution to theory, *Quarterly Journal of Economics* 31: 380–403.

1918, International trade under depreciated paper: a rejoinder, *Quarterly Journal of Economics* 32: 690–4.

1927, *International Trade*, New York, Macmillan.

Tinbergen, J. (ed.) 1976, *RIO Reshaping the International Order*, New York, Dutton.

Tirole, J. 1988, *The Theory of Industrial Organization*, Cambridge, Mass., Harvard University Press.

Turunen-Red, A. H. and Woodland, A. D. 1988, On the multilateral transfer problem, *Journal of International Economics* 25: 249–69.

Varian, H. R. 1992, *Microeconomic Analysis*, 3rd. edn., New York, W. W. Norton.

Viner, J. 1924, *Canada's Balance of International Indebtedness, 1900–1913*, Cambridge, Mass., Harvard University Press.

1955, *Studies in the Theory of International Trade*, London, George Allen & Unwin.

Welfens, P. J. J. 1992, German unification in perspective, *Intereconomics* 27: 174–81.

Wheatley, J. 1807, *An Essay on the Theory of Money*, in Viner (1955): 296–7.

Wicksell, K. 1918, International freights and prices, *Quarterly Journal of Economics* 32: 404–10.

Winters, A. L. and Venables, A. J. (eds.) 1991, *European Integration: Trade and Industry*, Cambridge, Cambridge University Press.

Woodland, A. D. 1982, *International Trade and Resource Allocation*, Amsterdam, North-Holland.

Yano, M. 1983, The welfare aspects of the transfer problem, *Journal of International Economics* 15: 277–89.

1991, International transfers: strategic losses and the blocking of mutually advantageous transfers, *International Economic Review* 32: 371–82.

Index